CAMBRIDGE
UNIVERSITY PRESS

CAMBRIDGE ENGLISH
Language Assessment
Part of the University of Cambridge

Cambridge English

EMPOWER

UPPER INTERMEDIATE STUDENT'S BOOK

B2

Adrian Doff, Craig Thaine
Herbert Puchta, Jeff Stranks, Peter Lewis-Jones

Contents

Contents

CAN DO OBJECTIVES

- Discuss people you admire
- Discuss a challenge
- Explain what to do and check understanding
- Write an article

UNIT 1
Outstanding people

GETTING STARTED

a Look at the picture and answer the questions.

1. Who do you think the man and the woman are? Where are they?
2. What are the people behind them doing?
3. What do you think the man and the woman have just said to each other? What's going to happen next?

b Discuss the questions.

1. On what occasions do you normally take photos? When was the last time you took a 'selfie'?
2. If you could take a 'selfie' with a famous person, who would you choose and why?
3. What role do you think celebrities and famous people play in modern society? How important is it that they should:
   – be good role models? – inspire other people?

1A She is an inspiring woman

Learn to discuss people you admire

G Review of tenses
V Character adjectives

1 READING

a What kinds of people do you admire most? Why?

b Look at photos a and b. What do you think these people have done that make other people admire them?

c Read *Apple's design genius* and *The woman who reinvented children's TV* quickly and check your answers.

d Read the texts again and answer the questions. Write JI (Jony Ive), JC (Joan Ganz Cooney) or B (both).

Who ... ?

1 had training in their area of work
2 carried out some research
3 set up their own company
4 was one of the first people in their role
5 initially found the work challenging
6 was interested in other people's learning
7 believes the things we use should be beautiful
8 has won prizes for their work

e Who do you think is more inspiring, Jony Ive or Joan Ganz Cooney? Why?

(a)

Apple's design genius

I've always loved great design. Ever since I can remember, I've been fascinated by the shape and look of objects. In my opinion, Apple Inc. is the number one company in the world for product design.

In the time that [1]**you're reading** this article, around 750 iPhones and 300 iPads will be sold internationally. These iconic devices generate millions of pounds a day for Apple, and the man behind their iconic look is known as a 'design genius'. In 2013, *Time Magazine* listed him as one of the 100 most influential people in the world, but can you name him?

If you said Steve Jobs, you'd be wrong, although it was Jobs who first recognised this man's talent. His name is Jony Ive.

Born in London, Jony Ive studied industrial design at Newcastle Polytechnic. After graduating, [2]**he helped** set up the London design agency Tangerine. In 1992, while [3]**he was working** at Tangerine, he accepted a job offer from Apple.

His first years in the job were tough and the design work wasn't very interesting. The company was also struggling to make money. However, when Steve Jobs returned to Apple in 1997 and saw the design work that Ive [4]**had produced**, he immediately recognised Ive's ability and promoted him. Ive's first success in his new role was the design of the original, colourful iMac in 1998, which was quickly followed by the first iPod in 2001. Thanks to Ive's simple, elegant designs, Apple became one of the most successful companies in the world. Since then, [5]**he has been** responsible for the iPhone, iPad and Apple Watch. Ive's design involves not only the way these products look but also the way they work. [6]**He believes** devices have to be both beautiful and practical.

Jony Ive's key contribution to Apple is now being recognised and he has received numerous awards. There is no doubt that Steve Jobs was a larger-than-life ideas man and businessman who created a hugely successful company. However, without Jony Ive's design talent, Apple may not have become such a huge success.

So what have I learnt from Jony Ive? That the best designs are often the simplest.

THE WOMAN WHO REINVENTED CHILDREN'S TV

I've always felt passionate about television's ability to entertain and educate. I grew up watching what I consider to be a master class in how you can combine these two aspects of television: *Sesame Street*. This is the programme that brought us Big Bird, Elmo, Cookie Monster and friends. They're all the invention of a woman I consider a genius: Joan Ganz Cooney.

In the mid-1960s, Ganz Cooney was working as a producer of television documentary programmes in America. She realised television could play an important role in the education of pre-school children. She researched this idea and, in 1967, she wrote an outline for *Sesame Street*.

Ganz Cooney presented her ideas to the TV channel she was working for at the time. However, the channel rejected her proposal, saying that they thought she didn't have the right experience to produce a TV programme for children. As a result, she set up Children's Television Workshop with a colleague, and two years later they had managed to raise eight million dollars to finance production. Even so, many people working in the television industry questioned her ability to manage such a project. This was during the 1960s, when the industry was largely controlled by men.

At first, Ganz Cooney didn't want to fight to keep her role as the director of the production company and the producer of the programme. However, her husband and a colleague encouraged her to do so, because they knew the project would fail without her involvement. This meant she became one of the first female television executives in America.

In 1969, two years after her initial research, *Sesame Street* went on air, and today it's still going strong. However, Joan Ganz Cooney didn't stop there. She continued to take an interest in early childhood education, and in 2007, she set up a centre to help improve children's digital literacy. I really admire the way she has quietly got on with helping young children. She's not a household name like Big Bird, but she's had a huge impact on the education of millions of children around the world.

Sesame Street Facts

- more than 120 million viewers worldwide
- shown in more than 140 different countries
- now has a production budget of around $17 million a year

2 GRAMMAR Review of tenses

a Match the verbs 1–6 in bold in *Apple's design genius* with the tenses below.

- ☐ present simple
- ☐ past simple
- ☐ present continuous
- ☐ past continuous
- ☐ present perfect
- ☐ past perfect

b Complete the sentences with the tenses in 2a.

We use the:

1 _____ to refer to an event that takes place at a specific time in the past.
2 _____ to refer to a temporary event in progress in the present.
3 _____ to refer to a state or action that began in the past and has continued until now.
4 _____ to refer to something that's generally true.
5 _____ to refer to an action that was in progress in the past when something else happened.
6 _____ to refer to a past action that occurred before another past action.

c Underline examples of the six tenses in the second text.

d Now go to Grammar Focus 1A on p.134

e Read the text about Nikola Tesla and circle the correct words.

f 1.3 Listen and check your answers.

Nikola Tesla

Not many people [1]*have heard / heard* of Nikola Tesla, who [2]*played / was playing* a key role in creating the alternating current (AC) supply of electricity we [3]*are having / have* in our homes today. Early in his career, Tesla [4]*has worked / worked* with Thomas Edison. He [5]*had emigrated / has emigrated* to the USA from Europe in 1884. While Tesla [6]*was working / had worked* for Edison, they had an argument over payment for an invention, so Tesla [7]*was deciding / decided* to work independently. It was then that he developed a motor that could produce an alternating current. Throughout his life, Tesla continued to conduct experiments and [8]*helped / was helping* develop X-ray radiography and wireless communication. There is no doubt that he [9]*has had / had had* a large impact on modern technology. Many of the gadgets that we [10]*are enjoying / enjoy* today would not have been possible without Nikola Tesla.

3 LISTENING

a 1.4 Listen to two colleagues, Amelia and Chloe, talking about a female scientist, Jocelyn Bell-Burnell. Tick (✓) the correct sentences.

1. She's always been famous. ☐
2. She isn't very well known. ☐
3. She made an amazing discovery. ☐
4. She created a new mathematical theory. ☐

b 1.4 Listen again. Are the sentences true or false?

1. Amelia's reading a non-fiction book about planets and stars.
2. Jocelyn Bell-Burnell discovered a particular kind of star.
3. She won a Nobel Prize for her discovery.
4. She did badly when studying science at high school.
5. Life wasn't easy for her when she made her discovery.
6. The press didn't treat Jocelyn Bell-Burnell seriously.
7. Amelia has been inspired by Jocelyn Bell-Burnell.

c Discuss the questions.

1. Could Jocelyn Bell-Burnell's story have happened in your country? Do you know any similar examples?
2. How popular is science in your country? Is it popular with both men and women?
3. Is it important what gender a scientist is? Why do you think it was important in the case of Jocelyn Bell-Burnell?

4 VOCABULARY
Character adjectives

a Underline the five adjectives that describe people's character in sentences 1–4. Which two adjectives have a similar meaning and what's the difference between them?

1. She's a respected physicist.
2. She is an inspiring woman.
3. She was really determined, but in a quiet way.
4. Well, you've always been motivated, that's for sure. And stubborn.

b 1.5 **Pronunciation** Listen to the pronunciation of the letter *e* in these words. Which two sounds are the same? What are the other two sounds?

r**e**sp**e**cted d**e**t**e**rmined

c 1.6 Look at the words in the box and decide how the underlined letter *e* is pronounced. Add the words to the table, then listen and check. Practise saying the words.

slept revise helpful serve desire
prefer identity university women

sound 1 /ɪ/	sound 2 /e/	sound 3 /ɜː/

d Complete the sentences with the character adjectives in 4a.

1. Once Dan gets an idea in his head nothing will change his mind. He's the most ________ person I know and it's really annoying.
2. I'm not the sort of person who gives up easily – I'm very ________ when I want to achieve something.
3. He's worked hard and has done some very interesting research. He's a highly ________ chemist who's known around the world.
4. Doing a PhD is hard work so you have to be quite ________ if you want to do one.
5. In my last year of high school we had a really ________ biology teacher. Her lessons were so interesting that we all worked very hard for her.

e Now go to Vocabulary Focus on p.154

5 SPEAKING

a Think of an inspiring person, who has influenced you in some way. It can be someone you know or it can be someone famous. Make notes about the person. Use the questions to help you.

- What is this person's background?
- What important things has this person done in their life?
- Why are they inspiring?
- How have they changed or influenced your life?

b Tell other students about your person. Ask questions.

My cousin Vera is an athlete. She trains really hard every day – she's really determined.

How does she stay motivated?

1B Are you finding it difficult?

Learn to discuss a challenge

G Questions
V Trying and succeeding

1 SPEAKING and LISTENING

a Look at photos a–c and read *The 30-day challenge*. Then discuss the questions.

1 What are the people in the photos doing? Have you ever taken up similar activities? If so, how successful were you?
2 Why do you think doing something for 30 days gives you a better chance of succeeding?

b 1.10 Listen to a podcast about the 30-day challenge. Tick the main point that Alison makes.

1 The 30-day challenge is a good way to give up bad habits.
2 It's difficult for the brain to adapt to new habits.
3 If you try something new for 30 days, you're more likely to keep to it afterwards.

c 1.10 Alison made some notes at the seminar. Complete her notes with one or two words in each gap. Listen again and check.

Seminar notes

- It takes the brain 30 days to adapt to a new [1]_____.
- 30 days isn't a [2]_____ time, so it's fun to do something new.
- Also a chance to try something [3]_____ – not just giving up bad habits.
- Two ways to do it:
  1 do something that doesn't get in the way of your [4]_____
  2 take time out to do something you've always [5]_____ do
- You need to make an [6]_____ !

The 30-day challenge

Have you ever started a new hobby, but given up after only a couple of weeks? Or started a course and stopped after the first few lessons? Most of us have tried to learn something new, but very few of us ever really get any good at it – it's just too difficult to continue doing something new.

But now there's some good news: did you know that if you can keep up your new hobby for just 30 days, you have a much better chance of succeeding? And you may learn something new about yourself too.

d What examples of 30-day challenges did you hear? Use words from both boxes for each challenge.

Cycle everywhere, even if it rains.

~~cycle~~ drink climb get up eat paint write

rise poem coffee new picture mountains ~~everywhere~~

e What do you think of the ideas Alison talks about? Make notes.

f Compare your ideas.

a

b

c

2 VOCABULARY
Trying and succeeding

a 1.11 Complete the sentences with the words and phrases in the box. Listen and check your answers.

give up have a go at keep it up keep to make an effort manage to successfully try out work out

1 Often if we try something new, we _____ after about a week or two because our brain hasn't adapted.
2 So if you _____ do something new for a month, you'll probably _____ it.
3 Maybe you wouldn't want to _____ for your whole life, but it might be fun to do it just for 30 days.
4 If you're successful it's great, but if it doesn't _____, it doesn't matter too much.
5 It's not just about giving up bad habits. The idea is really that you _____ something new.
6 Or you can take time out and _____ something you've always wanted to do.
7 Obviously to do something like that you need to _____.
8 They're all about half-way through and they've done it _____ so far.

b Match words and phrases from 2a with the meanings.

1 succeed _____, _____
2 stop trying _____
3 not stop trying _____, _____
4 try hard _____
5 try to see if it works _____, _____

c Complete the sentences below about 30-day challenges. Use the words and phrases in 2a and your own ideas. There is more than one possible answer.

1 He tried giving up coffee for 30 days. It wasn't easy, but he …
2 You've got up at 5.30 every day for three weeks now. You've only got one week to go, so …
3 30-day challenges sound fun. I want to do something different, so I think I'll …

d Work in small groups. Tell the group about a time when you:

- found something difficult but didn't give up
- made a real effort to succeed
- had a go at something unusual
- did something which worked out successfully
- tried to do something which didn't work out.

3 READING

a Look at challenges 1–3. Who do you think will find it easy and who will find it difficult?

b Read the interviews and check your ideas.

30-DAY CHALLENGE

Challenge 1: Farah decided not to eat meat.

What made you decide to become vegetarian, Farah?

Well, for quite a long time now I've been trying to eat less meat, partly for health reasons. I think vegetables are better for you.

1 ____

Yes, but I always thought I'd miss meat too much. The idea of being a vegetarian for 30 days was really good, because I could give it a try and then see how I feel.

2 ____

No, I feel really good. Actually, I don't miss meat at all, so I think I'll easily manage the 30 days and I might try carrying on longer. I certainly think I'm a bit healthier than I used to be.

Challenge 2: Mona decided to draw something every day.

Mona, why did you decide to draw something every day?

Well, I've never been very good at drawing, but I've always thought I'd like to start drawing things around me. It's one of those things that you think about doing, but you never get round to.

3 ____

All kinds of things. At the start I drew objects around me at home. Then I went out in my lunch break and started drawing things outdoors, like yesterday I drew a duck in the park – that was really difficult!

So do you feel it has been worthwhile?

Oh yes, definitely. I'm still not very good at drawing, but it's been lots of fun and it's very relaxing.

c Complete the interviews with the missing questions.

a And who do you practise with? Or are you just working alone?
b But didn't you ever think of being vegetarian before?
c And how do you feel? Are you finding it difficult?
d And do you think you'll carry on after the 30 days?
e What have you drawn pictures of so far?

d 1.12 Listen and check your answers.

Challenge 3: Steve decided to learn Italian.

Steve, what language did you decide to learn?

Well, I thought I'd choose a language that isn't too different from English, so I decided to try Italian.

Isn't it difficult to keep going with it?

Yes, it is. I've had to be very strict with myself. I'm using a book with a CD, so I usually try to cover one lesson a night.

4 ____________________

Well, there's an Italian restaurant just round the corner and I'm friends with the owner, so I go there and I chat to him. That's one reason I chose Italian.

5 ____________________

Maybe, or I might try a different language every month. I'm thinking of trying Japanese next.

4 GRAMMAR Questions

a Read the rules about questions. Find examples of each type of question in the interviews and 3c.

1 In questions, we usually put the auxiliary verb before the subject. If there is no auxiliary verb, we add *do* or *did*.
Are you *making dinner?* ***Have you*** *eaten?*
What ***did you*** *eat?*
2 If the question word (*who, what* or *which*) is the subject, we keep normal word order.
Who spoke *to you?* ***What happened*** *next?*
3 If a question has a preposition, it can come at the end:
You were talking to someone. → *Who were you talking* ***to****?*
4 To ask an opinion, we often ask questions starting with a phrase like *Do you think … ?*
Is it a good idea? → ***Do you think*** *it's a good idea?*

b Compare examples a and b.

a Did you see her at the party? b Didn't you see her at the party?

Which example … ?
1 is a neutral question (= maybe she was there, maybe not)
2 expresses surprise (= I'm sure she was there)

c Compare examples c and d.

c Which colour do you want? d What colour do you want?

Which example … ?
1 asks about an open choice (there may be lots of colours to choose from)
2 asks about a limited range (e.g. black, red or green)

d Now go to Grammar Focus 1B on p.134

e Work in pairs. You are going to role-play two of the interviews in 3b and continue with your own questions.

1 Choose one of the interviews.
Student A: Interview Student B. Add your own questions.
Student B: Answer Student A's questions using your own ideas.
2 Choose a second interview. This time Student B interviews Student A.

5 SPEAKING

a Work in pairs.

1 Write down three challenges you might do in the next three months.

1 Write a short poem every day
2 Get up at dawn
3 Go running

2 Look at your partner's challenges. Write some questions to ask about each one. Ask about:
- reasons for doing the challenge
- details of what he/she plans to do
- how he/she feels about it.

Are you planning to … ?
Do you think it will be … ?
How are you going to… ?

b Interview your partner about their three challenges. Do you think he/she will be successful?

1C Everyday English
Don't touch the sandwiches!

Learn to explain what to do and check understanding

S Breaking off a conversation

P Rapid speech

1 LISTENING

a Discuss the questions.

1 In your country, how do students manage financially? Do they … ?
   - rely on their parents
   - get a part-time job
   - use student loans

2 What do you think is the best way? Why?

3 If you had to do a part-time job to earn some money as a student, what job would you choose and why?

b Look at the photo of Tessa and Becky from Part 1. Who do you think they are?

1 tourists visiting a famous building
2 college students doing a course
3 journalists who have just done an interview

c 1.15 Watch or listen to Part 1 and check your ideas.

d 1.15 Watch or listen again. Answer the questions.

1 Are Becky and Tessa friends? How do you know?
2 Why does Becky have to go?

e 1.16 Watch or listen to Part 2. Are these sentences true or false?

1 Becky and Tom are married.
2 Becky is free this evening.
3 Becky is in a hurry.

2 CONVERSATION SKILLS
Breaking off a conversation

a 1.17 Look at these ways to break off a conversation and say goodbye.

1 I really must go now.
2 I must run.
3 I've got no time to talk now.
4 I'll see you tomorrow.

Listen to the speaker. Which words does she not use in 1–4?

b Look at some more ways to break off a conversation. Which words has the speaker not included?

1 Must be off now.
2 Talk to you later.
3 Can't talk just now.
4 Nice talking to you.

3 PRONUNCIATION Rapid speech

a 1.18 In rapid speech we often leave out sounds. Listen to the phrases below. Which sound is left out? Is it a consonant sound or a vowel sound?

1 must go
2 must run
3 got to go
4 can't talk

b Read the conversation. Put B's replies in order. Is more than one order possible?

A So how was your holiday?
B Got to go. / Sorry. / Can't talk now. / It was great.
A OK, well, have a nice evening.
B Bye. / See you tomorrow. / Yeah, thanks. / Must be off now.

c Work in pairs. Have short conversations.

Student A: Tell Student B about what you did last weekend. Continue until he/she stops you.
Student B: You're in a hurry. Use expressions in 2b and 3b to break off the conversation.

Then swap roles.

4 LISTENING

a 1.19 Watch or listen to Part 3. What happens to Becky? Choose the correct answer.

1 Becky meets Sam and learns how to make coffee.
2 Becky learns how to handle food and meets a café customer.

b 1.19 Watch or listen again. Answer the questions.

1 Sam explains two things to Becky. What are they?
2 What does Phil do in the café?
3 Why do they call him 'JK'?
4 Who is Emma?

c Discuss the questions with other students. Give reasons for your answers.

1 Do you think the others like Phil coming to the café?
2 Do you think Becky will be good at her new job?

d 1.20 Watch or listen to Part 4. Which of these topics do Tom and Becky mention?

coffee   food   Becky's new job   the reason Tom is here
Phil's book   their wedding plans

e 1.20 Watch or listen again. What do Tom and Becky say about each topic?

Becky and Sam

Becky and Emma

Phil

5 USEFUL LANGUAGE

Explaining and checking understanding

a Look at the expressions Sam uses to explain what to do. Put the words in italics in the correct order.

1 *most / thing / is, / the / important* don't touch the food.
2 *to / always / remember* use these tongs.
3 *is, / remember / thing / to / another* the tables are all numbered.

b 1.21 Listen and check your answers.

c Why does Sam use these expressions?

1 because he needs time to think
2 because he's not sure
3 to emphasise important points

d Look at these ways to check that someone has understood an explanation. Complete the questions with the endings in the box.

the idea?   got that?   clear?   I mean?

1 Is that …
2 Do you understand what …
3 Have you …
4 Do you get …

e 1.22 **Pronunciation** Listen to each question in 5d said in two ways. Which way sounds … ?

- friendly and polite
- unfriendly and not so polite

To sound friendly, does the speaker's voice go up (↗) or down (↘) at the end?

f Practise asking the questions in 5d in a friendly and polite way.

g Here are some other things Sam could explain to Becky. Imagine what he could say using language in 5a and 5d. What could Becky say to show she has understood?

1 how to clear and arrange a table when a customer leaves
2 what to do with the coffee machine at closing time
3 what to do if customers leave something behind

h Practise the conversation in 5g. Swap roles.

6 SPEAKING

a Choose a process you are familiar with or something you know how to do. It could be:

- something connected with a sport or a hobby
- how to use a machine or an electronic device
- how to make or cook something.

b You are going to explain the process to your partner. Prepare what you will say. Think how to emphasise the important points and check that your partner understands. Use expressions from 5a and 5d.

c Work in pairs. Take turns to explain the process to your partner and ask each other questions to check understanding.

Unit Progress Test

CHECK YOUR PROGRESS

You can now do the Unit Progress Test.

1D Skills for Writing
I really missed my phone all day

Learn to write an article

W Organising an article

1 SPEAKING and LISTENING

a Discuss the questions.

1 In your daily life, how much do you depend on technology?
2 What aspects of technology make your daily life easier?

b Look at the survey results below and discuss the questions.

1 Do you think people you know would agree with these results?
2 Do you agree with the results? Is there anything else you would like to add to the list?

MODERN LIFE IS RUBBISH!

A survey in the UK revealed the things that British people hate most about modern life. Here are the top five:

1 **self-service check-outs**
2 **sales calls**
3 **selfies**
4 **slow internet connection**
5 **mobile phone battery life**

c 1.23 Listen to Gitta and Derek talking about technology. Are they describing positive or negative experiences? Do they talk about the same device?

d 1.23 Listen again. What's the speaker's relationship with the other person in the story? What made the experience positive or negative? Why?

e Discuss the questions.

1 Do you agree with Gitta's reaction to her boss? Why / Why not?
2 Do you know people like Derek? Do you think they should try to change? Why / Why not?

f Work on your own. Think about the questions below and make notes.

- When has technology created a problem for you?
- When has technology helped you solve a problem of some kind?

g Discuss your experiences in 1f.

2 READING

a Read *Tech free!* Are any of the things in the survey mentioned?

b Read the text again. Are the sentences true or false?

1 Before the experiment, Sam was a bit worried by the idea.
2 Sam was annoyed that he had to chat to someone in the bank.
3 The bank teller was clearly surprised that Sam wanted to withdraw money.
4 Sam saved time by not using the self-service check-out at the supermarket.
5 Sam was able to work better when he wrote by hand.
6 As the day progressed, Sam thought less about using his phone.
7 Sam learnt something about the way we depend on technology.

c How would you feel if you had to live without using technology for one day? Discuss what you would enjoy and not enjoy.

3 WRITING SKILLS Organising an article

a How does Sam organise his article? Choose the correct summary. He …

1 explains his attitude towards technology, describes his day, requests readers to do the same thing
2 explains his level of dependency on technology, describes his day, finishes with an evaluation of the experience
3 explains his feelings about technology, describes his day, finishes by promising to repeat the experience

b How does Sam get the reader's attention at the beginning of the article?

TECH FREE!

by Sam Winton

Home | Blog | Follow me

[1]Have you ever wondered what it would be like to give up technology? I'm a TV journalist and I spend a lot of my working life in front of a computer or a TV. I decided to conduct my own private experiment: I would spend a day trying to manage without technological devices. What a scary thought!

[2]<u>The first thing</u> I usually do every day is reach for my smartphone to check the time and read any messages or emails. But I'd locked it away in a drawer the night before. Already I was feeling very cut off from the world, and it was only ... actually, I had no idea what time it was!

[3]After breakfast, I needed to get some cash. Inevitably, this meant a trip to the bank because cash points are technological devices. I had to queue, but I had a very nice conversation with a woman whilst I was waiting. Not surprisingly, the bank teller thought I was a bit strange withdrawing money this way. I think she thought I was a robber!

[4]Then it was on to the supermarket. You may be wondering what's technological about that Well, I had to make sure I avoided the self-service check-out and joined the queue for a normal one – with a real person. Naturally, it took longer, but I had a great chat with the guy who served me, and he told me about a new club that is opening up nearby. Would I have found out about that if I'd gone to the self-service check-out? No.

[5]Afterwards, I came home to have a go at writing a news story by hand. Strangely, I found it easier to concentrate on my writing. But my hand and fingers got really sore! And I have to confess – by this stage, I was having to make a real effort not to get my phone out and check my messages. I was starting to wonder what my friends were doing. Maybe they were making plans to go to that new club, and I would never know!

[6]All in all, I wouldn't say I could live without technology. Predictably, I really missed my phone all day. The worst part was not being able to check updates in the news or from my friends. I felt very out of touch. However, I kept to my promise of a tech-free day and I did have more face-to-face interaction. Undoubtedly, it made me realise just how addicted to technology we all are.

c Complete the tasks below.

1 In paragraphs 2–5, <u>underline</u> the linking word or phrase that sequences the events in Sam's day. The first one has been done for you.
2 In paragraph 6, what linking phrase shows that Sam is going to summarise his experience?

d Look at the example sentence from the article. The adverb *Inevitably* shows the writer's attitude. Find five other comment adverbs in the article.

Inevitably, this meant a trip to the bank because cash points are technological devices.

e Add the adverbs in the box to the sentences. (Sometimes there is more than one possible answer.)

amazingly naturally inevitably
(not) surprisingly

1 Why do some websites always ask you to change passwords? Having created a password for my bank account, I was asked to change it two weeks later.
2 I usually hate anything to do with technology. I quite like using the self-service check-out at the local supermarket.
3 I always expect IT products to be very expensive. The tablet I bought last week cost very little.
4 I find it very difficult to install new software. I've downloaded the latest version of a program and my computer has frozen.

f Which piece of advice is not correct for writing an article? Why?

1 Begin the article with a question to get the reader's attention.
2 Use direct questions to connect with the reader of your article.
3 Think about how you can structure the main part of the article. You can use a sequence of events or you could compare and contrast ideas.
4 Use linking words to guide the reader.
5 Be as objective as possible.
6 Use comment adverbs to show your opinions.
7 Summarise your experience or ideas and evaluate them.

4 WRITING

a Imagine you had to live for a week without a technological device you use in your daily life. Choose a device from the survey, the article or use your own ideas. Make notes about what the experience might be like.

b Discuss your notes.

c Write an article about your experience. Organise your article to follow the structure in 3a. Use the linking phrases and adverbs from 3c–e to help you.

d Swap articles with another student.
Does the article follow the advice in 3f?
Is the article interesting to read? Why?
What could make it more interesting?

UNIT 1
Review and extension

1 GRAMMAR

a Write verbs in the gaps in the correct tense.

My wife Anna and I first [1]_____ (meet) at a party while I [2]_____ (live) in London in the 1970s. When I [3]_____ (arrive) most people [4]_____ (already/leave). I [5]_____ (notice) Anna immediately. She [6]_____ (wear) a blue dress and she [7]_____ (chat) with a group of people on the balcony. I [8]_____ (go) up to her and we [9]_____ (start) talking. We both [10]_____ (feel) as if we [11]_____ (know) each other all our lives. Now we [12]_____ (be) both in our 70s. We [13]_____ (know) each other for 44 years.

b Read an interview with a famous actor about his life. Correct the mistakes in the questions.

1 *Where you grew up?*
In San Diego, in California. I left when I was 18.
2 *Did not you like living in San Diego?*
Yes, but there were more opportunities in San Francisco.
3 *How long for did you stay there?*
About eight years. Then I moved to New York.
4 *What did make you decide to move?*
I got an offer to act at the Apollo Theater in New York.
5 *Do you think was it a good decision?*
Oh yes. It was a chance to work with some great people.
6 *With who did you work?*
Oh, lots of good actors – Terence Newby, for example.

2 VOCABULARY

a Add an adjective to complete each gap.

1 The students are all keen to learn English. They're very m_____.
2 All Sophie's family and friends have warned her about marrying Fred but she's going to anyway. She's so s_____.
3 Everyone agrees the new president is a good leader. She's highly r_____.
4 My brother used to be very shy, but he's become much more s_____ since he left home.
5 I've always loved acting more than anything else. I'm p_____ about it.
6 Five thousand people came to hear him talk. He's a very i_____ speaker.
7 Try not to criticise his work. He can be very s_____ about it.
8 Just because they're rich they think they're better than everyone else. I hate a_____ people like that.

b Choose the correct answers.

1 I [1]*had / took* a go at running a café, but it didn't work [2]*up / out*. I didn't manage [3]*to make / in making* enough money so I had to sell it.
2 He's really [4]*doing / making* an effort to lose weight. He's on a diet and he's [5]*kept / held* it up for six weeks now. But I don't know if he'll [6]*stay / keep* to it for much longer.
3 There's only one way to find out if you can do something [7]*successful / successfully*, and that's to try it [8]*on / out*!

3 WORDPOWER *make*

a Match the remarks with the pictures.

a 'I can't make up my mind.'
b 'It really makes a difference to the room.'
c 'I can't make out what it is.'
d 'We'll have to make the best of it.'
e 'This is to make up for last night.'
f 'That doesn't make sense.'
g 'It wants to make friends with us.'

b 1.24 Listen to the conversations and check your answers.

c Add a word or phrase from exercise **a** after *make* in these sentences.

1 What was that? I can't make _____ what you're saying.
2 Why don't you drive faster? We need to make _____ lost time, or we'll be late.
3 So do you want to come with us? You need to make _____.
4 When the sun shines, it makes _____ to the way I feel.
5 I didn't buy any more food. You'll just have to make _____ of it.
6 He gave a long explanation but it didn't make _____ to me. I still don't understand.
7 Don't sit in front of the computer all day. You should go out and make _____ with people.

d What kind of person are you? Discuss these questions.

1 If you upset a friend, how would you make up for it? Would you buy a present, buy flowers, apologise ...?
2 When you buy clothes, do you make up your mind quickly or do you need a long time to decide?
3 You have to spend the night at an airport. Would you stay there and make the best of it, or would you pay money for a hotel?
4 You see a dog in the street. Would you try to make friends with it or would you keep out of its way?

REVIEW YOUR PROGRESS

How well did you do in this unit? Write 3, 2 or 1 for each objective.
3 = very well 2 = well 1 = not so well

I CAN ...

discuss people I admire	☐
discuss a challenge	☐
explain what to do and check understanding	☐
write an article	☐

CAN DO OBJECTIVES

- Discuss dangerous situations
- Give advice on avoiding danger
- Give and respond to compliments
- Write guidelines in a leaflet

UNIT 2

Survival

GETTING STARTED

a Look at the picture and answer the questions.

1 What do you think has happened here?
2 Who are the people in the picture?
3 What's the man on the phone saying?

b Discuss the questions.

1 What do you think are the worst kinds of natural disasters? Why?
2 Think of a natural disaster that has happened in your country. How effective was the response of the emergency services? How well did people cope?
3 Why do you think some people cope better with challenging situations than others?

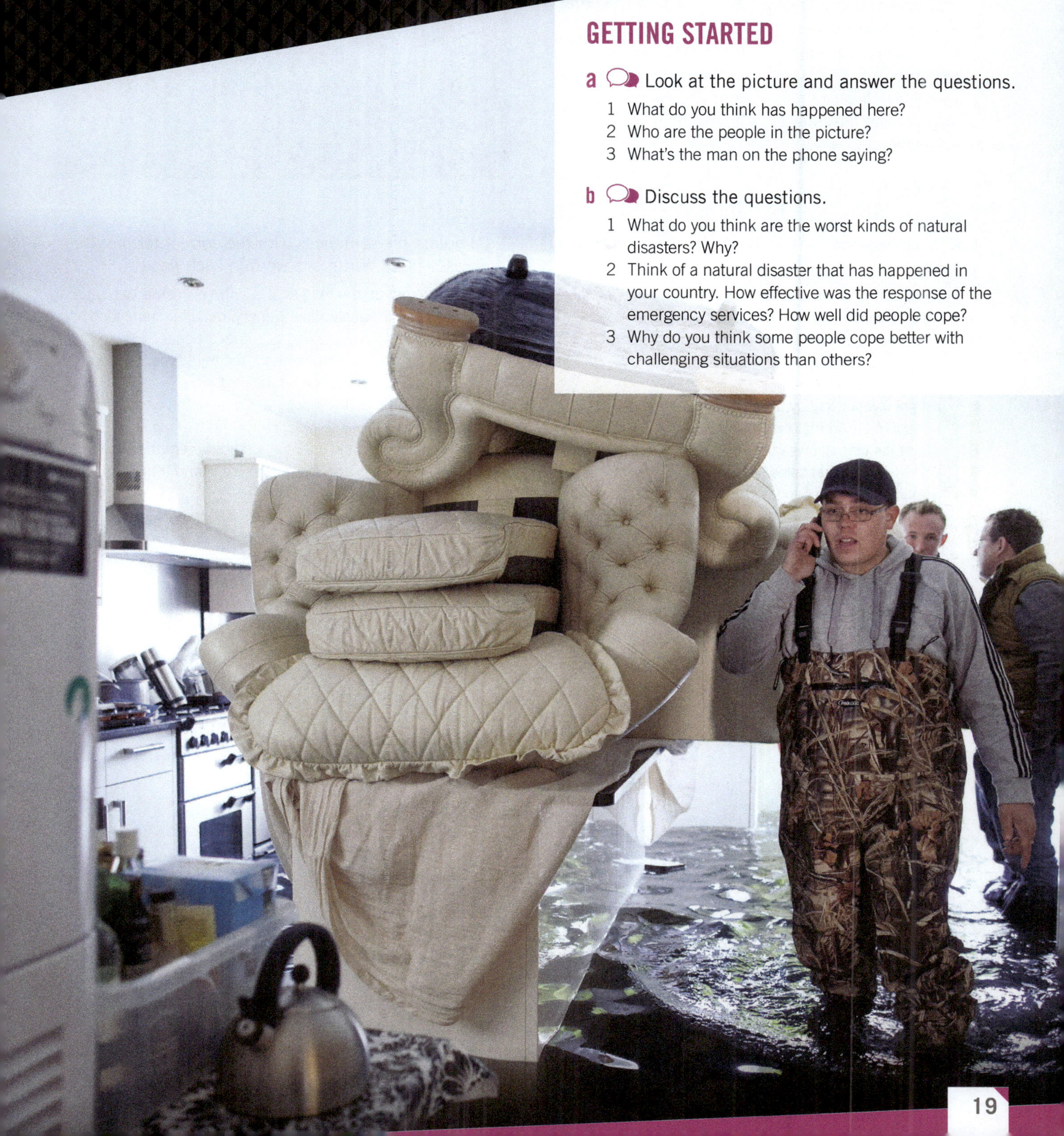

2A It was getting late and I was lost

Learn to discuss dangerous situations

G Narrative tenses
V Expressions with *get*

1 LISTENING

a Look at pictures a–d. What would you be most afraid of in each situation?

b 1.25 Listen to someone talking about their holiday. Which of the pictures is being described? Where was the holiday?

c 1.25 Listen again. Number events a–h in the order that they happened.

a bought a new surfboard
b lost the board
c waved to a life-guard
d swam against the current
e fell off the surfboard
f learnt to surf with instructors
g went surfing alone
h was rescued

2 VOCABULARY Expressions with *get*

a Match expressions 1–10 in bold with meanings a–j.

1 ☐ I can't wait to **get away**.
2 ☐ I've always wanted to learn how to surf and I'll finally **get to** do it.
3 ☐ I **couldn't get over** just how strong they are.
4 ☐ Actually, I **got into** a bit of **trouble** once.
5 ☐ I tried to **get hold of** it.
6 ☐ It **got swept away** by the wave.
7 ☐ I soon realised that I **wasn't getting anywhere**.
8 ☐ I **got the feeling** I was being pulled out to sea.
9 ☐ So I waved to **get someone's attention**.
10 ☐ I had a bad experience, but I soon **got over** it.

a make no progress
b go in a different direction in a powerful way
c have the chance to do something
d go somewhere else
e be very surprised by something
f find myself in difficulty
g take it in my hand
h recover from something negative that happened
i make someone notice
j have the sensation that

b Complete the sentences with the correct form of the phrases in 2a. Write one word in each gap.

1 She ran out on the road to _____ the policeman's _____.
2 They were exhausted and hungry, but after some food and sleep they soon _____ _____ the experience.
3 When he saw the same tree for the third time, he began to _____ _____ _____ that he was lost.
4 He went on a course about surviving in the woods and _____ _____ put into practice his fire-making skills.
5 They decided to ski off the main trail where the snow was fresh, but it was also quite dangerous and they soon _____ _____ _____.
6 The boat was sinking, but we all managed to _____ _____ _____ a life-jacket.
7 She was crossing the river, but the current was strong and she _____ _____ _____ by the water.
8 They had been walking for hours, but they'd only walked about two kilometres. They felt like they weren't _____ _____.
9 They were in such a rush to _____ _____ to the mountains, they left without taking sensible walking boots.
10 When they were in the water, they _____ _____ _____ how high the waves were.

c Now go to Vocabulary Focus on p.155

3 READING

a Read the article *Lost at sea* and answer the questions.

1 How long was Robert Hewitt in the water?
2 What problems did he have to overcome?

b Can you remember what these numbers refer to? Write sentences about each number. Then read the text again and check your answers.

1 200-metre
2 seven kilometres
3 fourth day
4 three hours
5 half a kilometre
6 third day

c Answer the questions.

1 What do you think most helped Robert to survive?
2 Do you think that Robert made the right decision on day one not to try to swim for shore? Give reasons.
3 What was the biggest challenge Robert had to overcome?
4 What would you have done in Robert's situation?

REAL DIVING

Stories *Articles* *Diving in NZ* *Shop*

LOST AT SEA

How long could you survive at sea? One day? Two? And when would you start to lose hope?

When Robert Hewitt came to the surface, he [1]**realised** straight away that something was wrong. He [2]**'d been diving** for sea urchins and crayfish off the coast of New Zealand with a friend, and [3]**had decided** to make the 200-metre swim back to shore alone. But instead, strong underwater currents had taken him more than half a kilometre out to sea.

Lying on his back in the middle of the ocean, Robert told himself not to panic. He was a strong swimmer and he [4]**was wearing** his thick wet suit. 'I'm not going to die. Someone will come,' he told himself. But three hours passed and still no one had come for him. Robert would soon have to make a tough decision.

He was now a long way from the coast and the tide was taking him further out, but he decided not to try to swim for shore. He felt it was better to save his energy and hold on to his brightly coloured equipment. But the decision was not an easy one. 'I just closed my eyes and said, "You've made the right decision. You've made the right decision" until that's all I heard,' he remembers.

As night approached, Robert established a pattern to help him survive in the water. To stay warm, he kept himself moving and took short naps of less than a minute at a time. Every few hours, he called out to his loved ones: 'Just yelling out their names would pick me up and then I would keep going for the next hour and the next hour and the next.'

When he woke the next morning, he couldn't believe he was still alive. Using his bright equipment, he tried to signal to planes that flew overhead. But as each plane turned away, his spirits dropped. He managed to drink water from his oxygen tank to keep himself alive, but as day turned to night again he started to imagine things.

Robert woke on the third day to a beautiful blue sky. Now seven kilometres off the coast, Robert decided he had to swim for it. But the sun was so strong and Robert quickly ran out of strength. Hope turned to disappointment yet again: 'I felt disappointed in myself. I thought I was a lot fitter. I thought I would be able to do it.' Robert then started to think he might not survive.

On the fourth day, the lack of food and water was really starting to affect him. Half unconscious, and with strange visions going through his head, he thought he saw a boat coming towards him with two of his friends in. Another vision, surely.

But no – 'They put me in the boat and I said something like "Oh, how's it going, what are you guys doing here?"' Then he asked them the question that he'd asked in all his visions: 'Can I have some water?' As they handed him the water and he felt it touch his lips, he knew. This was not a vision. He'd been found! After four days and three nights alone at sea, Robert had been found! Sunburnt, hungry and exhausted, but alive …

GLOSSARY

sea urchin

crayfish

4 GRAMMAR Narrative tenses

a Look at the verbs in bold in *Lost at sea* and match them with the uses a–d.

a a completed action that takes place before the main events in the story
b a background action in progress at the same time as the main events in the story happened
c a continuous activity that happens before the main events in the story and explains why the main events happen
d a completed action that tells you what happens at a specific time in the story

b 1.29 **Pronunciation** Listen to the three sentences. Underline the stressed verb in each sentence. How do we pronounce the words *had been*? Listen again and repeat.

He *had been* diving for seafood.
He *had been* swimming in the sea
He *had been* wearing a wet suit.

c Now go to Grammar Focus 2A on p.136

d Work in pairs. Student A: Read about Eric Le Marque. Student B: Read about Ricky Megee. Answer the questions about your text.

1 Where does the text take place?
2 Does the person survive?

e Underline the correct verbs in your text.

f You are going to tell your partner about your story. Make notes.

g Tell your partner your survival story. Use correct verb forms.

5 SPEAKING

a Think of a dangerous situation that you or someone you know was in, or it could be something you know about from a book or film. Make notes about the questions.

- Where and when did it take place?
- Who was involved?
- What was the scene or background to the story?
- What were the main events?
- How did you / the person feel?
- What was the outcome?

b Tell each other your story. Use different narrative tenses and expressions with *get*. Ask questions.

Student A: ERIC LEMARQUE

It was getting late and Eric LeMarque decided to have one final run on his snowboard. As he [1]*'d gone / was going* down the mountain, he [2]*came / was coming* across some thick fog and headed in the wrong direction. All of a sudden he was completely lost. All he had with him was his snowboard, some bubble gum and an MP3 player. Eventually, he [3]*remembered / 'd remembered* something he [4]*was seeing / 'd seen* in a movie about using an MP3 player as a compass. This meant he was able to get an idea of where he was and head in the right direction, up the mountain. Eric was missing for a week. During that time, he fell in a river, almost went down a waterfall and had to walk through snow that was four and a half metres deep! On the eighth day he was seen by a helicopter that [5]*had searched / had been searching* for him. He was completely exhausted but alive.

Student B: RICKY MEGEE

A farmer couldn't believe what he saw when he came across a stranger living on his farm. The man, Ricky Megee, [1]*lived / had been living* off the land in the Australian bush for two months. Ricky [2]*had been driving / had driven* near the border of Western Australia and Northern Territory. He [3]*stopped / had stopped* to help some people whose car had broken down and offered one of them a lift to a nearby town. Unfortunately, the passenger turned out to be a robber, who stole Ricky's car. Ricky was now completely lost in the bush. He [4]*ate / had eaten* insects, snakes and frogs and eventually managed to find a dam to provide him with water. He built a small shelter there and waited, hoping to be rescued. 71 days after being left, Ricky was found by the farmer. He [5]*'d lost / was losing* more than 50 kg in weight during his time in the bush.

2B If it runs towards you, don't run away

Learn to give advice on avoiding danger

G Future time clauses and conditionals

V Animals and the environment

1 READING

a Think of three wild places you know of.

- Would you be scared to go for a walk there?
- What dangers could you face?
- What would you do to get out of danger?

b Look at pictures a–e and answer the questions.

1 Which of the animals do you think are the most and least dangerous?

2 How good do you think your chances are of surviving an attack by these animals?

c Read the text and check your answers.

d Read the text again. Tick (✓) the correct sentences.

1 Some animals are less dangerous than people think.

2 If you go walking, you can't avoid meeting dangerous animals.

3 Not many animals attack without reason.

4 Having a weapon may help you survive an attack.

5 Most animals have a part of their body which is vulnerable.

6 It's better to run away than to try to fight.

e Do you think the text is ... ?

a a serious survival guide for travellers

b part of a scientific book about animals

c an article written mainly for interest and amusement

How to Survive ... an animal attack

YOU'RE WALKING IN A FOREST WHEN SUDDENLY A WILD ANIMAL APPEARS FROM NOWHERE AND IT DOES NOT LOOK FRIENDLY. WHAT DO YOU DO?

The first important point is that there's not usually much you can do, except hope it goes away again. With luck, you may never have to defend yourself against a wild animal, but it doesn't hurt to know what to do if an escaped leopard attacks you in your back garden, or if you're going for a country walk and you suddenly meet a family of wolves.

BE AWARE

The first thing is to know which animals are really dangerous. Many people are scared of animals that are in fact harmless, and not scared enough of animals that could kill you. Most animals won't attack people unless you do something to make them angry. Bears, for example, will usually move away as soon as they hear you and they'll only fight if they think you're attacking them or their young. Wolves won't normally attack unless they are very hungry, and then only if they're in a group. Tarantulas are horrible and hairy, but they aren't actually dangerous at all – you can let them walk over you. On the other hand, tigers and crocodiles are serious killers who will be happy to eat you for breakfast.

BE PREPARED

It's a good idea to take a stick, a knife or a pepper spray when you go for a walk in the wild in case you meet a dangerous animal. Have it in a place where you can easily find it. It may mean the difference between life and death.

KNOW YOUR ENEMY

If you ever find yourself face to face with a large and dangerous animal, you'll want to know their strong and weak points. Common weak points are:

- the nose
- the eyes
- the neck.

People have sometimes survived by punching sharks, large cats, and crocodiles on the nose, and pushing your thumbs into their eyes will also work well, as long as you press hard enough. Otherwise, you might just make them angry!

You can also try to get a psychological advantage. Provided you seem bigger and more dangerous than the animal, it will probably leave you alone, so make a lot of noise and try to make yourself look bigger.

WHAT NEXT?

If scaring them doesn't work, then you have two options: running or fighting. Remember that most animals are better at running and fighting than humans, so don't expect things to end well. But if you decide to fight, fight back with everything you have. Often during animal attacks people give up before the fight has even started. If you have any sharp objects or weapons, then use them. Hit the animal's weak points, keep shouting and make sudden movements. Good luck!

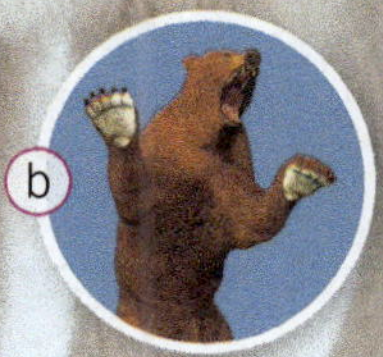

f Look at the ideas below for surviving attacks by three different animals. For each animal, decide which ideas are the best.

g **Communication 2B** Now go to p.127 to check your answers.

1 A wolf

a hit it on the nose with a stick
b look it straight in the eyes
c run away immediately

2 A shark

a swim away quickly
b swim towards it
c hit it in the eye if it bites you

3 A bear

a run straight uphill as fast as you can
b lie down and 'play dead'
c hit the trees with sticks if you think bears are nearby

2 GRAMMAR Future time clauses and conditionals

a Look at the words and phrases in bold in sentences 1–5 and answer questions a–e.

1 They'll only fight **if** they think you're attacking them.
2 They won't attack people **unless** they're trapped or provoked.
3 Bears, for example, will usually move away **as soon as** they hear you.
4 **Provided** you stay absolutely still, the bear will lose interest and go away.
5 **As long as** you don't panic, it will probably swim away.

a Which two words or phrases have a similar meaning to *if*?
b What does sentence 2 mean?
 1 A bear will only attack you if it's trapped or provoked.
 2 A bear will attack you anyway, even if it isn't trapped.
c What does sentence 3 mean?
 1 When bears hear you they will wait, then move away slowly.
 2 When bears hear you they will move away immediately.
d Look at these examples:
 If you stay still, the bear will go away (= something good will happen).
 If you move, the bear will attack you (= something bad will happen).
 In which example could we use *as long as* or *provided* instead of *if*?
e What tense is used after the words and phrases in bold? What tense is used in the other part of the sentence?

b Find one more example in *How to survive an animal attack* of each of these words and phrases:

1 as long as
2 unless
3 provided

c Now go to Grammar Focus 2B on p.136

d Complete the sentences. There is more than one possible answer. Compare with other students.

1 Sharks won't attack you unless …
2 Wolves will only attack if …
3 Tarantulas won't bite you provided …
4 If you hit a crocodile on the nose …

3 LISTENING and VOCABULARY Animals and the environment

a *The Tiger* by John Vaillant tells the true story of a hunter and a Siberian tiger. Use the words in the box to guess what happened.

tiger	mattress	attacked	
hut	forest	wounded	shot
killed	boots		

b 1.34 Listen to an interview about the book. Was the story similar to yours?

c 1.34 Which of these questions *doesn't* Miles answer? Listen again and check.

1. Is a Siberian tiger bigger than other tigers?
2. How far can it jump?
3. Have many people been killed by Siberian tigers?
4. Can tigers plan ahead?

d 1.35 Listen to the second part of the interview. Tick (✓) the things Miles talks about.

1. his own feelings about the tiger
2. life in Siberia
3. the relationship between humans and tigers
4. tigers as an endangered species
5. how to survive a tiger attack

e Do you think Miles would agree with statements 1–5? Write *Yes* or *No*. Then explain why.

1. It's a good thing they killed the tiger.
2. The tiger was just behaving naturally.
3. Tigers have always caused problems for people in Siberia.
4. In some ways, humans are more dangerous than tigers.
5. We should hunt more tigers to keep them under control.

f Which of the words in the box can we use to talk about ... ?

1 animals 2 places

at risk creature endangered environment extinct
habitats hunt natural protected rare species

g 1.36 Complete the sentences with the words in 3f. Then listen and check your answers.

1. ... in eastern Siberia, one of the wildest and most ________ ________ on Earth.
2. Imagine a ________ that is as active as a cat and has the weight of an industrial refrigerator.
3. Humans and tigers ________ the same animals and share the same ________.
4. Tigers are ________ because of humans.
5. Tigers have become extremely ________.
6. There are 40 million humans but only 500 tigers, so they really are an ________ ________, and although they're ________, they could easily become ________ in a few decades.

4 SPEAKING

a A visitor is coming to stay in your country. Make notes about:

- endangered species and where you can see them
- dangerous animals or other creatures (e.g. birds, fish, insects)
- other possible risks or dangers (e.g. diseases, dangerous places, travel, weather)

b Imagine what you could tell the visitor and what advice you could give. How could you use the words in the box?

if as soon as in case unless as long as provided

c Work in pairs. Student A, talk about your country. Student B, you are the visitor. Ask Student A questions. Then change roles.

Take malaria tablets in case you get bitten by a mosquito.

Be careful of dogs if you go jogging.

2C Everyday English
What a great shot!

Learn to give and respond to compliments

S Giving compliments and responding
P Agreeing using question tags

1 LISTENING

a Discuss the questions.

1 Do you like taking photos? Why / Why not?
2 In your opinion, what makes a good photo?
3 Do you think you are good at taking photos? Why / Why not?

b Look at photo a and answer the questions.

1 What is Becky doing?
2 Why do you think she needs Tessa to help?

c 1.37 Watch or listen to Part 1. Check your answers.

d 1.37 Are the sentences true or false? Watch or listen again to check.

1 Becky asks Tessa to help her check the height of the tripod.
2 Becky is happy with the shots she takes.
3 Tessa wonders if it's necessary to use a lot of equipment.
4 Tessa wants to take a photo of a small animal.

2 CONVERSATION SKILLS Agreeing using question tags

a 1.37 Watch or listen again. How does Tessa respond to Becky's comment 'It's quite difficult'?

b Choose the correct word.

1 We can use statements with question tags to *agree / disagree* with someone.
2 Using a different adjective in the answer is more *interesting / friendly*.

c Complete B's answers with the correct verb forms.

1 **A** I think she's a lovely person.
B Yes, she's very charming, ____ she?
2 **A** Their instructions weren't very clear.
B No, they weren't helpful, ____ they?

d Complete the rule.

If the sentence is positive, we use a ____ tag. If the sentence is negative, we use a ____ tag.

e Complete B's replies. Use an adjective from the box in the first gap and the correct verb form in the second gap.

welcoming	soaking	breathtaking	worried

1 **A** Your clothes are all wet.
B Yes, they're ____, ____ they?
2 **A** The scenery there is exceptional.
B Yes, it's ____, ____ it?
3 **A** They weren't a very friendly group of people.
B No, they weren't ____ at all, ____ they?
4 **A** He looks a bit anxious.
B Yes, he does look ____, ____ he?

3 PRONUNCIATION Tone in question tags

a 1.38 Listen to the examples. Does the tone go up (↗) or down (↘) on the question tag? What's the difference in meaning?

1 No, it isn't very quick, is it?
2 No, they weren't helpful, were they?
3 Yes, you need to make things easy, don't you?

b Practise saying the exchanges in 2e. Try to use the correct tone in the reply.

c Discuss people and things you and other students know – for example, a person, a café, a film or a car. Use the adjectives below and question tags to agree.

- amusing – funny
- cheerful – happy
- interesting – fascinating
- frightening – terrifying
- exhausting – tiring

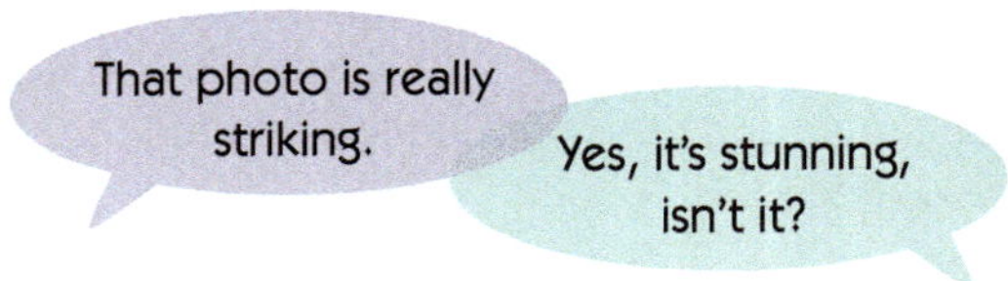

4 LISTENING

a Look at photo b of Becky and Tessa. Which approach to taking photographs would you prefer? Why?

b Look at the two photos of flowers. Which do you like best? Why?

Becky's photo

Tessa's photo

c 1.39 Watch or listen to Part 2. What are Becky and Tessa's opinions of their own photos?

d 1.39 Watch or listen to Part 2 again. Answer the questions.

1 How did Tessa start taking photos?
2 What do Becky and Tessa have trouble deciding?
3 What does Becky think about her photo of a squirrel? What does Tessa think?
4 Where do they go for coffee?

5 USEFUL LANGUAGE

Giving compliments and responding

a 1.40 Listen and complete the conversation.

BECKY _____ a _____ shot!
TESSA It's all _____.
BECKY You _____ just _____ to get a really good shot. The light is amazing.
TESSA Thanks. Guess it's _____ bad.

b Answer the questions about the conversation.

1 Do Becky's compliments sound excited?
2 Is Tessa's response grateful or neutral?

c Look at the bold words in compliments 1–4. Match them to the words and phrases in a–d.

1 That's a **lovely** picture!	a talented / skilled
2 You're so **good** at taking photos.	b excellent / amazing / beautiful / striking
3 I **love** the way you caught the light.	c were able to / succeeded in
4 You really **managed to** get it just right.	d really like / am impressed by

d Which of these responses are grateful and which are neutral?

Do you think so?
It's OK, I guess.
Thanks, I'm glad you like it.
I'm really pleased you like it.

e Work in pairs. Imagine you have both finished writing an essay and have read each other's essay. Use the ideas below to have a short conversation. Take turns to be A and B.

A

Tell your partner how easy/difficult it was to write the essay.

B

Agree with A using a question tag.

A

Say you've read your partner's essay and compliment him/her.

B

Respond gratefully.

6 SPEAKING

a Work alone. What compliments can you give to your classmates? Think about:

- things they do or make as hobbies
- their jobs
- things they have done in your English classes
- the clothes they are wearing.

b Talk to different students in your class. Give compliments and respond.

That's a really nice sweater you're wearing.
Thanks, It's not bad, is it?

Unit Progress Test

CHECK YOUR PROGRESS

You can now do the Unit Progress Test.

2D Skills for Writing
Make sure you know where you are going

Learn to write guidelines in a leaflet

W Organising guidelines in a leaflet

1 SPEAKING and LISTENING

a Discuss the questions.

1 When was the last time you went to some kind of natural environment?
2 What did you do there?
3 How did you prepare for your trip?

b 1.41 Listen to Luiza talking about an experience she had in Canada. Answer the questions.

1 Which natural environment does she talk about?
2 Near the beginning she says *I got in trouble*. What was the trouble?

c 1.41 Listen again and answer the questions.

1 Why did Luiza get lost?
2 How did she decide which way to go?
3 What helped her find the clearing?

d At the end, Luiza says: *I suddenly had this strange feeling I was not alone.* What do you think happened next? Discuss your ideas.

e 1.42 Listen to the continuation of Luiza's story. Were your ideas correct?

f 1.42 Listen again. Are the sentences true or false?

1 Luiza knew what to do.
2 She felt calm and wasn't afraid.
3 The helicopter saw Luiza the first time it flew over.
4 Luiza was surprised to find out she was close to the main track.

g What would you have done in Luiza's situation?

2 READING

a Think about Luiza's experience. Imagine you are going hiking in a forest. What do you need to remember in order to be safe?

b Read the leaflet *Be wise and survive*. Were your ideas similar? Put headings in spaces a–c in the leaflet. There is one extra heading.

1 In the forest
2 If you get lost
3 Identifying useful plants
4 Preparation

c Read the leaflet again. What should you ... ?

1 take with you when you go hiking
2 not do when you are hiking
3 do about food and drink if you are lost
4 do if you are lost: move around or stay in one place

Be wise and SURVIVE!

We all enjoy being in the great outdoors. There are lots of amazing environments, but some of them can be quite challenging, even dangerous, and it's important that you think about safety. Here are some simple guidelines to help you stay safe.

A ______________________________

1 Get a map of the area and make sure you know where you are going.
2 Check the weather forecast.
3 Wear clothes and shoes that are suitable for the conditions. If you think the weather may change suddenly, take extra clothing.
4 If you are going on a longer walk, take some emergency food with you.

B ______________________________

5 Provided you follow the signs, you shouldn't get into trouble.
6 Never take shortcuts unless you're absolutely sure where they go.
7 Allow plenty of time to get to your destination or get back before it gets dark.

C ______________________________

8 As soon as you realise you're lost, stop, keep calm and plan what you will do next.
9 Don't eat all your food at once. Have a little at a time.
10 Try to find a source of water you can drink from like a river or a stream. Being able to drink is more important than being able to eat.
11 Don't keep moving around. Find somewhere that is dry and get plenty of rest. It's easier for rescuers to find you if you stay in one place.
12 Always try to stay warm. You can cover yourself with dry plants.
13 If you need to keep moving, make sure you use rocks or pieces of wood as signs that show rescuers where you are going.
14 As long as you tell yourself you'll survive, you probably will!

3 WRITING SKILLS
Organising guidelines in a leaflet

a Notice these verb forms used in the leaflet.

1 ***Check** the weather forecast.* – positive imperative
2 ***Don't eat** all your food at once* – negative imperative
3 ***Never take** shortcuts …* – frequency adverb + imperative
4 ***If** you **think** the weather may change suddenly, **take** extra clothing.* – *if* + present tense + imperative

Find one more example of each verb form in the leaflet.

b Choose the correct answers.

1 What's the function of the verb forms in 3a?
  a to give advice
  b to make indirect suggestions
2 Why are those forms used?
  a to make the information clear and direct
  b to show hikers they have a strong obligation

c Correct the incorrect sentences.

1 Not eat any plants you don't recognise.
2 Never leave the main group of people you are hiking with.
3 If you will hear a rescue team, make lots of noise.
4 Always carries a pocket knife.
5 As soon as it starts getting dark, stop and think about what to do next.
6 If you have a map, take it with you.

4 WRITING

a Choose one of the situations in the box and make notes on advice you could include in a leaflet.

camping in a forest	backpacking in a foreign country
swimming in the sea	hiking in the mountains

b Write a leaflet for the situation you chose above. Remember to:

- use headings
- include the different imperative forms in 3a
- make the information clear and direct.

c Swap leaflets with another student. Does the leaflet include headings and different imperative forms? Is the information clear and direct? What improvements could be made?

d Give your leaflet to other students. Read other leaflets and decide which leaflet you think is the clearest and the most useful.

UNIT 2
Review and extension

1 GRAMMAR

a Complete the text with the verbs in brackets. Use the past simple, past continuous, past perfect or past perfect continuous forms.

The first time I [1] ______ (try) scuba diving [2] ______ (be) when I [3] ______ (live) in Cairns in North Queensland, Australia. I [4] ______ (travel) around the world and I [5] ______ (decide) to stop and work for a few months. I [6] ______ (be) on a gap year between finishing university and beginning work. Years before, someone [7] ______ (tell) me the best way to see the Coral Reef [8] ______ (be) by scuba diving. The diving I [9] ______ (do) on the Great Barrier Reef [10] ______ (be) fantastic. As I [11] ______ (dive) I [12] ______ (see) spectacular marine life.

b Make sentences by matching the halves. Put the linking expression in brackets in the correct place.

1 ☐ you won't find it difficult to learn to ski
2 ☐ you won't make much progress
3 ☐ you'll make steady progress
4 ☐ you won't be able to control your skis
5 ☐ you'll stay warm
6 ☐ you'll start making progress after a week

a	you can move your toes in your boots	(unless)
b	you're generally fit and healthy	(if)
c	you keep moving	(provided)
d	you choose an easy ski slope	(as long as)
e	you're patient with yourself	(provided)
f	you're prepared to fall down a lot at first	(unless)

2 VOCABULARY

a Correct the errors in the sentences.

1 I dropped my hat in the sea and it got swept by a wave away.
2 She couldn't get it over how hot it was.
3 He got trouble for being late.
4 I got feeling they didn't like guests.
5 She's now getting over it the shock of losing her job last week.
6 They're planning to get out to the countryside this weekend.

b Complete the words.

1 In North America, red wolves are considered an e __ __ __ __ __ __ __ __ __ s __ __ __ __ __ __ __.
2 In the UK, large blue butterflies are a __ r __ __ __ and are p __ __ __ __ __ __ __ __ __.
3 The New Zealand moa bird has been e __ __ __ __ __ __ __ for about six hundred years.
4 It's possible to find many Chinese alligators in zoos and research centres, but there are fewer living in their n __ __ __ __ __ __ __ h __ __ __ __ __ __ __.
5 In Australia, just over 20 per cent of the native plants are considered r __ __ __ and need to be conserved.

3 WORDPOWER *face*

a Match the examples 1–8 with the definitions a–h.

1 ☐ Although he said he enjoys the taste of the raw fish, he still **made a face**.
2 ☐ She **faced a difficult choice** between the two jobs she was offered.
3 ☐ Her **face fell** when I told her the painting was worthless.
4 ☐ I've been studying all day and I **can't face** doing my homework now.
5 ☐ It's not good news, but I feel I need to **say it to his face**.
6 ☐ We just have to **face the fact** that we haven't got enough money to buy a house.
7 ☐ I tripped on a loose brick and fell **flat on my face**.
8 ☐ I could tell my boss wasn't happy about the outcome. Now I have to talk to her and **face the music**.

a to be disappointed
b to accept another person's criticism or displeasure
c to accept an unpleasant situation
d to show from your expression that you don't like something
e to fall over badly and feel a bit embarrassed
f to make a difficult decision
g to say something directly to someone
h to not want to do something unpleasant

b In which of the expressions 1–8 is *face* used as a noun and in which as a verb?

c Which one of the following nouns doesn't collocate with *face*?

1 a problem	2 the truth	3 a difficult decision
4 the facts	5 a success	6 reality

d Add words to the gaps.

1 When did you last fall ______ on your face?
2 What was the last ______ choice you had to face?
3 What happened the last time you saw someone's face ______?
4 What's something difficult you've had to say ______ someone's face?
5 What can't you face ______ after class?
6 When was the last time you had to face ______ music?

e Ask and answer the questions in 3d.

REVIEW YOUR PROGRESS

How well did you do in this unit? Write 3, 2 or 1 for each objective.
3 = very well 2 = well 1 = not so well

I CAN ...

discuss dangerous situations	☐
give advice on avoiding danger	☐
give and respond to compliments	☐
write guidelines in a leaflet	☐

CAN DO OBJECTIVES

- Discuss ability and achievement
- Discuss sports activities and issues
- Make careful suggestions
- Write a description of data

UNIT 3
Talent

GETTING STARTED

a Look at the picture and answer the questions.

1 What are the people doing?
2 Why do you think three people are needed for the job?
3 What could the man on the left be thinking?

b Discuss the questions.

1 What makes something a work of art?
2 Do famous artists have natural talent? Or is their success due to luck, hard work or something else? Why do you think so?

3A I'm not very good in the morning

Learn to discuss ability and achievement

G Multi-word verbs
V Ability and achievement

1 LISTENING

a Think about how to learn something new. Do you agree or disagree with sentences 1–5? Why?

1 My teacher will get angry if I make mistakes.
2 Children learn faster than adults.
3 I must practise every day in order to make progress.
4 If something seems very easy, I must be doing it wrong.
5 Long practice sessions are best.

b 1.43 Listen to an experienced teacher talking about the same sentences. Are his ideas similar to yours? Do you agree with his ideas?

2 READING

a Discuss the questions.

1 How long does it take to learn something well?
2 What's the best time of day to learn something new?
3 How important is memory when we learn something new?

b Read *Learning to learn*. Match texts a–c with the questions in 2a.

c Read questions 1–6 from people who have to learn something. Use information in the texts to answer the questions.

1 I have to learn a lot of historical dates for an exam. What's a good way to do this?
2 I want to join a beginners' kickboxing class. Is it better to join the morning or afternoon class?
3 I know I have a natural talent for tennis. Do I need to practise hard to do well?
4 If I study first thing in the morning after my brain has rested, I'm sure I'll learn more. Do you agree?
5 I have to find out about the way car engines work, but the book I'm reading is really boring. Should I just stick with it?
6 I don't just want to be a good computer programmer – I want to be a brilliant one. What can I do to achieve that?

d Discuss the questions.

1 What information in the texts surprised you?
2 What information made sense to you?
3 Have you had any experience of the ideas discussed in the text?
4 Do you think you'll change your learning practice as a result of the information?

LEARNING TO LEARN

(a)

IT'S ALL ABOUT RHYTHM

Bodies and brains need time to warm up

'Early bird' or 'night owl', we all have different body clocks and rhythms. However, research is beginning to show that we're all quite similar in the way our minds and bodies behave at different times of the day. Understanding these rhythms helps us work out when's the best time to learn.

If learning means having to use your brain, the morning is the best time.

But not first thing. Our bodies and brains need time to warm up and our body temperature rises slowly from the moment we wake up. Between ten in the morning and midday, most people are at their best in terms of their ability to concentrate and learn.

If we want to learn something physical, then it pays to wait until the afternoon.

Between 2 pm and 6 pm our muscle strength is at its peak and our hand–eye coordination is very efficient. This means the afternoon is probably better for learning new sports or perhaps a new dance step.

3 VOCABULARY
Ability and achievement

a Look at the adjectives in bold and answer questions 1–4.

And when you look at all the people who are **outstanding** at what they do …
… they seem so much more **talented** …
…that's what it takes to become really **skilled**.
Those who became **exceptional** practised about two thousand hours more …
… in order to learn something and become very **successful** at doing it, all you'll need is about 10,000 hours!
Without a doubt, there are people who are **brilliant** at certain things …
All the musicians in the study had the **potential** to become world famous

1 Which two adjectives describe a good level of ability?
2 Which adjective describes a good level of achievement?
3 Which three adjectives describe a very high level of ability or achievement?
4 Look at the noun in bold in the last sentence. Are the musicians world famous now or are they likely to be in the future?

b Write the noun forms of the adjectives.

1 skilled ________
2 talented ________
3 brilliant ________
4 able ________

c Complete the sentences with the words in the box.

at for to (x2)

1 He's very talented _____ playing the guitar.
2 He has lots of potential _____ succeed in his career.
3 She's got a real talent _____ drawing.
4 She definitely has the ability _____ become a brilliant actor.

d Think of an example of someone who:

1 is skilled at some kind of sport or art
2 has a talent for some kind of musical instrument
3 is famous and you think is brilliant
4 you think is exceptional in their field
5 is the most successful person you know.

e Tell each other about your answers in 3d. Give reasons for your opinions.

b

GIVE ME STRENGTH
A new word suggests a picture

Isn't it strange how we can remember the words of a much loved poem that we learnt at primary school more than twenty years ago, but we can't remember where we left our keys about ten minutes ago? More than 130 years ago this problem caught the attention of the German psychologist Herman Ebbinghaus and he came up with a theory: the strength of memory.

Ebbinghaus believed that if we find new information interesting, then it'll probably be more meaningful to us. This makes the information easier to learn and also helps the strength of memory. It also helps if we associate the new information with something else. For example, a new word we learn might make us think of a picture. This association can also build memory strength.

Using associations to help us remember what we learn is known as 'mnemonics'. For example, some people are able to remember a long sequence of numbers because the shape of all those numbers reminds them of a specific physical shape such as a guitar. Mnemonic techniques are often used by competitors in the World Memory Championships held each year in London.

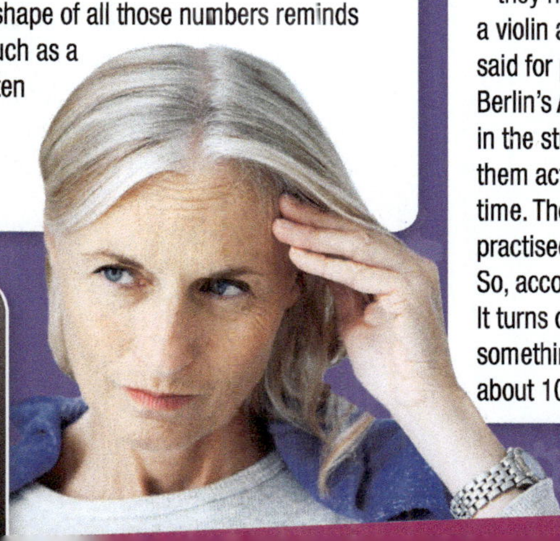

Popular spelling mnemonics:
BECAUSE
Big **E**lephants **C**an't **A**lways **U**se **S**mall **E**xits
HERE or HEAR?
We **hear** with our **ear**.

c

A QUESTION OF TALENT?
"All you'll need is about 10,000 hours!"

We've all had the experience of trying to learn something new only to find out that we're not very good at it. We look around at other people we're learning with and they seem so much more talented and are doing so much better. It seems to come naturally to them. And when you look at all the people who are outstanding at what they do – the really famous people who are superstars – all you see is natural ability. The conclusion seems obvious: talented people must be born that way.

Without a doubt, there are people who are brilliant at certain things – they have a talent for kicking a football around a field, or they pick up a violin and immediately make music. However, there's also a lot to be said for practice. Psychologist K. Anders Ericsson studied students at Berlin's Academy of Music. He found that even though all the musicians in the study had the potential to become world famous, only some of them actually did. What made the difference? The answer is simple: time. Those who became exceptional were more competitive and practised about two thousand hours more than those who only did well. So, according to Ericsson, that's what it takes to become really skilled. It turns out that practice really does make perfect, and in order to learn something and become very successful at doing it, all you'll need is about 10,000 hours!

4 LISTENING

a 1.44 Listen to Seamus, Fiona and Henry talk about their learning experiences. Answer the questions.

1 Who talks about … ?
   a the best time to learn
   b learning hours
   c the strength of memory
2 Do the speakers think the learning ideas they talk about work for them?

b 1.44 Listen again and make notes about the things they talk about.

1 Seamus
   a copying comics
   b friends
   c graphic design

2 Fiona
   a chemistry
   b system for remembering symbols
   c colleagues' attitudes

3 Henry
   a tour preparation
   b daily learning routine
   c results

c Whose ideas do you think make more sense? Why?

5 GRAMMAR Multi-word verbs

a What is the meaning of the multi-word verbs in bold? Which multi-word verb is most similar to the verb on its own?

1 All of my friends **were** also really **into** comic books, but none of them tried to **come up with** their own stories.
2 … so we decided to **try** it **out**

b Now go to Grammar Focus 3A on p.138

6 SPEAKING

a Think of something you've done that you have put a lot of effort into. For example:

- your job
- a free-time activity
- study of some kind
- playing a musical instrument
- learning a language

Make notes about these questions:
1 What special skills or talent do you need?
2 What level of ability do you think you have achieved?
3 How have you learnt new information necessary for this activity?
4 Do you need to remember a lot of things to do this well?
5 How much time have you put into it?

b Work in small groups. Tell each other about your activity. Ask questions.

c Who in your group do you think has put in the most effort? Who has been successful?

3B There are lots of good runners in Kenya

Learn to discuss sports activities and issues

G Present perfect simple and continuous
V Words connected with sport

1 READING

a Look at the pictures. What sports do they show? How many of the people do you recognise?

b What do you think makes a successful athlete or sportsperson? Choose the five things in the box you think are most important. Are there any you think are unimportant?

attitude   general level of fitness   luck
desire for money   genetic make-up
support from the community   technique
parents   training and practice

c Compare your ideas with other students.

d Read the text *Born to be the best* about professionals in four sports. In what way are they all similar?

e Read the text again and answer the questions about each sport.

1 What sport is it?
2 Who is given as an example?
3 What unusual features are mentioned?
4 What is the result?

f Which of the things in 1b are mentioned in the text? Do you think this is important for all sports activities or only for top professional players?

Born to be THE BEST

CHAMPION SKIER

Champion cross-country skier Eero Mäntyranta had an unusual gene which made him produce too many red blood cells. Cross-country skiers cover long distances and their red blood cells have to send oxygen to their muscles. Mäntyranta had about 65% more red blood cells than the normal adult male and that's why he performed so well. In the 1960, 1964, and 1968 Winter Olympic Games, he won a total of seven medals. In 1964, he beat his closest competitor in the fifteen-kilometre race by forty seconds.

RECORD HIGH JUMP

On the seventh high jump of his life, Donald Thomas cleared 2.22 m. The next year, after only eight months of training, Thomas won the world championships. How did he achieve this victory? Not from training. He had unusually long legs and an exceptionally long Achilles tendon, which acted as a kind of spring, shooting him high into the air when he jumped.

THE WORLD'S BEST RUNNERS

Why do so many of the world's best distance runners come from Kenya and Ethiopia? Because a runner needs not just to be thin, but also to have thin legs and ankles. Runners from the Kalenjin tribe, in Kenya – where most of the country's best athletes come from – are thin in exactly this way. Compared to Europeans, Kalenjins are shorter but have longer legs, and their lower legs are half a kilo lighter.

BASEBALL PRO

Professional baseball players have, as a group, remarkable eyesight. A typical baseball professional can see at seven metres what the rest of us can see at four metres. This means that, however much they trained, only a tiny proportion of the population would be able to do what professional baseball players can do naturally: see a ball that is travelling towards them at 150 km an hour.

2 VOCABULARY

Words connected with sport

a Find words in the texts which have a similar meaning to the words in italics.

1 Eero Mäntyranta was a cross-country skier *who often won competitions*.
2 He *did* so well because he had more red blood cells than most skiers.
3 He easily beat the closest *person competing with him*.
4 Before the world high jump *competition*, Thomas only had eight months of *practice*.
5 Thomas achieved a great *win*.
6 Most of Kenya's best *sportspeople* are from the Kalenjin tribe.
7 Baseball players *who play for a living* have very good eyesight.

b Now go to Vocabulary Focus on p.156

3 LISTENING

a 1.48 The texts in 1d are from a book called *The Sports Gene*. Listen to the first part of a programme in which people discuss the book. Answer the questions.

1 What do we know about Barbara McCallum?
2 What does she think of the ideas in the book?

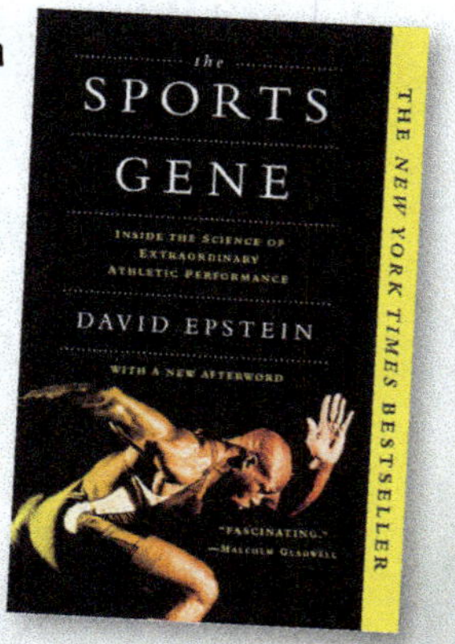

b 1.48 Answer the questions. Then listen again and check.

1 What is the main message of the book?
   a The best athletes are often genetically different from most other people.
   b There is a particular gene which makes you a good athlete.
   c Being a good athlete is mainly a question of luck.
2 Which of these factors does Barbara say are important in Kenyans' success in running?
   a They start running at an early age.
   b Many people have long legs.
   c Children learn to run in bare feet.
   d They train for hours every day.

c 1.49 Listen to the second part of the programme and answer the questions.

1 What do we know about Marta Fedorova?
2 What does she think of the ideas in the book?

d 1.49 Listen again and discuss the questions.

1 What does Marta notice about the people she has played against?
2 What conclusion does she reach from that?
3 In what way does she say sporting events like the Olympics are 'unfair'?
4 Do you agree with her conclusion? Why / Why not?

4 GRAMMAR

Present perfect simple and continuous

a Match sentences 1–4 with the uses of the present perfect simple and continuous (a–d).

1 ☐ You**'ve been playing** tennis since you were a child.
2 ☐ **I've** also **read** the book.
3 ☐ **I've been thinking** a lot about this recently.
4 ☐ **I've lived** in Kenya myself.

a to talk about a recent completed action, e.g. *I've lost my glasses.*
b to talk about an activity that started in the past and is still continuing, e.g. *We've been waiting since this morning.*
c to talk about an experience at some unspecified time in your life, e.g. *He's climbed Mount Everest.*
d to talk about a recent activity which continued for a while (which may or may not still be continuing), e.g. *I've been reading a lot of good books lately.*

b Now go to Grammar Focus 3B on p.138

c Add a sentence using the present perfect simple or continuous.

1 I don't think I could play squash any more. I …
I haven't played it for years.
2 She's really fit. She …
3 Of course I can play chess. I …
4 Why don't you buy a new pair of skis? You …

d Think about a sport (or other free time activity) that you have been doing for some time. Make notes about questions 1–4.

1 How good are you at it?
2 How long have you been doing it? Why did you start?
3 What are the main reasons you've become good at it (or haven't!)? Is it more to do with … ?
- your genetic make-up and natural ability
- developing technique and practising
- support from other people

4 Do you think any of the things you have read or heard in this lesson are relevant to the activity you've been doing?

e Tell other students about your activity

5 READING and SPEAKING

a Read about two famous US baseball players and answer the questions.

1 How are they similar?
2 How are they different?

b Think about the questions.

If 'sport isn't as fair as we like to think', should players be allowed to find ways to improve their performance? Which of these ways do you think are acceptable? Why?

- training hard
- having an operation (e.g. replacing arm muscles, improving eyesight)
- taking legal substances to enhance their performance (e.g. energy drinks)
- taking illegal substances to enhance their performance (e.g. drugs)

c Compare your ideas. Do you agree?

CASE STUDY: TOMMY JOHN

Tommy John is one of the best-loved figures in American baseball. In 1974, after an injury to his arm, he was the first player ever to have an operation to replace the muscles of his right arm with artificial ones. After his operation, he went on to win 164 games, more than he did before science helped to improve his performance. His 'bionic arm' enabled him to win at least 20 games a season. He had one of the longest careers in baseball history, retiring at the age of 46, and is regarded by the public as a sporting hero. Since then, at least a third of major-league baseball players have had the same operation, now known as 'Tommy John surgery'.

CASE STUDY: ALEX RODRIGUEZ

Alex Rodriguez is well known among baseball fans in the USA. He's one of the best baseball professionals of all time and the youngest player ever to hit 500 home runs. But he's also well known for a different reason. Between 2001 and 2003, under pressure to keep up his performance in the American League and to help him recover from an injury, he took steroids, which are an illegal drug under the rules of the League. He has since been suspended, but has tried to appeal against his suspension and return to the game. He is now one of the most hated figures in American baseball.

3C Everyday English
Who should we invite?

Learn to make careful suggestions

S Keeping to the topic of the conversation
P Consonant sounds

1 LISTENING

a Discuss the questions.

1 What kind of events do people usually celebrate?
2 Do you prefer small or big celebrations? Why?

b Look at photo a and answer the questions.

1 Where do you think Becky and Tom have been?
2 What do you think has happened?

c 1.51 Watch or listen to Part 1 and check your ideas in 1b.

d 1.51 Watch or listen again. Tick (✓) the topics that Becky and Tom talk about.

photographs Becky has taken   Tom's colleagues
dinner   Becky's café job   Tom's promotion
Becky's classmate, Tessa

e 1.51 Watch or listen again. What do they say about the topics?

f 1.52 Watch or listen to Part 2. What wedding plans do Becky and Tom talk about?

g 1.52 Watch or listen to Part 2 again and answer the questions.

1 What's the first decision they have to make?
2 Who seems more focused on wedding plans? Why do you think so?

2 CONVERSATION SKILLS Keeping to the topic of the conversation

a Read this conversation from Part 2. How does Becky return to the original topic of the conversation? Underline the expression she uses.

BECKY So when are you going to tell your parents about your promotion?
TOM At the weekend, I think. We're seeing them on Saturday, remember?
BECKY Oh yes. Anyway, as I was saying – about Tessa …
TOM Tessa, yes, your classmate …

b Join words from A and B to make expressions.

A	B
as I	were saying …
to go/get	back to …
just	was saying …
as we	getting/going back to …

c We can put two of these words before the expressions in 2b. Which words are they?

so   actually   oh   anyway

d Work in pairs. Have short conversations. You need to agree on an English language study plan and organise what to study, how much to study, when, etc.

Student A: Explain your ideas for your study plans. Make sure you keep to the topic of the conversation.
Student B: Answer your partner's questions about the study plans, but keep trying to change the topic of conversation to something else.

Swap roles.

I think we should start with vocabulary.
Why don't we go to the café first?
As I was saying, we should start with …

3 PRONUNCIATION

Sounds and spelling: Consonant sounds

a Look at the examples from Parts 1 and 2. Underline words that begin with the sounds in the box.

/b/ /f/ /g/ /k/ /p/ /v/

1 I've gradually got better …
2 … guests, a venue for the reception, the cake.
3 But don't you agree that she'd be perfect …
4 We'll need a photographer.

b 1.53 Listen to these two words. Which begins with a voiced sound? Which begins with an unvoiced sound?

better people

Do you use your lips differently in the /b/ and /p/ sounds?

c 1.54 Listen to six words. Which word do you hear in each pair?

1 bill / pill	3 van / fan	5 lap / lab
2 goat / coat	4 leave / leaf	6 bag / back

d Work in pairs. Take turns saying one word from each pair. Which word does your partner say?

4 LISTENING

a 1.55 Watch or listen to Part 3. What is the main topic of Becky and Tom's conversation?

1 food for the wedding
2 their wedding clothes
3 the guests they'll invite

b 1.55 Watch or listen again. What do they say about the topics below? Make notes.

1 Aunt Clare
2 Uncle Fred
3 Tom's colleagues
4 Regent's Lodge
5 after they get married

5 USEFUL LANGUAGE

Making careful suggestions

a 1.56 Becky and Tom make careful suggestions to each other. Can you remember the missing words?

BECKY We ______ ______ invite them to the evening reception.
TOM But don't you agree that it'd ______ ______ not to invite them?

Listen and check.

b Why do Becky and Tom make careful suggestions? Choose the best answer.

1 They feel the subject-matter is a bit sensitive and they don't want to offend each other.
2 The wedding won't happen for a few months, so it doesn't feel real to them.

c Look at these examples of careful suggestions. Match the examples to the correct uses below.

a Don't you think it's a good idea to … ?
b How does it sound if we/I … ?
c Another idea might be to …
d I think maybe we should …
e I thought maybe we could …

1 Putting forward an idea carefully
2 Asking the other person to give their point of view

d Correct the careful suggestions.

1 Another idea might to be booking a DJ for the reception.
2 Don't you think a good idea to invite more people?
3 Maybe I thought we could get married at home.
4 How does it sound we only have a small cake?

e Communication 3C Student A: Go to p.131. Student B: Go to p.129.

6 SPEAKING

a You are going to have a class party. Work alone and think of ideas for the party.

- when
- where
- party theme and music
- food and drinks

b Discuss your ideas and make careful suggestions. Make sure everyone keeps to the topic of the conversation.

We could always do it at college.

Another idea might be to rent a hall.

Unit Progress Test

CHECK YOUR PROGRESS

You can now do the Unit Progress Test.

3D Skills for Writing
It doesn't matter what sport people choose

Learn to write a description of data

W Describing data

1 SPEAKING and LISTENING

a Discuss the questions.

1. What's the most unusual sport you've ever seen or heard of? Have you tried it?
2. What do you think are the most popular sports in your country to participate in? Why do you think they are popular?
3. How do you think new sports become popular?

b Look at photos 1–3. What are the names of the sports? Which of these sports have you tried? Which would you like to try?

c 1.57 Marco talks to three people at a sports complex: Lizzie, Barry and Patricia. Listen and match the speakers to the sports in the photos.

d 1.57 Listen again and make notes for each speaker:

1. reasons for choosing their sport
2. experience of the sport
3. future plans

e Are any of these sports popular in your country? Why / Why not?

2 READING

a Look at the bar chart. Are the sentences true or false?

1. The data only shows information about people who take part in sports.
2. The data doesn't give information about children's sport participation.
3. The data shows every year between 2005 and 2013.
4. Most of the sports have more participation in 2012/2013 than in 2005/2006.

Once-a-week sport participation – top five UK sports. 18 years and over.

b Read the article *A nation of armchair athletes*. Does the article give the same information as the bar chart?

c Read the article again and answer the questions.

1. Does the writer think the major sporting event encouraged people to take part in sports?
2. Does the information represent only five sports?
3. What piece of information did the writer not expect?
4. What possible reason does the writer give for the increased interest in cycling?
5. What change does the writer mention in the final paragraph?

3 WRITING SKILLS
Describing data

a Match the summaries with the paragraphs (a–e) in the article. Which paragraph ... ?

1. ☐ states the main conclusion you can draw from the data
2. ☐ adds extra information not shown in the data
3. ☐ interprets the data in more detail
4. ☐ outlines the issue that the article and the data is about
5. ☐ explains what the bar chart is about

b Look at paragraph d in the article again and complete the table.

	Adjective	Noun
there is a/an	1_____	increase
	obvious	2_____
	3_____ / 4_____	decrease
	Verb	Adverb
the number(s)/ size	has/have increased	5_____ / 6_____
	7_____	significantly

c Notice *This* in paragraph d in the text. Answer the questions.

1 Does it refer back or forward to other information in the paragraph?
2 How is information organised in the paragraph?
   a data followed by a comment
   b a comment followed by data

d Use the data about a British city to write sentences. Use language from 3b.

1 People playing tennis: 2014 = 18%; now = 22%
2 Number of football teams: 1 year ago = 53; now = 39
3 Gym memberships: 2014 = 21%; now = 33%
4 Number of volleyball teams: 2 years ago = 26; now = 23

4 WRITING

a Look at the bar chart and read the notes below. What does the information show?

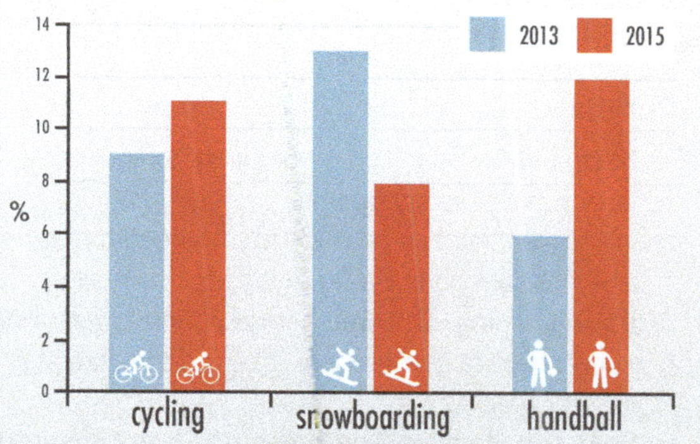

Once-a-week sport participation – top three sports at Market Street Sports Complex. 14 years and over.

cycling – now more popular in the UK
snowboarding – snowboards quite expensive and expensive to go abroad
handball – local teams have been winning games

b Work in pairs. Plan an article about the data and notes in 4a. Then write your article.

c Swap your article with another pair. Does the article use language from 3b correctly? Does it include verbs and nouns? Does it have the same organisation as 3a? Was it easy to understand?

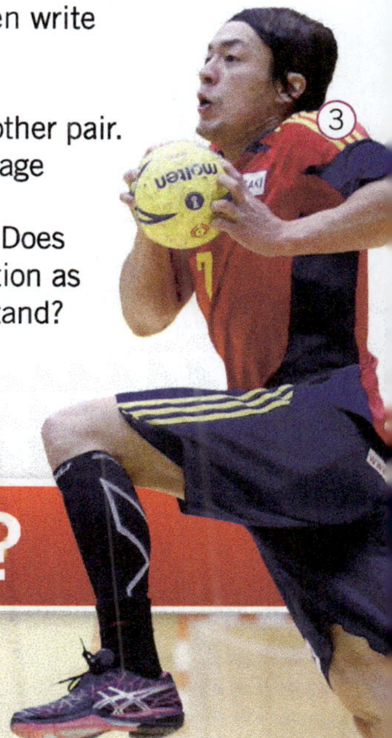

A nation of armchair athletes?

ᵃThere's no doubt that international sporting events are good for sport. There's always huge interest in them and people are glued to their TV sets watching different events. Of course, this is all about watching sports, but does it also mean that people get off the sofa and actually take part in sports?

ᵇThe bar chart looks at the five most popular sports in the UK in terms of people participating – not just sitting around and watching them on TV. One point to note is that all these sports include a range of activities. So, for example, 'swimming' also includes the sports of diving, water polo and deep water diving, while 'football' includes five-a-side games as well as full teams. The results in the graph show percentages of people who actively participate in that sport at least once a week.

ᶜThe blue and the red columns make a direct comparison between the year from October 2005 to October 2006 and a similar period in 2012/2013, just after a major sporting event. As you can see, the statistics show there has been no sudden increase in British people getting actively involved in sport.

ᵈIn fact, most surprising of all, there's a significant decrease in the number of people getting involved in swimming, the number one sport in the UK. You can see that there has also been an obvious change in the number of people wanting to go out and kick a football. There's a slight decrease in the number of people playing golf although participation hasn't decreased significantly. The most noticeable increase in sport participation can be seen in athletics. Perhaps this is because athletics features regularly at international sporting events. It also requires very little equipment initially, so can be a low-cost sport. Interest in cycling has also increased slightly. *This* might be because cycling includes BMX and cross-country, which makes this a very varied sport. Cycling enthusiasts have reported that interest in different kinds of cycling has increased noticeably in recent years.

ᵉIt's important to remember that the information in the table only focuses on the five most popular sports in the UK. Recent reports show that British people are becoming interested in a wide range of sports and are taking up activities like snowboarding and handball. It doesn't really matter what sport people choose to get involved in – the key thing is that they get out of their armchairs and take part.

UNIT 3
Review and extension

1 GRAMMAR

a Put the words in italics in the correct order.

1 I didn't know Spanish before I went to Mexico but I managed to *up / pick / it* very quickly.
2 I'm just as good as you. There's no need to *me / down / look / on* just because I didn't go to university.
3 It's still raining. This weather is starting to *get / down / me*.
4 I don't believe she was ever married to a film star. I think she *it / up / making / is*.
5 She's very creative. She keeps *up / with / coming* new ideas.
6 I don't know how to do this task. I just can't *out / figure / it*.

b Choose the correct verb tenses in these conversations.

1 **A** Come in. Sorry the flat is such a mess.
B What have you [1]*done / been doing*? There are things all over the floor.
A I've [2]*sorted / been sorting* things out but I haven't quite [3]*finished / been finishing* yet.
2 **A** How are things? I haven't [4]*seen / been seeing* you for ages. What have you [5]*done / been doing*?
B Oh, nothing much. I've got exams next month so I've [6]*studied / been studying* most of the time.

c Think of things you could say in answer to these questions using the present perfect simple or continuous.

- What have you been doing these days?
- How's your family?
- You're looking fit. Have you been doing a lot of sport?
- So what's new?

d Have conversations, starting with the questions in 1c.

2 VOCABULARY

a Rewrite the sentences, using the word in brackets, so that they keep the same meaning.

1 We're looking for someone who can lead a team of researchers. (ability)
2 She can design things very well. (skilled)
3 The members of the band all play music extremely well. (outstanding)
4 He could become a very good politician. (potential)
5 He's better than most goalkeepers. (exceptional)
6 My sister can cook very well. (brilliant)

b Give a different form of the words in italics to complete the definitions

1 Someone who *trains* sportsmen is a trainer.
2 A person who *competes* in a sport is a ________ .
3 The sporting activity that *athletes* do is called ________ .
4 Someone who does sport as a *profession* is a ________ sportsperson.
5 If you *perform* well, you give a good ________ .
6 A team that wins a *victory* is ________ .

3 WORDPOWER *up*

a Match the comments with the pictures. Where are the people and why are they saying this?

1 ☐ '**Drink up**. We need to go.'
2 ☐ 'Could you **speak up**? We can't hear you.'
3 ☐ 'I've **used up** the shampoo. Is there any more?'
4 ☐ 'Let me see the bill. I think they've **added** it **up** wrongly.'

b Adding *up* often gives an extra meaning to a verb. In which examples in 1a does *up* mean … ?

a to the end b together c louder

c What does *it* mean in each example below?

a suggestion a language a glass a word

1 You dropped it so I think you should **clear** it **up**.
2 I don't know. I'll have to **look** it **up**.
3 It was easy. I **picked** it **up** in about six months.
4 Why don't you **bring** it **up** at the meeting?

d 1.58 Listen and check your answers. What was the problem in each case?

e Here are some more multi-word verbs with *up*. Match the two parts of the sentences.

1 Walk more slowly! I can't	**look up to** him.
2 He's a good father. His children really	**turned up**.
3 We invited 50 people, but only a few	**put up with** it.
4 He's so rude. I don't know why people	**keep up with** you.

f Match the multi-word verbs in 3e with these meanings.

a tolerate
b go at the same speed
c appear or arrive
d admire or respect

g Work in pairs. Choose two of the multi-word verbs in 3a, c or e. Think of a situation and write a short conversation which includes both verbs.

h Act out your conversation. Can other students guess your situation?

REVIEW YOUR PROGRESS

How well did you do in this unit? Write 3, 2 or 1 for each objective.
3 = very well 2 = well 1 = not so well

I CAN …

discuss ability and achievement	☐
discuss sports activities and issues	☐
make careful suggestions	☐
write a description of data	☐

CAN DO OBJECTIVES

- Discuss events that changed your life
- Discuss and describe rules
- Describe photos
- Write an email to apply for work

UNIT 4

Life lessons

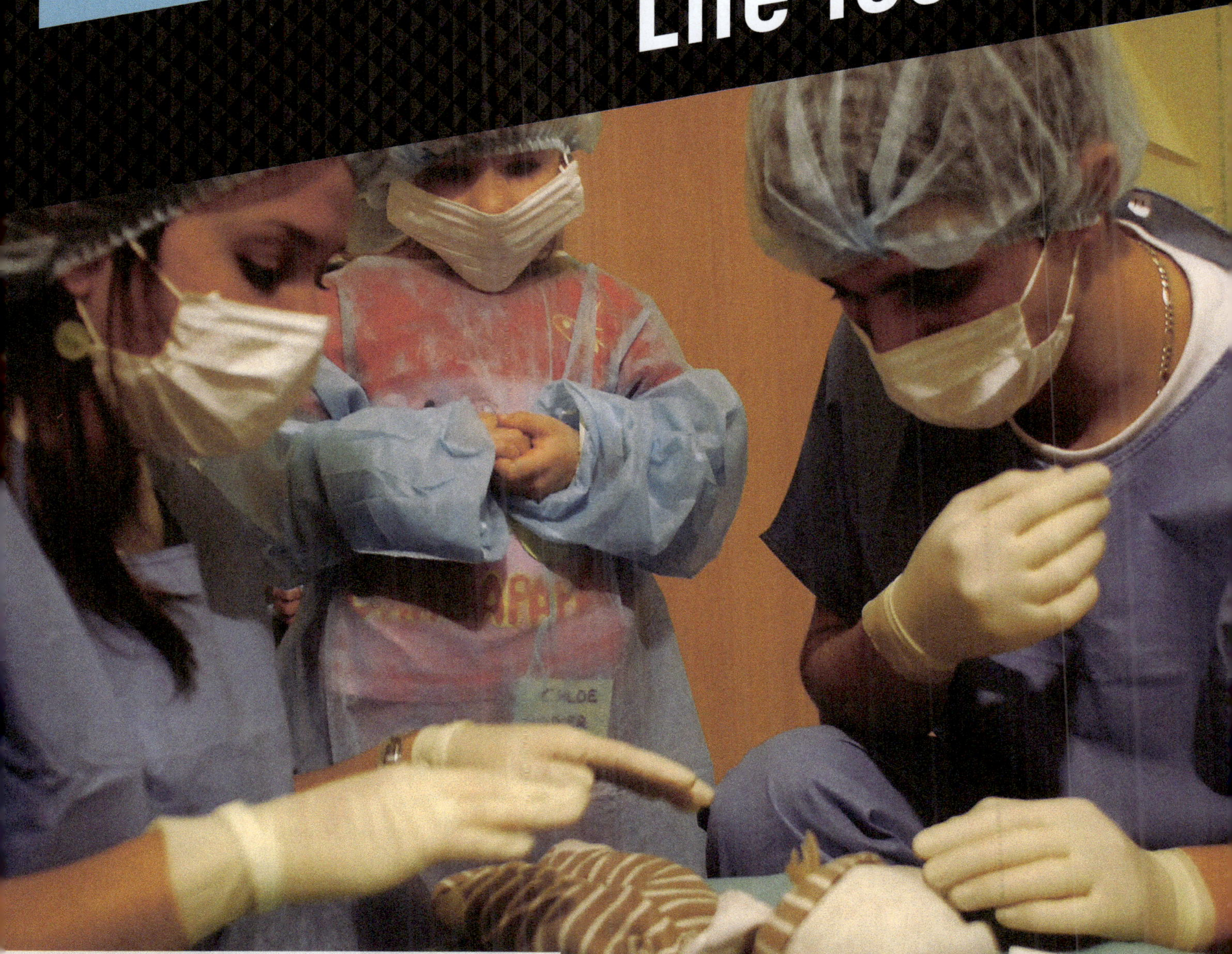

GETTING STARTED

a Look at the picture and answer the questions.

1 Where are these people? What are they doing?
2 What is the girl thinking?
3 Why do you think they're doing this?

b Discuss the questions.

1 Is it important to help children prepare for what might happen to them later in life. Why?
2 Which of your childhood experiences have had an impact on your adult life?
3 In general, how far do you think experiences in childhood influence the choices you make in your life?

4A She's happier now than she used to be

Learn to discuss events that changed your life

G *used to* and *would*

V Cause and result

1 SPEAKING

a Imagine you suddenly became very rich, either by winning or inheriting money. How would you spend the money if you had … ?

a $10,000 b $100,000 c $1,000,000

b Read the headlines a–c.

1 What do you think happened to these people?
2 Do you know anyone (either people you know or people you have read about) who has won or inherited money? What did they do with the money?

(a) **£1.8 MILLION LOTTERY WIN WRECKED MY LIFE**

(b) **'HOW I SPENT MY PRIZE MONEY'**
Nigerian Idol Season III winner, Moses Obi

(c) **HOMELESS BROTHERS INHERIT $7 BILLION**
Zsolt Pelardi: 'Maybe we can finally have a normal life'

2 READING

a Read the first part of two texts about people who won the lottery. What do you think the people did? Which person do you think spent the money most wisely?

b The words in the boxes give an outline of each story.

Sharon Tirabassi:
wild shopping huge house family friends electric bike happier kids pay day family values

Ihsan Khan:
taxi driver dream number Mercedes mansions mayor earthquake school satisfied parliament

Find words in the boxes which mean:

1 the day when you get money from your job
2 large luxury houses
3 a sudden movement of the earth
4 the people who make the laws of the country
5 children
6 pleased that you have got what you wanted
7 the leader of the city government
8 traditional principles of being honest and decent

c What do you think each person's story is?

HOW TO SPEND A $10 MILLION LOTTERY WIN IN LESS THAN THREE YEARS

Nine years after winning $10.5 million in the lottery, Sharon Tirabassi is back catching the bus to her part-time job. She's working to support her kids in their rented house in northeast Hamilton, USA. Tirabassi, one of this city's biggest lotto winners, has gone from being super rich to living from week to week.

LOTTO WINNER TAKES HOME FORTUNE TO PAKISTAN

People who win the lottery usually spend their money on things they've always wanted: a dream holiday or a beautiful house. But Ihsan Khan had a different idea. He kept his money and brought it back to Battagram, the town in Pakistan where he grew up.

d ▶ **Communication 4A** Student A: Read the story of Sharon Tirabassi on p.128 and answer the questions. Student B: Read the story of Ihsan Khan on p.130 and answer the questions.

e Work in the same pairs. Take turns to tell your stories and include the keywords in 2b. Ask questions about your partner's story to check anything you don't understand.

f Discuss the questions.

1. What sensible decisions do you think Sharon and Ihsan made? What poor decisions did they make?
2. Why do you think they made these decisions?
3. Which moral or 'message' comes out of these stories for you? Write it down and compare your idea with other students.

Be careful what you wish for!

Believe in your dreams.

If you have lots of money, don't go to Las Vegas!

3 GRAMMAR

used to and *would*

a Look at sentences a–c and complete the rules with the words in the box.

a Ihsan Khan **used to** work as a taxi driver and security guard in the USA.
b He **used to** think he could use his money to fix everything.
c She **would** regularly go on shopping trips where she **would** buy anything she fancied.

now	past	used to (x2)	would (x2)

We use *used to* and *would* to talk about things in the [1]_____ which are no longer true [2]_____.
To talk about states, thoughts and feelings in the past, we can only use [3]_____, not [4]_____.
To talk about habits and repeated actions, we can use either [5]_____ or [6]_____.

b Find and underline other examples of *used to* and *would* in the texts.

c Look at the sentences and answer the questions.

a Today, the Tirabassi family **don't** live in a huge house **any more**.
b He used to think he could use his money to fix everything, but he **no longer** believes that.

1. What do the words in bold mean?
   (a) things are the same as before
   (b) things are different now
2. Rewrite sentence a with *no longer* and sentence b with *not any more*. How does the word order change?

d ▶ Now go to Grammar Focus 4A on p.140

4 LISTENING

a You are going to listen to an interview with Monica Sharpe, a researcher into the psychology of money. How do you think she will answer these questions?

1. Does winning lots of money make you behave badly?
2. Does having lots of money make you happy?
3. Does buying things make you happy?

b 2.5 Listen and check your answers.

c 2.5 Tick (✓) the points Monica makes. Listen again and check.

1. Most people who get a lot of money spend it all quickly.
2. We enjoy hearing stories about people who won the lottery and then lost all their money.
3. Suddenly having lots of money usually has a negative effect on you.
4. Most people feel much happier just after they win money.
5. In the long term, being rich doesn't always make you happier.
6. It's better to spend money on things you can own, like houses and cars.

d Which of the points in 4c do you agree with? Can you think of examples from people you know or have heard about?

5 VOCABULARY Cause and result

a 2.6 Underline the correct expressions in bold. Then listen and check your answers.

1 Of course people like to believe that winning money leads **into** / **to** disaster.
2 The idea that winning a lot of money **causes** / **is caused by** misery is actually a myth.
3 Suddenly having a lot of money is just as likely to have a positive effect **on** / **to** you as a negative effect.
4 They measured how happy people are as a result **from** / **of** winning the lottery.
5 Getting richer doesn't actually **effect** / **affect** how happy you are.
6 But spending money on experiences usually results **in** / **on** longer-term happiness.

b Answer the questions about the expressions in 5a.

1 Which expressions have a similar meaning to 'causes'?
2 Which expression has a similar meaning to 'caused by'?
3 What is the difference between *affect* and *effect*?
4 Look at sentences 4 and 6. In which sentence is *result* a verb and in which is it a noun?

c Complete the sentences with the words in the box.

affect effect cause lead result (x2)

1 He's much friendlier than he used to be. Getting married has had a positive _____ on him.
2 Having no money at all can often _____ to problems in a relationship.
3 I hear John and Barbara have split up. I hope it won't _____ our friendship with them.
4 It's well known that smoking can _____ cancer.
5 Hundreds of villagers' lives were saved as a _____ of Ihsan Khan's help.
6 Be careful! Borrowing large amounts of money can _____ in serious financial problems.

d Think about an important event in your own life, and another event that happened as a result. Write three sentences about it using expressions in 5a.

e Read your sentences to each other and ask questions.

6 LISTENING

a Look at the information about Alphonso and Dragana. How do you think their lives have changed? Think about:

lifestyle attitude to life daily routine work money leisure

b 2.7 Listen to Alphonso and Dragana. Which of the topics in 6a do they talk about?

c 2.7 Are the sentences true or false? Correct the false sentences. Listen again and check.

Alphonso
1 They both used to work.
2 They didn't have much money.
3 The baby hasn't changed his attitude to life much.

Dragana
4 She's from a big city in Croatia.
5 She didn't enjoy being in Berlin.
6 The experience has changed her attitude to other cultures.

7 SPEAKING

a Think about yourself now and how you have changed in the last 10 years. Make notes on some of these topics:

- work
- free time
- attitude to life
- daily routine
- family and relationships
- money

b Tell each other how you think you have changed using *used to* / *would*.

4B We weren't allowed to talk in class

Learn to discuss and describe rules

G Obligation and permission
V Talking about difficulty

1 SPEAKING

a Look at photos a–d. What kind of training do you think is needed for these jobs? Which training would be the hardest?

b Read what these people say about training. Do you agree with their opinions?

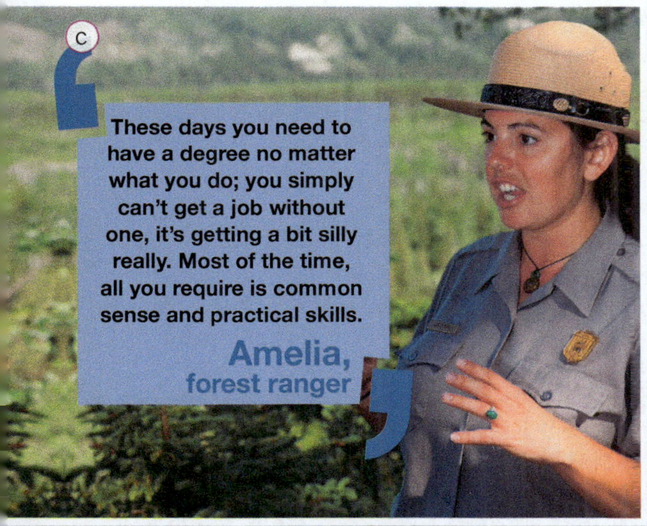

2 GRAMMAR 1 Modality review

a Underline all the modal verbs or phrases (e.g. *can*, *have to*) in the quotes.

b Complete the rules with the correct modal verb or phrase in 2a.

1 We use ________, ________ and ________ when we talk about something that's necessary.
2 We use ________ to talk about something that isn't necessary.
3 We use ________ when we talk about something that's possible.
4 We use ________ to talk about something that's not possible.

3 READING

a Look at photos a–d and answer the questions.

1 What jobs are shown in the photos?
2 What kind of training might you need for this work?

b Read the texts. Were your ideas correct?

c Read the texts again. Who do you think would say this, someone at the Peking Opera School (P) or someone doing Swiss Guard training (S)?

1 The easiest class was learning how to act.
2 I feel part of an on-going history.
3 I had no problems being accepted as I'm very tall.
4 I often feel exhausted.
5 I can't remember the words of that song.
6 My parents didn't have to pay for my training – I did later on.
7 I get asked some very silly questions.
8 This sword is very uncomfortable to wear.

d Which of the two kinds of training seems harder to you? Which one would you choose to do? Why?

4 VOCABULARY Talking about difficulty

a All the adjectives in bold, except for one, describe something that is *very* difficult. Which adjective is not as strong as the others?

The training was **punishing**.
Discipline was very **strict**.
Teachers could be quite **tough**.
He described his time at school as '**arduous**'.
It's not likely to be quite as **gruelling** as Jackie Chan's training.
Those lucky enough to be selected go through **rigorous** training.
Sometimes they might need to use force to resolve a **tricky** situation.

TRAINING TO BE THE BEST

BECOMING JACKIE CHAN

How do you get to be the next Jackie Chan? Most people think you should find a martial arts master and learn all their secrets. Jackie Chan's training was in a Peking Opera School in Hong Kong. These schools used to train people for traditional Chinese theatre and apart from the acrobatics and martial arts, students also learnt speech, song and dance.

The training was **punishing**. Students would rise at 5 am and train for at least ten hours. Discipline was very **strict** and teachers could be quite **tough**.

Jackie Chan, who did his training in the 1960s, described his time at school as '**arduous**'. Students had to repeat exercises again and again until they got them right. At the same time, they would need to learn traditional character roles used in Chinese theatre.

Students were sent to Peking Opera Schools when they were children. They would stay at the school and were given food and accommodation as well as training. This meant that they built up a debt that they had to repay once they began performing in Chinese theatre. They were forced to sign a contract agreeing to this.

During the 1960s, interest in traditional Chinese theatre declined and the schools closed down. Today there are still academies in China that offer a mixture of the study of and training in Peking opera. However, it's not likely to be quite as **gruelling** as Jackie Chan's training.

THE VOICE IS A WEAPON

Imagine getting up each day and going to work back in the sixteenth century. That's probably what it feels like for guards around the Vatican City, the people who are dressed in the amazing uniforms from the Renaissance that you can see in the pictures.

These people are part of a 500-year-old tradition. All the guards are Swiss and they are there to protect the Vatican and the Pope. They're the oldest military unit that still exists today and is still active.

Getting into the Swiss Guards isn't easy. You need to be a Swiss male between the ages of 19 and 30 and you need to be at least 1.74 metres tall. You also have to have completed basic military training with the Swiss Army and have some kind of professional qualification like a degree or diploma.

Those selected go through **rigorous** training. They start by learning about the history of the Swiss Guards and how to recognise key people around the Vatican. At the same time, there is weapons training. Vatican Swiss Guards have to learn to handle old-fashioned weapons such as swords.

However, Swiss Guards also learn that the very first weapon they should use is their voice. Guards often have to deal with difficult tourists who want to explore parts of the Vatican not open to the public, so their training involves lessons in both Italian and English. Of course, sometimes they might need to use force to resolve a **tricky** situation, so they are trained in self-defence, a mixture of karate and judo developed specially for the Guards.

In this day and age, it's difficult to think of a job where you learn languages, martial arts and how to use a sword. It's no easy task, but in order to wear one of the most striking uniforms in the world, that's what the Swiss Guards have to do.

a

b Which adjective in 4a means ... ?

1 something is so hard you have to push yourself almost to the point of hurting yourself
2 something is very difficult because the training is very thorough and detailed
3 something is difficult because there are rules that must be obeyed

c Ask and answer the questions. Give extra details.

1 Imagine you have to run a marathon. Would it be tough or punishing for you?
2 Can you remember a teacher you had at school who was very strict?
3 What's a job that requires rigorous training?
4 Have you ever been in a tricky situation? What happened?

d Now go to Vocabulary Focus 4B on p.157

5 LISTENING

a 2.10 Listen to Miranda, who trained at a drama school, and Fred, who trained at a football academy. Which sentence describes their experience best?

1 They both enjoyed the training, but felt they missed a part of growing up.
2 They weren't sure about the training, but they know they'll do well anyway.
3 They weren't sure about the selection process, but they feel they did well during the training.

b 2.10 Listen again. Are the sentences true or false?

Miranda

1 During the audition process she had to perform scenes from plays twice.
2 She was confident she would get into drama school.
3 All her tutors were tough.
4 The school was flexible when she wasn't sure if she wanted to continue training.

Fred

5 His parents were unsure whether he should join the academy.
6 They knew they would have to sacrifice a lot of time to help Fred.
7 He was surprised to find that he enjoyed analysing football matches.
8 He felt disappointed for his friend, Jack.

c Do you think the kind of sacrifice that Miranda and Fred made was worth it? Why / Why not?

6 GRAMMAR

Obligation and permission

a Look at the words and phrases in bold in sentences 1–6. Which show obligation (O) and which show permission (P)?

1 I **was supposed to** prepare a song as well, but they forgot to let me know.
2 ... there was a workshop for a day where they **made** us work on new scenes from plays ...
3 ... in her class we **weren't allowed to** talk or use our voices in any way.
4 ... they could see this was a pretty unique opportunity, so they **let** me do it.
5 ... we **were allowed to** see the games for free.
6 ... there were some boys who **were forced to** give it all up ...

b Now go to Grammar Focus 4B on p.140

7 SPEAKING

a Think of a time (at school, university or work) when you had to do some training and follow rules. Make notes about the questions.

What was the situation?
Who made the rules?
Were some of the rules very strict?
Were there some rules you didn't follow?
How did you feel about the experience?

b Discuss your experiences. What similarities and differences were there?

4C Everyday English
Thank you, you've saved my life

Learn to describe photos

P Contrastive stress

S Expressing careful disagreement

1 LISTENING

a Discuss the questions.

1 How do you feel about showing your work to other people? Do you … ?
   a always show other people what you've done
   b only show your work if you think it's good
   c never show your work unless you really have to
2 How do you feel about people commenting on it or criticising it?

b Look at photo a from Part 1. Where do you think Becky and Tessa are? Who are they talking to?

c 2.13 Watch or listen to Part 1 and check your ideas.

d 2.13 Answer the questions. Watch or listen again and check.

1 Whose photos are they?
2 What does the tutor especially like?
3 What's the topic for the next assignment?

a

2 USEFUL LANGUAGE Describing photos

a Which of the expressions below could describe the photos? Write *1*, *2*, *n* (*neither*) or *b* (*both*).

1

2

1 ☐ And here's a close-up of some leaves.
2 ☐ We tried to get a closer shot with this photo.
3 ☐ Here's a more distant shot of the tree.
4 ☐ And this is the same tree, but from further away.
5 ☐ Here's another shot of the tree, but from a different angle.
6 ☐ As you can see, there are mountains in the background.
7 ☐ That's my car in the foreground.
8 ☐ This one's a bit out of focus!

b 2.13 Which underlined expressions in 2a did Becky use? Watch or listen again and check.

c Communication 4C Student A: Go to p.128. Student B: Go to p.131.

d Work in pairs (one student from A and B in each pair). Take turns to show your photos to your partner and discuss them. Ask questions about your partner's photos.

e Discuss the photos. In what ways are the photos similar? In what ways are they different?

3 LISTENING

a 2.14 Watch or listen to Part 2. Answer the questions.

1 What are Becky and Tessa talking about?
2 Where is Becky going next?

b Who thinks these things, Becky (B) or Tessa (T)?

1 Bridges are an interesting topic.
2 The theoretical part of the course is boring.
3 She is missing information for the essay.

4 CONVERSATION SKILLS Expressing careful disagreement

a 2.15 Look at the exchange between Tessa and Becky. Then listen to what they actually say. What is the difference?

TESSA Yes, bridges. So boring.
BECKY I don't agree. They're not at all boring.

b Why does Becky use careful ways to disagree?

c The sentences below are replies to what another person said. What do you think each speaker is talking about? Match the replies with the topics in the box.

a football match   a film   bank managers
a restaurant meal   a party

1 Really, did you think so? I thought he played quite well.
2 I'm not sure about that. It doesn't seem that expensive.
3 I know what you mean, but on the other hand it's a very responsible job.
4 Oh, I don't know. I think it could be quite good fun.
5 Maybe you're right, but I enjoyed some bits of it.

d 2.16 Listen to the conversations and check your answers.

e How could you disagree with the comments below? Prepare replies using underlined expressions from 4c. Then take turns to reply.

1 I love Café Roma. It's a great atmosphere
2 I'd never want to have a cat. All they do is sit around and sleep.
3 I don't know why people play golf. It's such a boring sport.

5 PRONUNCIATION Contrastive stress

a 2.15 Listen again to Becky's reply and answer the questions below.

TESSA Yes, bridges. So boring.
BECKY Oh, I don't know. **It's not that boring.**

1 Underline the word which has the strongest stress in the **bold** sentence.
2 Does the sentence mean … ?
   a They're not all boring.
   b They're not as boring as you think they are.
   c They're not as boring as other kinds of architechture.

b Reply to the comments below using *not that*.

1 I thought that was a really interesting lecture.

Oh, I don't know. …

2 I find photography a very difficult subject.
3 Look at that bridge. It's so unusual.
4 I thought the questions in the exam were incredibly easy.

c 2.17 Listen and check. Were your replies similar?

6 LISTENING

a 2.18 Watch or listen to Part 3. Which of these is the best summary of what happens?

1 Becky gives Tessa a coffee and some books she found in the library. Then they talk about the wedding. Then Tessa notices Phil and asks who he is.
2 Becky gives Tessa her lecture notes then they talk about the wedding. Then Tessa meets Phil and they talk about his book.

b Are the sentences true or false? Discuss the false sentences – what actually happens?

1 Becky gives Tessa her lecture notes and some photos.
2 Tessa is grateful to Becky for her help.
3 Becky wants Tessa to be their wedding photographer.
4 Tessa refuses because she thinks she's not good enough.
5 Phil finishes typing and saves what he's written.
6 Phil asks who Tessa is.
7 Tessa wants to read Phil's novel.

7 SPEAKING

a **Communication 4C** Student A: Go to p.130. Student B: Go to p.132.

b Present an opinion on one of the topics to the rest of the class. Do they agree with you?

Unit Progress Test

CHECK YOUR PROGRESS

You can now do the Unit Progress Test.

4D Skills for Writing
I'm good at communicating with people

Learn to write an email to apply for work

W Giving a positive impression

1 SPEAKING and LISTENING

a If you go to live in a different country, do you think it's important to … ?

- learn the local language
- make friends with local people
- go somewhere beautiful with a good climate

Why do you think these things are important or not important?

b 2.19 Listen to three people talking about living in the places in the photos. Which topics do they mention?

meeting people   the climate   food and drink
the culture of the country   speaking the language

c 2.19 Listen again. Answer these questions about each speaker.

1 What did they like?
2 What did they find difficult?
3 How was it different from their own country?

d Which speakers make these points? How did their own experience support these opinions?

1 It's important to learn the local language.
2 Beautiful cities aren't always the best places to live.
3 The weather influences the way people live.
4 Foreigners often don't make an effort to get to know the local culture.
5 Living abroad can be worthwhile even if you don't always have a good time.

e The speakers say that meeting local people is important when you live in a different country. Think of three ways you could meet local people. Which is your most interesting idea? Why?

2 READING

a Read the leaflet about becoming an international student 'buddy' in London. Answer the questions.

1 What is a 'buddy' and what does he/she do?
2 What are the advantages of becoming a buddy?
3 What kind of person are they looking for?

BE A BUDDY FOR THE INTERNATIONAL STUDENTS' CLUB

Are you curious about other cultures? Are you eager to get to know and meet new people from all over the world?
Volunteer to offer assistance and friendship to international students as a 'buddy' at your university or college.

Responsibilities
After an international student has been assigned to you, you will show them around during the first weeks of their stay. You'll give them an insight into the student life in your area and generally help them out.

What we offer you

- free membership and benefits of belonging to the International Students Club
- free training courses which will look great on your CV (a certificate of participation awarded)
- the opportunity to get a wide range of cross-cultural experience

b Paulo wrote an email applying to be a buddy and saying why he is suitable. Which of the reasons below do you think he should use?

he understands the needs of foreign students
he loves living in London he's outgoing and sociable
he's interested in other cultures
he speaks several languages
he has plenty of free time he knows London well

Read the email and check your answers.

Dear Sir/Madam,

1 I saw the information about international student buddies on your website and I am writing to apply for the role.

2 I am a Brazilian student at Birkbeck College, London, where I am studying international law. I am fluent in English, Spanish, French, and Portuguese, which would help me to communicate with students from different countries. I am also very sociable and good at communicating with people, which I am sure would help me to establish a good relationship with new students.

3 As a foreign student in London myself, I am in an excellent position to understand the needs of students coming from other countries. I have a thorough knowledge of the city and the student life here. I am confident that I would be able to help students to feel at home and find their way around.

4 I have always been very keen on learning about other cultures and my own circle of friends in London is completely international. I strongly believe we should encourage people from different cultures to come together to help promote intercultural understanding.

5 I would be more than happy to give up my free time to work as an international student buddy and I'm certain I could make a valuable contribution to your programme.

I look forward to hearing from you.

Yours faithfully,

Paulo Figueiredo

3 WRITING SKILLS

Giving a positive impression

a Paulo uses phrases in his email which give a positive impression. Underline the phrases which have these meanings.

1 I *speak* English *well*.
2 I *like being with other people*.
3 I *have no problem talking to people*.
4 I *am able to* understand the needs of students.
5 I *know* the city *well*.
6 I have always *been interested* in learning about other countries.
7 I would be *willing* to give up my free time.
8 I could *help* your programme.

b Paulo writes *I am sure this would help me …* instead of *I think …* in order to sound more confident. Find four more expressions like this in the email.

c What is the advantage of using the expressions in 3a and 3b when applying for a job? Which answer is not correct?

1 They make the writer sound positive and enthusiastic.
2 They make the email more interesting to read.
3 They give the impression that the writer could do the job well.

Qualifications
You're open-minded and interested in other cultures.
You have a knowledge of English as well as other languages.

4 WRITING

a Plan an email applying to do voluntary work. Choose one of these situations. Make a list of reasons why you would be suitable.

- A website is advertising for volunteers to work in an international summer camp and organise activities for teenagers.
- A voluntary organisation wants helpers to make contact with English-speaking families living in your country and help them to adapt to your culture.
- A large secondary school in your area wants volunteers to give talks to pupils about different jobs and to help them decide on a future career.

b Write the email. Include:

- an opening sentence, explaining why you are writing
- two or three paragraphs, explaining why you are suitable
- phrases from 3a and 3b
- a final sentence to conclude the email.

c Work in pairs. Look at your partner's email. Does it … ?

- make it clear why he/she is suitable
- have a clear structure
- use expressions from 3a and 3b to give a positive impression

d Swap your email with other students. Would they choose you as a volunteer?

UNIT 4
Review and extension

1 GRAMMAR

a Use the words in brackets to rewrite the sentences. Make sure the meaning doesn't change.

1 I was a nurse but now I work for a drug company. (used to)
2 I don't do shift work now. (no longer)
3 When I was a nurse I sometimes slept in, but now I always get up early. (would)
4 I no longer take my lunch to work because there's a cafeteria at the drug company. (any more)
5 I don't wear a uniform in my new job so I can now wear my own clothes. (used to)
6 I don't have to deal with difficult patients now. (no longer)
7 I'm much happier than I was before. (used to)

b Correct five obligation and permission expressions in the text.

I went to a very strict primary school when I was a child. I wasn't allowed to do about two hours homework every night which meant there was little time to play with my friends. But often my parents told me just to study for an hour and wrote a note for the teacher excusing me from homework. In class we weren't let to talk to each other when we were working on a task because teachers didn't like noisy classrooms. However, we allowed to put up our hand and ask our teacher a question as she felt it was good to help students. We weren't allowed to do some kind of physical exercise every day after lunch, but that made us very tired in the afternoon. One good thing is that they supposed us learn a musical instrument and I learnt to play the clarinet, which I still enjoy doing.

2 VOCABULARY

a Complete the sentences with a preposition followed by your own idea.

1 Tiredness is usually caused _____ ...
2 A sunny day always has a positive effect _____ ...
3 Too much exercise can result _____ ...
4 Visiting a foreign country can lead _____ ...
5 As a result _____ learning English, I ...

b Work in pairs. Compare your ideas. Ask your partner why they completed the sentences in that way.

c Which word in the box collocates best with the nouns?

rigorous tough punishing strict arduous tricky

1 __________ training programme / schedule
2 __________ laws / parents
3 __________ plastic / teachers
4 __________ journey / task
5 __________ testing / training
6 __________ situation / question

d Discuss three examples from 2c that you have experience of.

3 WORDPOWER *as*

a Replace the underlined words with *as* expressions in the box.

as a whole as far as restaurants are concerned
as for as a matter of fact as far as I'm concerned
as far as I know as if as follows

1 I'm glad you're happy. But speaking of Alan, it's impossible to please him.
2 All students in the class are improving their speaking.
3 I'm not English. To tell you the truth, I'm from Denmark.
4 My list of complaints are below: 1) There was no hot water ...
5 It felt like we had always lived there.
6 In my opinion, the cost of food here is very high.
7 Thinking about restaurants, there are some excellent ones in our neighbourhood.
8 From what I've seen and from what people tell me, she's usually on time.

b Add a word to the gaps in 1–8 and then match to a–h.

1 ☐ The key reasons for our success are as _____
2 ☐ As far as I _____
3 ☐ I'm fit and well. As _____
4 ☐ As far as I _____
5 ☐ The team as _____
6 ☐ She's not boring. As _____
7 ☐ It looks as _____
8 ☐ As far as sport is _____

a ... whole played very well.
b ... they make the best coffee in town.
c ... concerned, I go running twice a week.
d ... matter of fact, she's a really interesting person.
e ... my husband, he's got the flu.
f ... football is more about the money than the sport.
g ... 1. We trained very hard ...
h ... it's going to be a sunny day.

c Complete the sentences with your own ideas.

1 As far as I'm concerned ...
2 As far as I know ...
3 It looks as if ...
4 Our class as a whole ...
5 As far as English is concerned ...

d Tell another student your sentences and ask questions.

REVIEW YOUR PROGRESS

How well did you do in this unit? Write 3, 2 or 1 for each objective.
3 = very well 2 = well 1 = not so well

I CAN ...

discuss events that changed my life	☐
discuss and describe rules	☐
describe photos	☐
write an email to apply for work	☐

CAN DO OBJECTIVES

- Discuss possible future events
- Prepare for a job interview
- Discuss advantages and disadvantages
- Write an argument for and against an idea

UNIT 5
Chance

GETTING STARTED

a Look at the picture and answer the questions.

1 What kind of place do you think this is? Why do you think so?
2 Why is it an unusual place to jump?
3 What could the man be thinking?
4 Imagine you're on the beach below. What could you be thinking?

b Discuss the questions.

1 Why do you think some people like doing extreme and dangerous things?
2 Do you think they do these things in spite of the risk or because of the risk?

5A You could live to be a hundred

Learn to discuss possible future events

G Future probability

V Adjectives describing attitude

1 READING

a Read the quiz and answer the questions.

Are you an optimist or a pessimist? Test yourself!

As you read each question, try to imagine yourself in each situation. Think of how you would react (be honest!) and then choose a) or b).

1 You bought a book, but you left it on the bus on the way home. Do you think you will get it back?
a) Yes, probably – I'll call the bus station.
b) Not very likely – someone probably took it.

2 You want to buy a shirt/dress that you've seen in a shop. You find they've just sold the last one. Do you think:
a) Oh well, I can probably find something similar.
b) Why am I always so unlucky?

3 You get an 'A' in an exam. Do you think:
a) Wow, I'm really good!
b) I was lucky with the questions.

4 You're crossing the road. A driver gets annoyed and shouts at you. Do you think:
a) He/She must be having a difficult day.
b) People are so rude!

5 You're trying to figure out a problem with your computer. Do you think:
a) There must be some simple solution to this.
b) I just don't understand computers. I give up.

6 You start a new fitness programme and you're really tired the next day. Do you think:
a) Wow, I worked hard yesterday – it'll be easier next time.
b) Wow, I must be really unfit!

7 A friend you haven't seen for months says 'You're looking good.' Do you think:
a) Yes, he's right. Nice of him to notice.
b) Does he really mean it or is he just being nice?

b Work in pairs. Compare your answers to the quiz. Did you have mostly a or mostly b answers?

c **Communication 5A** Now go to p.131.

d Read the article *Why we think we're going to have a long and happy life* quickly. Choose the correct words to complete the summary.

Most people are naturally *optimistic / pessimistic* and this is generally *an advantage / a disadvantage* for the human race, because it helps us to be *realistic about the future / more successful.*

WHY WE THINK WE'RE GOING TO HAVE A LONG AND HAPPY LIFE

Researchers have found that people all over the world share an important characteristic: optimism. Sue Reynolds explains what it's all about.

WE'RE ALL ABOVE AVERAGE!

Try asking a 20-year-old these questions:

- What kind of career will you have?
- How long do you think you'll live?

Most people think they'll be able to earn above-average salaries, but only some of the population can be in that top half. Most young men in Europe will say they expect to live well into their 80s, but the average life expectancy for European men is 75. Most people will give an answer that is unrealistic because nearly everyone believes they will be better than the average. Obviously, they can't all be right.

Most people are also optimistic about their own strengths and abilities. Ask people 'How well do you get on with other people?' or 'How intelligent are the people in your family?' and they'll usually say they're above average. Again, they can't all be right. We can't all be better than everyone else, but that's what we think.

LOOKING ON THE BRIGHT SIDE

There is a reason for this. Research has shown that, on the whole, we are optimistic by nature and have a positive view of ourselves. In fact, we are much more optimistic than realistic and frequently imagine things will turn out better than they actually do. Most people don't expect their marriages to end in divorce, they don't expect to lose their jobs or to be diagnosed with a life-threatening disease. Furthermore, when things do go wrong, they are often quick to find something positive in all the gloom. Many people who fail exams, for example, are quite sure they were just unlucky with the questions and they'll do better next time. Or people who have had a serious illness often say that it was really positive, because it made them appreciate life more. We really are very good at 'looking on the bright side'.

Even if our optimism is unrealistic and leads us to take risks, without it we might all still be living in caves …

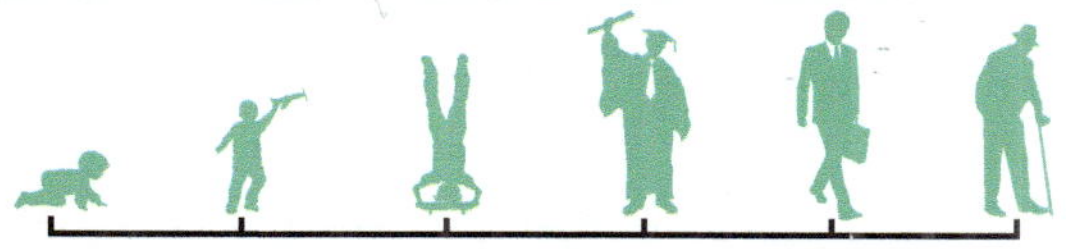

THE OPTIMISM BIAS

This certainty that our future is bound to be better than our past and present is known as the 'Optimism Bias' and researchers have found that it is common to people all over the world and of all ages. Of course, the Optimism Bias can lead us to make some very bad decisions. Often, people don't take out travel insurance because they're sure everything will be all right, they don't worry about saving up for old age because the future looks fine, or they smoke cigarettes in spite of the health warnings on the packet because they believe 'it won't happen to me'. Or on a global scale, we carry on polluting the planet, because we're sure that we'll find a way to clean it up some day in the future.

OPTIMISM IS GOOD FOR YOU

But researchers believe that the Optimism Bias is actually good for us. People who expect the best are generally likely to be ambitious and adventurous, whereas people who expect the worst are likely to be more cautious, so optimism actually helps to make us successful. Optimists are also healthier because they feel less stress – they can relax because they think that everything is going to be just fine. Not only that, but the Optimism Bias may also have played an important part in our evolution as human beings. Because we hoped for the best, we were prepared to take risks such as hunting down dangerous animals and travelling across the sea to find new places to live and this is why we became so successful as a species. Even if our optimism is unrealistic and leads us to take risks, without it we might all still be living in caves, too afraid to go outside and explore the world in case we get eaten by wild animals.

e Read the article again. Tick (✓) the five points made in the article.

1 Pessimists usually have fewer friends than optimists.
2 Humans are naturally positive about their future.
3 Reality is often worse than we imagine it to be.
4 People who live in warmer countries are usually more optimistic.
5 We often act (or don't act) because we're confident everything will work out.
6 If we imagine a better future, we will take more risks.
7 Optimists spend a lot of time daydreaming.
8 Optimism about the future makes us feel better in the present.

f Discuss the questions.

- Look again at your results in the quiz. Do you think you have the 'Optimism Bias'?
- Do you agree that it's better to be optimistic than realistic? Why / Why not?
- How do you see yourself in 20 years' time?

2 VOCABULARY

Adjectives describing attitude

a Find adjectives in *Why we think we're going to have a long and happy life* which mean:

1 expecting the future to be good
2 seeing things as they are
3 not seeing things as they are
4 prepared to take risks
5 not prepared to take risks
6 wanting to be successful

b Which of these adjectives best describe you?

c Now go to Vocabulary Focus 5A on p.158

3 LISTENING

a Read the statistics and guess which numbers complete the sentences.

8,000	6	18 million	1 million	4

WHAT ARE YOUR CHANCES?

Chance of living to be 100 (man):
1 in ______

Chance of living to be 100 (woman):
1 in ______

Chance of having a road accident:
1 in ______

Chance of winning the lottery:
1 in ______

Chance of being in a plane crash:
1 in ______

b 2.23 Listen and check your answers. Do you think any of the statistics would be different for your country?

c 2.23 According to the speaker, how can you increase your chances of doing these things? Listen again and check.

1 surviving a plane crash
2 getting to the airport safely
3 living to be 100

4 GRAMMAR Future probability

a 2.24 Complete the sentences with the words in the box. Then listen and check.

likely unlikely could may probably (x2) certainly (x2) chance

1 It's very ______ that your plane will crash.
2 Even if it does you'll ______ be fine, because 95% of people in plane crashes survive.
3 So, if you're worried about getting on that plane, don't be, because you'll almost ______ survive the journey.
4 You're more ______ to have an accident in the car going to the airport.
5 You have quite a good ______ of living to be 100.
6 Modern medicine ______ well make the chances higher still during your lifetime.
7 You ______ won't die in a plane crash and you ______ live to be 100.
8 But the bad news is, you almost ______ won't win the lottery.

b Find phrases in 4a which mean ... ?

1 it's certain / nearly certain
2 it's probable
3 it's possible
4 it's not probable

c Which words in the box in 4a are used in these patterns?

1 *will* ______ (+ verb)
2 ______ *won't* (+ verb)
3 *is/are* ______ to (+ verb)
4 It's ______ that ...
5 There's a ______ that ...

d Change these predictions, using words from 4a.

1 I'll meet someone famous in my life – 70%.
2 I'll have children – 50–60%.
3 I'll fall in love at least once in my life – 90%.
4 I'll become a millionaire – 0.05%.
5 Someone will steal from me – 80%.
6 I'll live in the same place all my life – 20%.

e Now go to Grammar Focus 5A on p.142

5 SPEAKING

a Do you think these things will happen in your lifetime? Decide if each event is certain, probable, possible, unlikely to happen, or if it will certainly not happen. Then add a question of your own.

1 Will we find a cure for cancer?
2 Will people go to live on Mars?
3 Will the level of the oceans rise?
4 Will there be another world war?
5 Will people stop using cars?
6 Will Chinese become the world language?

b Ask other students their opinion.

c Tell the class what you found out.

- How many people agreed with your opinion?
- What were the most interesting comments?
- Are people in your class generally optimistic, pessimistic or realistic?

5B I'll be settling into my accommodation

Learn to prepare for a job interview

G Future perfect and future continuous
V The natural world

1 READING

a Look at the pictures of Antarctica and answer the questions.

1 What can you see in the pictures?
2 What do you know about Antarctica?
3 Would you like to go there? Why / Why not?

b Do the quiz. Then compare your answers with a partner.

THE UNKNOWN CONTINENT

① HOW BIG IS ANTARCTICA?
(a) the size of Russia
(b) the size of the USA and Mexico
(c) the size of Australia

② HOW MUCH OF ANTARCTICA IS COVERED BY ICE?
(a) 98% (b) 86% (c) 77%

③ WHICH OF THE FOLLOWING CAN'T YOU FIND IN ANTARCTICA?
(a) rivers (c) trees
(b) deserts

④ WHICH OF THESE ANIMALS CAN YOU FIND THERE?
(a) polar bears
(b) seals
(c) wolves

⑤ WHO WAS THE FIRST PERSON TO REACH THE SOUTH POLE IN 1911?
(a) Richard Byrd (American)
(b) Robert Scott (British)
(c) Roald Amundsen (Norwegian)

c **Communication 5B** Now go to p.132.

d Read the first part of an article about working in Antarctica. What would your reaction be to a job advert like this?

My life ON ICE

Imagine you saw a job advertised with the following conditions:

- no leaving your place of work for 6 months – you must stay inside
- work six days a week, but always be available
- socialise only with your colleagues – no contact with other friends and family

You'd be mad to apply, wouldn't you? Probably. But if you want to work in Antarctica during the winter, this is what you'll have to put up with.

e Discuss the questions.

- Why do you think people want to work in Antarctica?
- What kinds of jobs can people do there?
- What kinds of leisure activities do they do during the winter months when it's difficult to go outside?

f Read *Cooking in Antarctica*. Does it include any of your ideas from 1e?

g Read the article again. Make notes about:

- Fleur's background
- her role at the base
- her free time
- her thoughts about Antarctica
- her colleagues at the base

h What do you think are … ?

- the advantages of a job like Fleur's
- possible frustrations in this kind of job

Would you ever consider doing a job like this?

2 VOCABULARY The natural world

a Cover the article *Cooking in Antarctica*. Match words from A with words from B to make collocations.

A	B
rough	environment
environmentally	energy
solar	atmosphere
fragile	footprint
ecological	weather
global	change
carbon	warming
climate	impact
the Earth's	friendly

b Check your answers in the article.

c Complete the sentences with the collocations in 2a.

1. We're going to change our energy supply to ______ ______ to reduce our ______ ______.
2. When the steam engine was invented, not many would have thought about the ______ ______ of burning so much coal.
3. Our boat trip was cancelled due to ______ ______.
4. The factories on the outskirts of town burn their waste and release toxic gases into ______ ______. I think they should be shut down.
5. If there is an oil spill from a ship, it will damage the ______ marine ______ in this bay.
6. Most scientists agree that irregular weather patterns are evidence of ______ ______ and ______ ______.
7. Travelling by train is slower but it's far more ______ ______ than going by plane.

Cooking in ANTARCTICA

When she saw an online advertisement for a Chef Manager at the British Antarctic Survey (BAS) base in Rothera, chef Fleur Wilson was certainly given food for thought. Fleur, in her mid-thirties, felt it was time for an adventure and a life experience that really was different.

Fleur is part of a group of key support staff at Rothera. The main focus of BAS is scientific research into the climate, the oceans and ecosystems of Antarctica. In order to carry out this research successfully, scientists need the help of people like Fleur to make their lives as comfortable as possible.

A key responsibility for Fleur is keeping everyone happy, and one of the best ways of doing this is by keeping them well fed. This doesn't mean preparing high-end restaurant food, but it does mean organising lots of social events to boost the mood. However, everyone has to play their part, and Fleur makes sure no one escapes doing the dishes.

One thing that all staff at BAS share is their love of the continent. 'I don't mind the rough weather,' Fleur says, 'and I've always found landscapes with ice and snow amazingly beautiful. Sure, I don't get to see much for six months of the year, but for the other six months there's plenty of light and the scenery is stunning.' But, quite apart from admiring the natural beauty of Antarctica, the staff all have a clear understanding of the fact that it's a fragile environment because, compared to the rest of the world, it is largely untouched. They're aware that the presence of human beings can have a significant ecological impact on the continent and, therefore, they treat it with care. BAS research stations use solar energy to heat air and hot water. 'We try to be as environmentally friendly as possible,' says Fleur; 'we don't want to leave a carbon footprint down here.'

As Fleur notes, 'Antarctica can tell us a lot about what's happening in the world. It can tell us a lot about global warming and climate change. In an extreme climate like this, you can really notice if things are changing.'

During the winter months, all Rothera staff try to keep themselves entertained either by making mid-winter gifts for each other or creating a murder mystery event. Fleur has also taught herself Spanish to intermediate level. However, during the summer months she does cross-country skiing and enjoys trips to do some penguin and whale watching.

Fleur realises that living and working in Antarctica isn't for everyone. 'If you're the kind of person that likes shopping, going out for dinner and clubbing, then forget it.' She's now in her fourth year here and still finds it a unique and rewarding experience.

'I was mad enough to apply for the job and I've been mad enough to stay. But it's a job that's given me so much – I've worked with some remarkable people and I'm living in a unique and fascinating part of the world.'

d Work on your own. Answer the questions and make notes.

- Are there any environments in your country that are considered fragile? What kind of environments are they?
- What different human inventions have a negative ecological impact?
- What kind of things could you do to reduce your carbon footprint?

e Discuss your answers.

3 LISTENING

a 2.27 Martha's going to Antarctica to do research on Adelie penguins. She talks to her friend Joe about her work. Listen and answer the questions.

1 How well does Joe understand Martha's research?
2 Are his questions serious or light-hearted?
3 What do we learn about the personality of the penguins?
4 Why is the research important?

b 2.27 Listen again. Number the actions in the correct order from 1 to 5.

- ☐ the eggs are laid
- ☐ tags are put on the penguins
- ☐ penguins get into pairs
- ☐ Martha arrives in Antarctica
- ☐ penguin chicks are born

4 GRAMMAR
Future perfect and future continuous

a Look at these future verb forms from the conversation in 3a and match them to the uses a–c below.

1 … this time next week **I'll be settling** into my accommodation.
2 … I think **I'll be doing** similar things every day.
3 … by the time I arrive **the penguins will already have got** into pairs.

a talk about an action that will be in progress at a specific time in the future
b talk about an action that will be completed before a specific time in the future
c talk about planned actions in the future

b Now go to Grammar Focus 5B on p.142

c Work on your own. Make notes about the questions.

- Where do you think you'll be living this time next year?
- What do you think you'll have achieved in five years' time?

d Tell each other your answers to 4c and ask follow-up questions.

5 SPEAKING

a Read the job advert. Would you like this job?

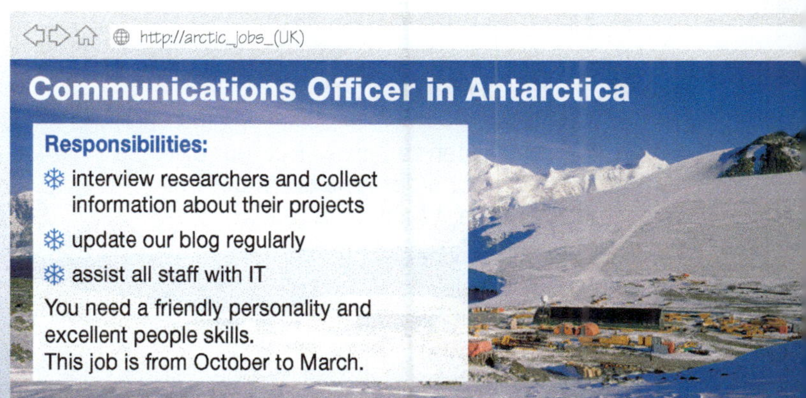

b Prepare a job interview role play for the job in 5a.
Student A: You want to apply for the job. Imagine you have the skills and experience that make you a suitable job applicant. Think of questions you can ask the interviewer.
Student B: You are the interviewer. Think of questions you can ask the applicant. Think of any useful information you can tell the applicant.

c Work in pairs. Do the role play.
Student A: Do you still want the job?
Student B: Do you think Student A is suitable for the job? Why / Why not?

5C Everyday English
We're not making enough money

Learn to discuss advantages and disadvantages

- **P** Tone groups
- **S** Responding to an idea

1 SPEAKING and LISTENING

a Discuss the questions below.

- What kind of cafés are there near where you live? e.g traditional, modern, part of a chain
- What kind of cafés do you like? Why?
- What do you usually do in a café?

b 2.30 Watch or listen to Part 1. Put four of these events in the correct order. One event doesn't appear in the scene. Which is it?

- ☐ Sam talks about money.
- ☐ Becky offers to help.
- ☐ Phil finishes his chapter.
- ☐ Phil asks about Tessa.
- ☐ Phil suggests staying open longer.

c 2.30 Answer the questions. Watch or listen again and check.

1. Why is Sam worried?
2. What are the problems with serving meals?
3. Why does Phil think serving meals is a good idea?
4. What does Phil want to know about Tessa?

2 LISTENING

a 2.31 Look at photo b of Sam and Emma. Which of these topics do you think they're talking about? Listen to Part 2 and check.

money problems staying open later Sam's birthday
hiring a cook investing money in the café

b 2.31 Watch or listen again. Make notes about the ideas Sam and Emma discuss. What are the positive and negative points for each idea?

3 USEFUL LANGUAGE
Discussing advantages and disadvantages

a Sam and Emma discuss the advantages and disadvantages of making changes to the café. What do you think they say? Complete the sentences.

1. Of course, the ________ is we'd have to invest even more money.
2. Yes, but the ________ is, it might be a way to get more business.

b 2.32 Listen and check.

c Which of these words/phrases could you use in the sentences in 3a?

problem advantage disadvantage
best thing drawback

d 2.33 Add prepositions from the box to the expressions. Then listen and check.

of (x2) with (x2) about

one good thing ________
the advantage/disadvantage ________
the only drawback ________
another problem ________
the trouble ________

e Look at some people's ideas for the future. Use an expression from 3d in each second sentence.

1. 'I might sell my car and go everywhere by bike. I'd get fit.'
2. 'I'd love to live in London. It would be very expensive.'
3. 'I could work in China for a year. I don't speak the language.'

4 PRONUNCIATION Tone groups

a 2.34 Listen to these sentences. Answer the questions.

The good thing about it is it might be a good way to get more business.

The trouble is it means investing even more money.

1 Where do you hear a slight pause?
2 Which words are stressed in the **bold** phrase?
3 Does Sam's voice go up (↗) or down (↘) on the word *is*?

b 2.35 Listen to these sentences. Practise saying them, pausing after *is*.

1 The trouble is we don't have enough money.
2 The point is we still owe money to the bank.
3 The problem is we'd need to employ more staff.
4 The advantage is we'd attract more customers.

5 LISTENING

a 2.36 Watch or listen to Part 3. Who suggests doing these things (Sam or Emma) and what do they say about it?

1 have live music
2 get students to play music
3 have photo exhibitions
4 ask people to read poems and stories

b Which of these adjectives and phrases describe Emma? Which describe Sam?

full of ideas   cautious in making decisions
enthusiastic   worried about the future
careful with money   fair to other people

6 CONVERSATION SKILLS Responding to an idea

a Read what the speakers say. Complete the replies with the words in the box.

bad   possibility   lovely   worth

1 **A** I don't know, it's a big risk.
B I think it's a ______ idea.
2 **B** Well, how about entertainment? We could have live music, get locals to play at the weekend.
A That might be ______ a try.
3 **B** Or display paintings or photos.
A That's not a ______ idea.
4 **B** Or readings. Have poetry readings.
A Yeah, that's a ______.

b 2.37 Listen and check. Which of the replies is … ?

1 more enthusiastic   2 more cautious

c Look at these ways to respond to an idea. Order them from 1–6 (*1* = very cautious, *6* = very enthusiastic).

☐ It's an idea, I suppose.
☐ Yes, that makes sense.
☐ That's a great idea.
☐ What a brilliant idea!
1 Mm, I don't know about that.
☐ Yes, good idea.

d You want to do something with the whole class at the end of the course. Write down three ideas.

We could go on a day trip

e Work in groups. Take turns to suggest your ideas. Respond to other students' ideas, using expressions in 6a and 6c. Which idea is the best?

(b)

7 SPEAKING

a ▶ Communication 5C Now go to p.128.

b Take a class vote. Whose café sounds the best?

Unit Progress Test

CHECK YOUR PROGRESS

You can now do the Unit Progress Test.

5D Skills for Writing
The weather is getting more extreme

Learn to write an argument for and against an idea

W Arguing for and against an idea

1 SPEAKING and LISTENING

a Discuss the questions.

1 What extreme weather events are shown in photos a–d?
2 What kinds of extreme weather might affect your country or region? What can people do to protect themselves against it?

b 2.38 Listen to the news reports and match them with photos a–d. What key words helped you decide?

c 2.38 What did the news reports say about these topics?

1 farmland – cattle – villages – rivers
2 around Boston – the Boston to New York highway – residents
3 the weather in March – emergency supplies – the rice harvest
4 winds – residents – food and shelter

Re-tell the reports. Listen again if necessary.

d Discuss the questions.

1 Have you ever heard a news report like those in 1b about your own country or a country you know? What happened?
2 Which of these statements do you agree with most and why?
   - 'The climate does seem to be changing, but it's probably just a natural process.'
   - 'The weather is getting more extreme all over the world. This is clearly a sign of man-made climate change.'
3 What action (if any) do you think governments and world leaders should take to manage climate change?

a

b

c

Are extreme weather events a sign of
CLIMATE CHANGE?

Leon

[1] People have always complained about the weather, but the number of extreme weather events – such as droughts, hurricanes and heavy snow – seems to have increased in recent years. Naturally, people are worried about this. But are these events a sign that our climate is changing?

[2] Many people believe that extreme weather is part of a general pattern of climate change. Scientists predicted that global warming would lead to more unstable weather and this is exactly what seems to be happening. Furthermore, most scientists agree that these changes are happening faster than expected and that they are a direct result of human activity. Many scientists also warn that this is only the beginning and things will almost certainly get worse if we don't take action.

[3] However, not everyone agrees with this point of view. Some people point out that there have always been extreme weather events, but we are simply more aware of them now. They say it's not certain that climate change is a result of human activity, so we should try to find out the facts before we spend millions on fighting it.

[4] On balance, it seems that extreme weather is probably linked to climate change, but we can't be completely sure about this. My own view is that we can't take the risk of waiting until we are absolutely certain about climate change, as by then it will be too late to stop it. It's far cheaper to invest in cleaner forms of energy now than to fight climate change in the future, and rich countries should lead the way doing it.

d

2 READING

a Leon wrote an essay discussing the topic of climate change. Read the essay and answer the questions.

1 Which of these sentences best summarises the essay?
   a He considers arguments for and against climate change and then draws a conclusion.
   b He sets out to prove that climate change is really happening.

2 What is his conclusion?
   a We don't know enough about it to act now.
   b We should act against climate change now or it will be too late.

b Read the essay again and make notes on the points Leon makes for and against extreme weather being a sign of climate change.

3 WRITING SKILLS Reporting opinions

a Match four of the descriptions below to paragraphs 1–4 in the essay.

- Introduction – stating the problem
- Introduction – giving Leon's point of view
- Arguments against the existence of climate change
- Arguments for the existence of climate change
- Conclusion – re-stating the problem
- Conclusion – summarising the main points and giving Leon's point of view

b Answer the questions.

1 Why does Leon ask a question in the first paragraph?
2 How does Leon make his arguments seem more objective (i.e. not just his own opinion)?

c Find linking expressions in the essay that mean:

1 considering the various arguments
2 I think
3 also
4 but

d Notice how Leon uses expressions like these to report people's opinions.

Most scientists agree that …
Many people believe that …

Find more expressions in the essay that:

1 report what scientists say or think (x2)
2 report what other people say or think (x4)
3 report how people feel (x1).

e Write sentences for and against these questions, using expressions from 3d. Compare your sentences with other students.

Should investment in cleaner forms of energy continue?
Is the climate changing faster now than ever before?
Is it already too late to stop climate change?

4 WRITING

a Work in pairs. Choose one of the essay topics below.

Should air fares be increased to discourage people from travelling by plane?
Does recycling household rubbish really make any difference to the planet?
Is building nuclear power stations the best way to provide 'clean' energy?

b Discuss the topic you chose and make notes on possible arguments for and against. Then decide on your conclusion.

c Work on your own. Plan your essay using the structure in 3a.

d Compare your notes with your partner and explain roughly what you plan to write.

e Write the essay in about 150–200 words, using expressions in 3b–3d.

f Swap essays with another student. Does the essay … ?

1 have a clear structure
2 set out the arguments in a clear way
3 use suitable expressions for reporting opinions

Do you agree with the conclusion?

UNIT 5
Review and extension

1 GRAMMAR

a Change these sentences using the words in brackets, so that the meaning stays the same.

1 Cities will probably become more dangerous over the next 50 years. (likely)
2 Scientists will probably find a way to delay the ageing process soon. (chance)
3 It's quite possible that the Democratic Party will win the election. (could well)
4 There are bears in this forest, but you probably won't see one. (unlikely)

b Complete the gaps with the verbs in brackets. Use either future continuous (*will be* + *-ing*) or future perfect (*will have* + past participle).

I'm in my 20s, but I sometimes imagine my life at 70. When I'm 70, I'll [1]_____ (retire), so I won't [2]_____ (work) and I'll have plenty of free time. But I will [3]_____ (have) a successful career and I will [4]_____ (save) lots of money, so I'll be rich. I will [5]_____ (get) married in my 30s and we will [6]_____ (have) two or three children. By the time we're 70 we'll have a nice house by the sea, and our children will [7]_____ (live) nearby.
Of course, my life could turn out quite differently, but it's always good to have positive dreams!

c Imagine yourself 30 years from now. What will you be doing? What will you have done?

2 VOCABULARY

a What adjective could describe these people? Use words from the box.

well-organised critical adventurous
reliable sympathetic realistic

1 Dana has started a rock group but she knows she probably won't ever become famous.
2 Ivana always keeps her desk tidy and she knows where to find everything.
3 Tom listens to people's problems and knows how to make them feel better.
4 Pierre gave up work for six months to travel through Central America on a motorbike.
5 Christine's very hard to please. If you get something wrong, she'll notice it and she'll tell you.
6 If you ask Hamid to do a job, he'll always do it well and on time.

b What is the opposite of these words?

1 reliable	3 responsible	5 well-organised
2 sensitive	4 thoughtful	6 realistic

c Work in pairs. Which words in 2b (or their opposites) are true of people you know? Tell your partner and give a few examples of things the people do or don't do.

3 WORDPOWER *side*

a Look at these examples and match the word *side* with the meanings in the box.

group or team point of view part of a person's character

1 She's friendly but she also has a rather unpleasant **side**.
2 He usually plays for Liverpool but today he's playing for the national **side**.
3 We need to look at both **sides** of the argument.

b Here are some common expressions with *side*. Use them instead of the underlined parts of the sentences.

on your side look on the bright side
to one side from side to side on the side
side by side see the funny side

1 They sat on the bench <u>next to each other</u> without talking.
2 We think he was wrong. We're all <u>supporting you</u>.
3 Well, let's <u>see things positively</u> – we're both still alive.
4 I didn't earn much as a taxi driver, but I made quite a bit of money <u>doing other work.</u>
5 I was very embarrassed at the time, but now I can <u>laugh about what happened</u>.
6 She took me <u>away from the other people</u> and said quietly, 'I'll phone you this evening.'
7 As the sea got rougher, the lamp in my cabin started swinging <u>from left to right</u>.

c Read these extracts from stories. Which sentences from 3b do you think go in the gaps?

(1)
The first few days of the voyage were calm, but then the weather changed. _____
I lay in my bed watching it, feeling sick.

(2)
She saw a man approaching. It was Tom. 'OK if I sit here?' he asked. She nodded. _____
Then he turned to her and said, 'Do you still have the letter?'

d Work in pairs. Choose another sentence from 3b. Imagine it's from a story, and write a sentence before and after it.

e Read out your sentences. Which were the most interesting?

REVIEW YOUR PROGRESS

How well did you do in this unit? Write 3, 2 or 1 for each objective.
3 = very well 2 = well 1 = not so well

I CAN ...

discuss possible future events	☐
prepare for a job interview	☐
discuss advantages and disadvantages	☐
write an argument for and against an idea	☐

CAN DO OBJECTIVES

- Discuss choices
- Discuss changes
- Introduce requests and say you are grateful
- Write a travel blog

UNIT 6

Around the globe

GETTING STARTED

a Talk about the photo. What do you think?

1 Where are the man and the boy and why?
2 Why aren't they talking to each other?
3 What's on the man's phone? What's on the boy's phone?

b Discuss the questions.

1 Do you prefer travelling alone or with other people? Why / Why not?
2 What do you usually do while you're waiting in an airport or a train/bus station?
3 What are the positives and negatives of going on long journeys?

6A I'm not going to try to see everything

Learn to discuss choices

G Gerunds and infinitives

V Travel and tourism

1 READING and LISTENING

a Look at photos a–d and read about the four tourist attractions. Have you visited any of these places? Which one would you most like to visit?

b Read the tourist comments. Which are positive and which are negative?

1. "To see all these amazing things in gold and silver with precious stones like diamonds, and to know they've been used by kings and queens – it was wonderful!"
2. "It sort of felt like a lot of rooms with too much furniture in them. I mean, it was historic and interesting, especially if you like gardens, but it was too much in one visit."
3. "All these beautiful old religious objects – they were in glass cases and too far away. I wanted to get much closer than that."
4. "I've never seen so many beautiful paintings in one place – it was extraordinary."
5. "We spent hours exploring the gardens with lovely statues and fountains – I could have stayed longer."
6. "We had to keep walking and couldn't stop and look at the crown. It felt like high-pressure tourism."
7. "Absolutely fascinating – I learnt so much about the Ottoman Empire."
8. "Over-crowded – and everyone rushing to take a photo of just one famous painting – not a pleasant experience."

c Match comments 1–8 with the tourist attractions in 1a.

d 2.39 Listen to two tourists, Di and Bernie. Which places in 1a do they mention? Do they have the same idea about sightseeing tours?

a

The Louvre, Paris

- dates from the 12th century
- home to one of the world's largest art collections
- more than 8 million visitors a year

b

The Tower of London

- dates from 1080
- home of the British Crown Jewels
- about 2.5 million visitors a year

e 2.39 Listen again and answer the questions.

Di

1. Why did Di join a tour?
2. What was her impression of the organisation of the tour?
3. Where did she want to spend more time?
4. What did she and her friend Sue do in Italy?

Bernie

1. How many people did Bernie go travelling with?
2. What was the problem with guidebooks and maps?
3. Why did they almost have an accident in Paris?
4. What was disappointing about the Mona Lisa?

f Discuss the questions.

1. Have you had experiences similar to Di and Bernie?
2. How do you prefer to go sightseeing?
3. Di and Bernie and some of the tourists in 1b mention some negative aspects of tourism. What others can you think of?
4. Do these negative aspects stop you from wanting to see traditional tourist sights? Why / Why not?

2 GRAMMAR Gerunds and infinitives

a 2.40 Underline the correct verbs. Listen and check.

1 … it would be easy *to meet* / *meeting* people …
2 … we took off together *travel* / *to travel* around Europe.
3 *Drive* / *Driving* in Paris was really hard work …
4 Before *arriving* / *to arrive* in Rome, I became friendly with a woman, Sue.

b Match rules a–d to sentences 1–4 in 2a.

a We use gerunds after prepositions.
b We use gerunds when it is the subject of a sentence.
c We use *to* + infinitive after adjectives.
d We use *to* + infinitive to talk about the purpose or reason for something.

c Match the verbs in bold with meaning a or b in each pair of sentences.

1 … the people organising these tours **try** to include too much in the timetable.
2 I might **try** going on a tour of some kind.
a do something to see what effect it has
b attempt to do something (often unsuccessfully)

3 I **remember** visiting this really beautiful palace …
4 … **remember** to be back at 10.30.
a have a memory of doing something
b not forget to do something

d Where do the objects (in brackets) go in these sentences?

I could hear setting up their market stalls. (the sellers)
I noticed waving their arms at us. (all these people)

We can use this pattern with *see, watch, observe, listen to, feel, smell.* What kinds of verbs are they?

e Now go to Grammar Focus 6A on p.144

f Complete the sentences with the correct form of the verbs in brackets.

1 _____ (see) the Pyramids for the first time was a magical experience.
2 You can't leave London without _____ (visit) the British Museum.
3 Why don't you try _____ (speak) to him in Spanish? He obviously can't understand you.
4 It's not possible _____ (go) to the museum in the evening. It closes at 5.00pm.
5 When you visit the Hermitage, remember _____ (look for) the two paintings by Leonardo da Vinci.
6 I heard the guide _____ (have) an argument with another tourist.
7 _____ (discover) Topkapi Palace in Istanbul was the highlight of my trip.
8 We went to Rome _____ (visit) the Colosseum and Roman Forum, but we found the Baroque architecture just as interesting.
9 It was a small restaurant and I could smell our dinner _____ (be) cooked – delicious!
10 I remember _____ (see) the Sagrada Familia for the first time – it was so original.

g Discuss the questions.

1 Why do you think we all like visiting the same tourist attractions?
2 Do you think it's important to see all the famous sights and landmarks if you visit a new place?
3 How do you think tourism will change in the future?

3 READING

a Read the information from a tourism website about three destinations. Answer the questions.

1. What countries are the tourist destinations in?
2. Are the places well known?
3. Is the main tourist attraction in each place part of nature or is it man-made?

b Read the texts again. Are the sentences true or false?

1. Uruapan is an ancient city.
2. The Paricutin volcano is still active.
3. Colin and his girlfriend left Hanoi because of bad food.
4. The people of Ha Long Bay don't live on the islands.
5. The wooden constructions on Kizhi Island were built in the 1950s.
6. Emmy and her friends felt that visiting Kizhi Island was a special experience.

c Which place do you think sounds most interesting? Which place sounds least interesting? Why?

WHERE TO GO?

We all know about the world's most famous tourist attractions, but what about those places we haven't heard of? Tell us about your favourite places and send us a photo.

URUAPAN

I agree that people always go to the same places. I live in Mexico and tourists always visit places like Mexico City and Acapulco. Not many tourists come to my hometown, Uruapan. It's one of the oldest cities in Mexico. A beautiful river – it's called 'The river that sings' – runs through it, and there are spectacular waterfalls on the outskirts of the city. However, the most amazing feature you can see here is the nearby volcano, Paricutin. It really is quite **impressive**. You can go trekking up the volcano (it's about 420 metres high). The volcano is extinct so it's perfectly safe. So for some history and some really **remarkable** scenery, Uruapan is a good choice.

Teresa

HA LONG BAY

It's interesting that not many people talk about Vietnam as a holiday destination. Last year my girlfriend and I went there for the first time. We loved it – the people were great and the food was **superb**. Hanoi is a busy city, but there are lots of more **exotic** places you can escape to in Vietnam. The place we loved the most was Ha Long Bay where everyone lives on a floating house! On top of that, all around the bay there are **astonishing** islands made of limestone. Some of them look like beautiful towers – they're really quite **breathtaking**. And there are lakes and caves on some of the islands, as well as some very cheeky monkeys. Ha Long Bay is **dramatic** and beautiful. But best of all, there aren't thousands of tourists – not yet anyway!

Colin

KIZHI ISLAND

If you want to see something original and **unique**, you should go to Kizhi Island in Russia. The whole island is like a museum of **stunning** wooden constructions that look like they are straight out of a fairy tale. The island's in the middle of Lake Onega in Karelia, Russia. In the 1950s, lots of historic wooden buildings were moved from different parts of Karelia on to the island in order to save them. A couple of years ago, a group of us went to St Petersburg first, then on to Kizhi Island. It's the most **memorable** holiday I've ever had, and I felt like I'd been transported to another world. Although it's a UNESCO site, not too many people know about it so you won't meet loads of tourists.

Emmy

4 VOCABULARY
Travel and tourism

a Look at the adjectives in bold in the text. Do they have a positive or negative meaning?

b Answer the questions about the adjectives.

1. If something is *remarkable*, is there something special about it or is it quite normal?
2. If you see something *memorable*, is it something that stays in your mind for a long time or do you forget it easily?
3. If you think something's *exotic*, does it seem foreign and unpleasant or foreign and interesting to you?
4. If a landmark is *breathtaking*, is it exciting and surprising or really high up?
5. If you feel that something's *impressive*, is it something you admire or just something that's very big?
6. If something's *unique*, how many are there of them in the world?
7. If you think something's *superb*, do you believe it's very spicy or of very high quality?
8. If you see something *astonishing*, are you very bored or very surprised?
9. If something's *stunning*, does it feel almost as though you've been hit by its beauty or does it mean you think it's quite old-fashioned?
10. If you think scenery is *dramatic*, is it pleasant and interesting or beautiful and exciting?

c 2.45 **Pronunciation** Look at these adjectives from the text and mark the stress. Then listen and check.

impressive	stunning	breathtaking
remarkable	dramatic	memorable
superb	exotic	
astonishing	unique	

d Think of some interesting and beautiful things you've seen as a tourist. Choose adjectives from 4c to describe them. Then tell each other about the things you've seen.

e Now go to Vocabulary Focus 6A on p.159

5 READING and SPEAKING

a **Communication 6A** Student A: Go to p.130 Student B: Go to p.128.

b Tell the class what you decided.

6B About half the world's languages will disappear

Learn to discuss changes

G The passive

V Describing change

1 READING and LISTENING

a Work in small groups. Do the quiz together.

b 2.49 Listen to the first part of an interview with a language expert and check your answers. Then answer these questions.

1 What languages are most in danger of disappearing?
2 What is a 'language hotspot'?

How much do you know about … ?

LANGUAGES OF THE WORLD

Can you answer these questions?

1 How many independent countries are there in the world?

a) 120 b) nearly 200 c) nearly 500

2 How many spoken languages are there in the world?

a) around 500 b) around 3,000 c) around 7,000

3 Which one of these languages has just over 400 million native speakers?

a) Arabic b) English c) Spanish

4 What percentage of the world's population speaks Mandarin Chinese?

a) 4% b) 14% c) 24%

5 On average, how many languages die out every year?

a) 5 b) 25 c) 120

2 VOCABULARY Describing change

a Match the verbs in the box with the meanings.

be lost decline decrease deteriorate die out disappear increase preserve revive

1 keep as it is
2 stop existing (x3)
3 become more
4 become less or go down (x2)
5 bring back into existence
6 get worse

b Complete the sentences with the correct form of a verb in 2a and the information from 1b.

1 The number of people who speak English is ______.
2 The number of minority languages is ______.
3 Many languages are in danger of ______.
4 Educating children may help to ______ a language.

c 2.50 **Pronunciation** Listen to the verb and noun forms of these words. Which are pronounced differently?

verb: increase decrease decline
noun: increase decrease decline

d 2.51 Say the words in bold in sentences 1–4. Then listen and check.

1 There has been a steady **increase** in world literacy.
2 The number of different English dialects is slowly **decreasing**.
3 There has been a gradual **decline** in student numbers.
4 The number of bilingual children has **increased** over the last 50 years.

e What is the noun form of these verbs? Choose the correct ending in the box. What changes do you need to make?

-al -ance -tion

1 disappear 2 deteriorate 3 revive 4 preserve

f Think of three things which have increased or decreased in your country recently. Then compare with a partner.

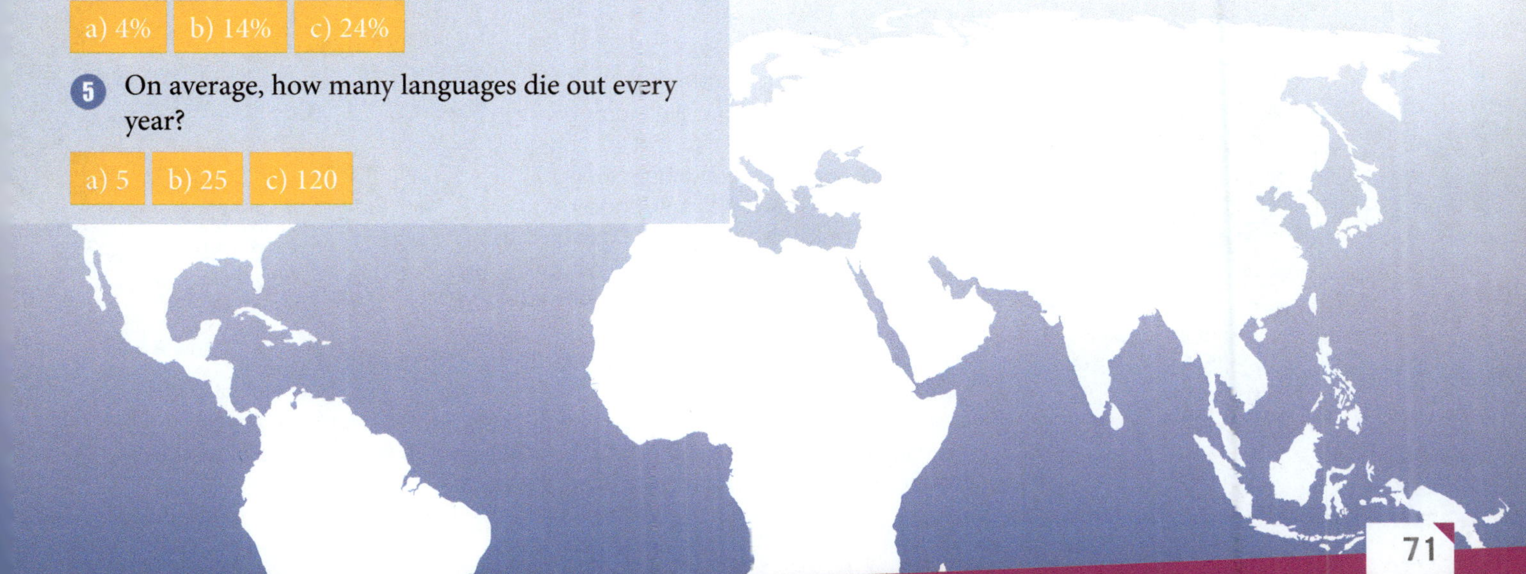

3 READING

a Read about three languages. In what ways are they similar? In what ways are they different?

DANGER!
DYING LANGUAGES

About half the world's languages are in danger of dying out, and many have already been lost, sometimes without any written record to show what they were like. We look at three languages: one dead, one dying and one which is being brought back to life thanks to one woman's dream.

BO In 2006, the last speaker of Bo, an ancient tribal language, died in the Andaman Islands, off the coast of India, breaking a 65,000-year link to one of the world's oldest cultures. Boa Sr was the last native who was fluent in Bo, which had been spoken since pre-Neolithic times.

Though the language was being studied and recorded by researchers, Boa Sr spent the last years of her life as the only speaker of the language, so she was unable to converse with anyone in her mother tongue. The Bo songs and stories which the old woman told couldn't be understood even by members of related tribes.

N|U Hannah Cooper is one of the few remaining speakers of a southern African language called N|u (the vertical line represents a clicking sound made with the tongue). N|u is now only spoken by about eight people. Now most young people have no interest in learning N|u, which they see as an 'ugly language, just for old people'. Although efforts are being made to save the language from dying out by recording stories and by giving language classes for children, it seems unlikely to survive as a spoken language for more than a few years.

Hannah remembers: 'We all used to get together and speak the language. We gathered together, we discussed issues, we laughed together in N|u.'

WAMPANOAG When the first European settlers landed in North America in 1620, they were helped by a Native American tribe called the Wampanoag, who showed them how to plant corn. The language died out in the early 19th century and there were no fluent speakers of Wampanoag for more than 150 years.

However, one night a young woman called Jessie Little Doe dreamed that her ancestors spoke to her in the Wampanoag language. Inspired by this, she first studied the language herself and then started a programme to revive the language, using old written records and books written in the language. She and her husband are raising their three-year-old daughter entirely in Wampanoag, and every summer they organise a 'language camp', which is attended by a group of about 50 young people and where only Wampanoag is spoken. This is the first time a language with no living speakers for many generations has been revived in a Native American community, and there's a good chance that it will be spoken more widely by future generations of Wampanoag.

b Read the text again and make notes about each language:

1 number of speakers
2 increasing or decreasing?
3 other important facts

c Imagine you could ask each of the three people mentioned in the text a question. What would you ask? What answer do you think they would give?

4 GRAMMAR The passive

a Match examples 1–8 with the passive forms a–h.

1 Many languages **have** already **been lost**.
2 Bo was a local language which **had been spoken** since pre-Neolithic times.
3 The language **was being studied** by researchers.
4 Her songs and stories couldn't **be understood** even by members of related tribes.
5 N|u **is** now only **spoken** by about eight people.
6 Efforts **are being made** to save the language from dying out.
7 They **were helped** by a Native American tribe called the Wampanoag.
8 There's a good chance that it **will be spoken** more widely by future generations.

a Present simple passive
b Past simple passive
c Present perfect passive
d Future passive
e Present continuous passive
f Past continuous passive
g Past perfect passive
h Passive infinitive form

b How do we form the passive?

a *be* + past participle
b *have* + past participle
c *be* + infinitive

c Find and underline other examples of the passive in the text. What tense are they?

d Now go to Grammar Focus 6B on p.144

e Rewrite the paragraph using the passive, so that the subject remains 'the N|u language'.

The N|u language is in serious danger because people only speak it in a few small villages. In the past people spoke it in a large region of South Africa and Namibia. Linguists have now recorded it and they've written it down and teachers who have learned the language themselves are teaching it to children in schools.

f Think about languages in your own country and discuss the questions.

1 What languages are spoken? What about dialects? Is there one 'official' language or more than one?
2 Which languages or dialects do you think are increasing and which are declining? Why?
3 Do you think people should be encouraged to use their own language, dialect or accent? Why / Why not?

5 LISTENING and SPEAKING

a You are going to listen to the rest of the interview with Professor Barnett, who tries to preserve endangered languages. How do you think he will answer these questions?

1 Does it matter if small languages die out … ?
   - to the people who speak that language
   - to the wider world
2 Isn't it a good idea for everyone to learn a global language?
3 Is it possible to stop languages from dying out?

b 2.54 Listen and check your ideas.

c 2.54 Listen again. Tick (✓) the points he makes.

1 No one feels happy about their language dying out.
2 Languages are just as important as buildings.
3 You can translate everything from one language to another.
4 You can learn a 'big' language and still keep your own language.
5 It's not good for children to be bilingual.
6 Children are the key to keeping languages alive.
7 Technology can stop languages dying out.

d Which points in 5c do you agree with? Are there any you disagree with? Why?

e **Communication 6B** Work in two pairs. Pair A: Go to p.133. Pair B: Go to p.131.

f Work with a partner from the other pair. Have a discussion, using the arguments you prepared. Report back to the class which points you agree on.

6C Everyday English
It's time you two had a break together

Learn to introduce requests and say you are grateful

S Introducing requests
P Consonant sounds

1 LISTENING

a Discuss the questions.

1 When was the last time you had to ask a friend or a family member for a favour?
2 What kind of favour was it?
3 How do you feel about asking someone a favour?

b Look at photo a. Who do you think is asking for a favour? What do you think they're saying?

c 2.55 Watch or listen to Part 1. Were your ideas in 1b correct? What is the favour?

d 2.55 Watch or listen to Part 1 again. Answer the questions.

1 What do Sam and Emma want to do?
2 How does Sam feel about asking Becky?
3 How do Sam and Emma feel afterwards?

2 CONVERSATION SKILLS Introducing requests

a 2.56 Read the conversation below and then listen to an excerpt from Part 1. What is the difference?

SAM Becky?
BECKY Yes, Sam.
SAM Could you look after the café this weekend?
BECKY Yes, that's fine.

b 2.56 Sam and Emma go through four steps to introduce the request. Put the steps in the correct order. Listen again and check.

1 They make the request.
2 They show that they realise they're asking a big favour.
3 They say they want to make a request.
4 They give a reason for needing to make the request.

c Why do Sam and Emma introduce their request carefully? Choose the correct answer.

1 They don't know Becky very well.
2 Sam and Becky had an argument recently.
3 They realise they're asking Becky a big favour.
4 They're worried about paying her overtime.

d Complete the beginnings in A with a word in the box. Then match A and B to make expressions that introduce requests.

like if mind to if

A	B
1 Do you mind ____ …	a … ask you this, but …
2 I'm really sorry ____ …	b … you wouldn't mind … ?
3 There's an idea I'd ____ …	c … I ask you something?
4 I was wondering ____ …	d … my asking, but …
5 I hope you don't ____ …	e … to run past you

e Answer the questions about the requests in 2d and the replies below.

1 What do you say to the requests to encourage the speaker? *Yes* or *No*.
2 Which two replies can be used with requests 1–2 and 4–5?
3 Which reply matches request 3?

What is it?
No, that's fine.
No, not at all.
Go right ahead.

3 USEFUL LANGUAGE
Showing you are grateful

a Sam thanks Becky and then shows how grateful he is. Complete Sam's sentence.

Thank you. That's ____ ____ of you.

2.57 Listen and check.

b Put the words in the correct order to make expressions.

1 really it appreciate we
2 really grateful we're
3 it's of kind you so
4 don't to I thank know you how

c Look at these replies to the expressions in 3b. Which one is not suitable? Why?

1 Oh, don't worry about it.
2 I'm happy to help.
3 It's no trouble at all.
4 I'm glad you're grateful.
5 It's not a problem.
6 My pleasure.

4 LISTENING

a Look at photos b and c and discuss the questions. Why do you think … ?

1 Tessa has come to visit Becky at the café
2 Phil is saying 'great'
3 Becky is saying 'sorry'

b 2.58 Watch or listen to Part 2 and check your answers.

c 2.58 Watch or listen again. Are the sentences true or false?

1 Tessa is interested in science fiction.
2 She asks Phil if she can read his book.
3 Tessa suggests that she and Becky begin their photography project.
4 Tessa offers to make sandwiches at the café.
5 Becky suggests that Tessa works in the café every Saturday.

5 PRONUNCIATION
Sounds and spelling: Consonant sounds

a Notice the **bold** consonant sounds. Match the underlined sounds a–h with consonant sounds 1–8.

1 /θ/ **th**irty
2 /ð/ **th**ey
3 /s/ **s**ay
4 /z/ **z**ero
5 /ʃ/ **sh**op
6 /ʒ/ u**s**ually
7 /ʧ/ **ch**oose
8 /ʤ/ **j**eans

a I'm really sorry to ask you …
b My pleasure …
c Do you think it'll be a problem?
d I need to check with Becky …
e I'm quite into science fiction.
f It's time you had a break together.
g … this project photographing bridges.
h I could close up on Friday.

2.59 Listen and check.

b Find a sound from 5a in the following words:

1 ideas
2 earth
3 television
4 jewel
5 bother
6 sugar
7 science
8 future

2.60 Listen and check. Then practise saying the words.

6 SPEAKING

a Think of a big favour to ask your partner. Think of a reason why you need to ask this favour.

b Take turns making your requests. Make sure you introduce your request carefully. If your partner agrees to your request, show that you're grateful.

I hope you don't mind my asking.
No, not at all.
I know that you're usually really busy at weekends …
Well, this weekend looks OK at the moment.

Unit Progress Test

CHECK YOUR PROGRESS

You can now do the Unit Progress Test.

6D Skills for Writing
The scenery was fantastic

Learn to write a travel blog

W Using descriptive language

1 SPEAKING and LISTENING

a Look at the photos of the top five tourist attractions in the USA. What do you know about them? Why do you think people want to see them? Which place would you most like to visit? Why?

b 2.61 Listen to Kirsten and John telling a friend about a trip to the Grand Canyon. Which of these topics do they not talk about?

the people the views camping birds
cars the desert cowboys meals

c 2.61 Listen again and answer the questions.

1 How did they travel?
2 What is unusual about the Mojave Desert?
3 Where did they stay: the first night? the second night? What do they say about it?
4 What two events did they watch at the Grand Canyon?
5 Where did they go next?

d Work on your own. What do you think are the top tourist destinations in your country?

e Compare your destinations with other students' ideas. Why do you think tourists find these places interesting?

2 READING

a Read Kirsten's travel blog about their trip. What information does it contain that was not in the recording?

Around the GRAND CANYON

Driving up to the Grand Canyon was an experience in itself. On the historic Route 66, we passed through the heart of the Mojave Desert, which is a huge, flat, salt desert – it was the first time we had seen salt plains. We stopped off at a small town called Williams, where we saw cowboys and a re-enactment of an old shootout that had taken place here in the 1800s.

It was late when we finally found a restaurant, where they let us put up our tents behind the building. To our horror, the airbed had a hole in it, so we had another uncomfortable night's sleep. I could feel stones pressing into my back all night! In the morning, we woke and drove the final 20 kilometres to the Canyon. It was literally breathtaking … it's hard to describe in words the grandeur and beauty of this natural phenomenon – it was the experience of a lifetime. We drove around the South Rim, which has superb views down into the canyon itself, until we found a campsite. Luckily we found a spot even though it was peak season. We ate, then went to the Desert Drive Watch Tower to watch the sun going down – just amazing.

At 4.45am, we woke and took a walk to watch the sun rise, which was a whole new experience as the light and the shadows made everything look different. After breakfast, we headed up to the village where a bus service took us round the other part of the South Rim. We took a short walk and we were very lucky to see a condor, as their numbers have declined and there are now only about 30 left – they are huge and very impressive. We watched it circling right above our heads. Again, the scenery was fantastic and we saw the canyon from a few different viewpoints.

After that we drove to Lake Mead for a few days to relax before the madness of Las Vegas. Vegas – here we come!

This is me walking in the salt desert (or trying to – it was 35°).

John looking down into the canyon.

3 WRITING SKILLS Using descriptive language

a Kirsten says the sunset was *amazing*. Find five other adjectives in the blog that mean *very beautiful* or *very big*.

b Look at the adjectives and phrases in the box. Which of them have a positive meaning and which have a negative meaning?

disappointing fabulous awesome
uninspiring mind-blowing ordinary
unbelievable out of this world dull
awe-inspiring unforgettable

c Which adjectives/phrases in 3b can be used to complete these sentences?

1 The scenery was absolutely ______.
2 The scenery was very ______.

Can you think of adverbs to replace *absolutely* and *very*?

d Change these sentences to make the meaning stronger. Use adjectives and phrases from 3a and 3b.

1 Manhattan was good and I thought the buildings were very nice.
2 The Niagara Falls were beautiful. We went on a boat below the Falls – it was very good.
3 People say that Las Vegas is a nice place to visit, but I thought it was not very good.

e Kirsten also uses three expressions with *experience* to describe the trip. Find the examples in 2a and complete the expressions below.

1 It was an experience ______.
2 It was the experience ______.
3 … which was a whole ______ experience.

f Think of a place you have visited. Write sentences about your experience using language from 3a–e. Then discuss it.

4 WRITING

a Choose one of the photos, or think of one of your own travel photos. Plan a travel blog around this photo. Make notes on:

- where you went
- what you did
- what you saw
- what it was like

b Write the travel blog. Include language from 3a–e.

c Swap travel blogs with other students. Ask and answer questions. Do the descriptions make you want to visit the place? Why / Why not?

UNIT 6
Review and extension

1 GRAMMAR

a Correct the mistakes in these sentences.

1 Do you find it easy relax at the weekend?
2 What kind of things do you do for help you relax?
3 Do you have a series of household tasks you need to remember doing?
4 In your neighbourhood, do you notice people to do the same kinds of thing as you do?
5 Do you remember to do the same kinds of things at the weekend when you were a child?

b Ask each other the questions.

c Put the verbs in brackets in the correct passive or active form.

This small pot 1_____ (give) to me by my great-grandfather about 10 years ago. It's Egyptian. He 2_____ (buy) it about 60 years ago. Apparently it 3_____ (discover) in the desert by an Egyptian farmer. Then it 4_____ (see) by an English soldier during the war. He 5_____ (pass) through a village where the pot 6_____ (clean). My great-grandfather 7_____ (say) the pot 8_____ (sell) for the price of a packet of cigarettes. He 9_____ (pay) about £50 for it after the war. It 10_____ (value) recently by an expert and it's now worth more than £2,000.

2 VOCABULARY

a Put the correct adjective in the gap.

1 We had a fantastic meal followed by a brilliant concert. It really was a m_____ evening.
2 They have a really i_____ collection of old movie posters – I've never seen so many.
3 I come from Tahiti so for me somewhere like England is e_____.
4 She paid a lot of money for her new evening dress. But it was worth it – she looks s_____ in it.
5 My favourite act in the circus was the high-wire acrobats. They were so skilled – their performance was b_____.

b Choose the correct word in italics.

'Robinsons' used to be my favourite department store. However, in the past few years I've noticed there's been a 1*decreasing / deterioration* in service. Years ago, the owners used to walk around the store and chat with customers, but not now. I wish they'd 2*revive / increase* that and 3*preservation / preserve* those old traditions with a personal touch. However, the Robinson family have all 4*died out / been lost* now and the store's owned by some anonymous company. They've 5*declined / decreased* the number of shop assistants who can help you. Instead there's been an 6*increased / increase* in self-service check-outs and face-to-face contact has 7*been lost / revived*. I think it's a shame.

3 WORDPOWER *out*

a 2.62 Listen to the short conversations. What multi-word verb with *out* is used to replace the underlined phrase?

1 Yes, if I keep working 14-hour days, I'll <u>get sick</u>. _____ out
2 I feel like I'm going to <u>faint</u>. _____ out
3 I just need to <u>calculate</u> the total cost. _____ out
4 I've <u>argued</u> with my brother and we're not speaking. _____ out
5 I think we've <u>got no</u> milk <u>left</u>. _____ out
6 But of all the applicants Maria really <u>is noticeably better</u>. _____ out
7 But he's <u>become</u> a very nice young man. _____ out
8 I'm going to lie by the swimming pool with a cold drink and just <u>relax</u>. _____ out

b Put an *out* multi-word verb in each gap. Think carefully about the correct verb form to use.

1 The weather was terrible this morning, but it's _____ to be a beautiful day.
2 His way of _____ is to play video games and forget daily life.
3 She was getting annoyed with the bad behaviour of the class and her patience was beginning to _____.
4 All the staff are saying that they're going to _____ if they keep working so hard.
5 This model really _____ as being more economical than all other cars of this size.
6 I'm trying to _____ how much tax I have to pay, but it's really hard.
7 The sight of blood makes him _____.
8 He always _____ with his friends – he's very difficult to get on well with.

c Make notes about the following questions.

1 Have you ever fallen out with another family member? Why?
2 What do you like to do to chill out?
3 Have you ever passed out? If so, how did it happen?
4 Who's a famous person that you think really stands out? Why do you think so?
5 What kinds of jobs do you think could result in burn out?

d Discuss your answers to the questions.

REVIEW YOUR PROGRESS

How well did you do in this unit? Write 3, 2 or 1 for each objective.
3 = very well 2 = well 1 = not so well

I CAN ...

discuss choices	☐
discuss changes	☐
introduce requests and say I am grateful	☐
write a travel blog	☐

CAN DO OBJECTIVES

- Discuss living in cities
- Discuss changes to a home
- Imagine how things would be
- Write an email to complain

UNIT 7
City living

GETTING STARTED

a Look at the picture and answer the questions.

1 Look at the new building. How is it different from the older building beside it? How is it similar?
2 What do you think of it? Do you think it is … ?
interesting   outrageous   ridiculous   amusing   ugly   harmonious
3 What do you think the architect was aiming to achieve? How successful was he/she?

b Discuss the questions.

1 Think of modern buildings that you know. What do you like / not like about them?
2 Do you think new buildings should fit in with their surroundings or stand out from them? Why?
3 Do you think it's right to develop and alter city neighbourhoods or should they be preserved?

7A There's very little traffic

Learn to discuss living in cities

G *too/enough; so/such*

V Describing life in cities

b

1 SPEAKING

a What type of stress do photos a and b show? How do you think the people in the pictures feel?

b Imagine a third photo of city life. What might it show? Discuss your ideas.

a

2 READING

a The article below is from an online group called *The Slow Movement*. What do you think they believe?

1 Success isn't as important as people think.
2 You shouldn't let your work take over your life.
3 Modern life is bad for our health.

Quick – slow down!

Speed worship

We love speed. When it comes to doing business and connecting with people, speed is important. We need to get our work done faster. We worry that we're too slow, that we aren't efficient enough or productive enough to succeed. We need to get there first. How do we do this? We speed up. Why? Because we seem to associate 'slow' with failure, inefficiency and perhaps worse: laziness.

City life

Many people complain that they don't have enough time. They have too much work to do every day and there are always too many things that they haven't done. There is pressure to be available 24/7 – to colleagues, clients and friends. We spend around 13 hours a week on emails and an average of three hours a day on social networking sites. City living can make things worse – we spend 106 days of our life looking for a parking space and up to three days a year in traffic jams. We have less time to relax, and this make us more impatient and less polite. Even birds are affected by the pace of urban living – blackbirds in cities get up earlier and go to sleep later than rural blackbirds.

RULES FOR SLOWING DOWN

1 Put your feet up and stare idly out of the window. (Warning: Do not attempt this while driving.)
2 Think about things, take your time. Do not be pushed into answering questions. A response is not the same as an answer.
3 Yawn often. Medical studies have shown that yawning may be good for you.
4 Bright lights and screens before bed will make sleeping difficult. So avoid gaming and social networking late in the evening.
5 Spend more time in bed. When it's time to get out of bed in the morning, don't. Sit there for half an hour and do nothing. Then get up slowly.
6 Read long, slow stories.
7 Spend more time in the bath.
8 Practise doing nothing. (Yes, this is the difficult one.)

b Read *Quick – slow down* quickly and check your ideas.

c Read the article again. What connection does the writer make between … ?

1 speed and business
2 slowness and laziness
3 time and city life
4 relaxing and our mood
5 work and sleep
6 'sleep debt' and alcohol
7 tiredness and health

d How could you live more slowly? Compare your ideas.

e Read *Rules for slowing down*. Were they the same as your ideas in 2d? Which ones are … ?

- things you do already
- things you don't do, but you think are a good idea
- things you think are a bad idea

Time poverty and sleep debt

Economist Juliet Schor calculated that people in most jobs now work the equivalent of a full month more each year than they did two decades earlier. In addition to this, scientist Russell Foster says that people get about two hours less sleep than they did 60 years ago.

This results in 'sleep debt', in other words people have so little sleep over such a long period of time that they are permanently tired. Studies done on doctors who hadn't had enough sleep showed that they had the same reaction speed as people who had drunk two glasses of beer. Being so tired can also seriously affect your health – scientists have discovered a link between sleep debt and cancer, heart disease, diabetes, infections and obesity.

Slow seeing

We are in such a hurry that we are creating big problems for ourselves. The answer to this is simple: slow down! Slowing down gives us the opportunity to see things more clearly and make the right decisions, and in the end it may help us to have better ideas and a healthier life. Einstein, one of the greatest scientific minds of all time, spent a lot of time daydreaming, and psychologists agree that this helps us to be more creative. So sit back and do nothing for a little while – your brain and body will thank you for it.

3 GRAMMAR *too/enough; so/such*

a Put *too, too much, too many* or *enough* in the correct place in each sentence. Then check your answers in the article *Quick – slow down!*

1 We worry that we're slow.
2 We aren't efficient or productive to succeed.
3 Many people complain that they don't have time.
4 They have work to do every day.
5 There are always things that they haven't done.

b Look at the sentences in 3a again. Did you put the words before or after … ?

1 an adjective 2 a noun

c Complete the rules with the words in the box.

an adjective countable after
a noun before uncountable

1 We use *too* before ____, but *too much* or *too many* before ____.
2 We use *too much* before ____ nouns and *too many* before ____ nouns.
3 *Enough* always comes ____ an adjective but ____ a noun.

d Complete the sentences with *so* or *such*.

1 People have ____ little sleep over ____ a long period of time that they are permanently tired.
2 Being ____ tired can also seriously affect your health.
3 We are in ____ a hurry that we are creating big problems for ourselves.

e ▶ Now go to Grammar Focus 7A on p.146

f Find and correct the mistake in each sentence.

1 I have such much work to do that I often have to work at weekends.
2 You spend too many time in front of the computer.
3 We don't have money enough to buy a new car.
4 He doesn't like his job, but he's too much lazy to look for a better one.
5 Cheer up! Why are you always in so a bad mood?
6 I'll have to draw the plan again. It isn't enough clear.

g Write four sentences about your everyday life and work/studies. They can be true or false. Include *too, enough, so* or *such*.

I've got so many clothes that I never know what to wear.

h Work in groups. Read your sentences. Can your group guess which sentences are true and which are false?

4 READING and LISTENING

a Look at the cities in photos a–d. What do you think the expression 'smart city' means?

b 3.6 Listen to the interview. What are the two main ideas of a 'smart city'? Choose two of the answers below.

1 People in it have a good quality of life.
2 It responds to people's needs.
3 It encourages people to have new ideas.

c 3.6 Listen again. What new information do you hear about … ?

1 traffic in London, UK
2 parking in Dublin, Ireland
3 energy use in Masdar, UAE
4 daily life in Songdo, South Korea

5 VOCABULARY
Describing life in cities

a Read the audio script on p.171. Find words or phrases which mean:

1 the level of enjoyment and health in someone's life
2 the people in a particular area
3 the problem of too many vehicles in the streets
4 a place to leave your car
5 the process in which a city grows or changes
6 buses, trains, trams, etc.
7 damage caused to the air by harmful substances
8 areas where people live without offices and big shops

b Cover your answers to 5a. Match the words 1–7 and a–g to make collocations.

1 ☐ quality	a development
2 ☐ local	b pollution
3 ☐ traffic	c transport
4 ☐ parking	d of life
5 ☐ urban	e congestion
6 ☐ air	f spaces
7 ☐ public	g residents

c Use two or three of the collocations in sentences about the place where you are now.

d Read out your sentences. Do other students agree?

SMART CITIES:
Are these the cities of the future?

In London, UK, cars pay to enter the city centre, and you only need a single card for the whole public transport system.

Masdar, UAE, is built in the desert and solar panels provide all its energy needs.

Songdo, a new city in South Korea, is built around a large central park with lakes.

In Dublin, Ireland, they have a system which can tell drivers where there's a free parking space.

6 LISTENING

a 3.7 Listen to Daniela and Richard talking about the cities they live in. Answer the questions.

1 Do they like living there? Why / Why not?
2 Do they think it fits the idea of a 'smart city'?

b 3.7 Which of these points do Daniela and Richard make? Listen again to check.

Daniela

1 In many American cities, people work in the centre but live outside the city.
2 The centre of Munich is quite a relaxing place to be.
3 Munich has serious problems with traffic congestion.

Richard

4 Bangkok is disorganised but full of life.
5 It's easy to find places to sit and relax in the city centre.
6 The centre of Bangkok is too expensive for ordinary people to live there.

7 SPEAKING

a Think about the town you're in now. In what ways does it fit the idea of a 'smart city'? What are the good and bad points about living there? Make notes.

b Discuss your ideas, using the expressions in 5b. Does everybody agree?

7B I could have it done by a professional

Learn to discuss changes to a home

G Causative *have/get*

V Film and TV; Houses

1 READING

a Look at photo a and answer the questions.

- Where is the woman?
- Why do you think she's there?
- What do you think she's doing?

b **Communication 7B** Now turn to p.133.

c Discuss the questions.

1 What kinds of reality TV programmes are there in your country?
2 Do you enjoy these programmes? Why / Why not?

d Read the article quickly. What is the main point the critic wants to make about reality TV? Choose the correct answer.

1 We no longer need stories for entertainment. Real people are more interesting.
2 Reality TV is in danger of creating unreal expectations about life.
3 A lot of the 'reality' in reality TV programmes is invented.

e Read the article again. In what way does the writer think reality is managed in these kinds of TV programmes?

- survival
- cooking
- home renovation
- garden makeover

f If what the writer says is true … ?

- does this make the programmes less enjoyable
- are TV producers and directors being dishonest

WHO PUTS THE 'REAL' IN REALITY TV?

These days we like our entertainment to be real. We watch people go off to extreme environments to see who's the most successful survivor. We can't get enough of chefs fighting it out to prove they're the best. Then there are the people who transform their homes, their gardens or even themselves in front of a TV camera. But what's really going on in these programmes?

Let's imagine someone called Julie. She isn't a real person – I've made her up – but she could be real. She's the kind of person who might appear on a reality TV show. You know, she's someone who lives a quiet life in a small town somewhere but then she decides to do something really extreme and dangerous on TV. Of course, it helps that she has got one or two big fears hiding under that quiet exterior – the type of thing that's going to come to the surface when, like the woman in the picture above, she's lost in the forest with no map … But, of course, we tend to forget the film crew that's filming all this. I'm sure they're very helpful. It's also possible that the director asked Julie to crawl through the bushes more than once – just so he could get a better shot.

What about those cooking programmes? They're all good cooks, aren't they? Well, yes, they are. But that's not always why they get chosen. TV producers want drama so they need a range of personalities on the show. Imagine a cooking competition where the cooks all got on really well and co-operated. In other words, no conflict. Is that the kind of reality we want to watch on TV?

A NEW LIFE IN 5 MINUTES

And then there's the makeover programme – you know, the new home, the new garden or the new-look you. Haven't you ever stopped to wonder how people on these programmes miraculously have a new kitchen after just one weekend? Remember your family's kitchen renovations? They took forever. On these programmes they like to speed up reality just a bit. While many of these programmes use professional tradespeople, others claim the renovation is all the work of the contestants. But did Julie really manage to repaint those walls between morning tea and lunch by herself? No, the director had some of it done by a professional painter. It probably would have taken Julie all weekend.

And wasn't Julie clever coming up with such a beautiful design for her garden? It's so good you would almost think that a landscape architect had done it. The chances are that's exactly what happened – the TV company got the design done by an expert.

DISASTER STRIKES … OR DOES IT?

Finally, let's not forget those little crisis moments along the way. Julie would love to be able to buy that designer fridge because it would make all the difference to her home makeover. But no, she's only got so much to spend and this just might blow her budget. Don't panic, dear viewer, the TV production company has got lots of money, and there's nothing to stop them increasing Julie's budget. The production company can afford to let Julie buy ten designer fridges without stopping to think about it.

TV production companies would like us to believe that what we see on TV actually happens. Well, it does, but only sort of. What we're really seeing is a kind of managed reality. Real reality on TV would probably be like real life – a bit slow and boring.

2 VOCABULARY Film and TV

a Look at the highlighted words in *Who puts the 'real' in reality TV?* With a TV programme, who … ?

1 organise(s) everything
2 tell(s) the actors what to do
3 work(s) as a technical team
4 watch(es) the programme

b Match the words in bold in 1–4 to definitions a–d.

1 ☐ There are only eight characters in the film – that means a small **cast**.
2 ☐ It's a very well-written film with a great **script** – there are some very funny scenes.
3 ☐ I loved everything about the film except for the **soundtrack** – too much jazz for my taste.
4 ☐ The film opens with a long **shot** of the main character walking along the edge of a cliff.

a the sounds and music
b a piece of film
c the story the actors act out
d all the actors in a production

c ▶ Now go to Vocabulary Focus 7B on p.160

3 GRAMMAR Causative *have/get*

a Look at the examples from *Who puts the 'real' in reality TV?* What is the meaning of *have* and *get*? Choose the correct answer.

The director ***had** some of it* done by a professional painter.
The TV company ***got** the design* done by an expert.

1 someone arranges for another person to do something
2 someone has done something later than planned

b ▶ Now go to Grammar Focus 7B on p.146

c Discuss these jobs. What things do you do yourself? What things do you have/get done?

personal appearance | household jobs | vehicles you own

I have my hair cut once a month.

My father has his car serviced twice a year.

I always decorate the house myself.

4 VOCABULARY Houses

a Use the words to label the picture.

cottage passage attic chimney cellar/basement fence
terrace detached semi-detached terraced bungalow

b Discuss the questions.

1 Does the house or apartment you live in have a cellar or basement? What do people keep there?
2 What are different uses of attics?
3 In your country, what kinds of homes have chimneys?
4 Do you prefer fences or walls around gardens?
5 What kinds of houses are there most of in your country: detached, semi-detached, cottages or bungalows?
6 Is a terrace and a terraced house the same? What's the difference?
7 Where could you find passages in your country? Are they common?

5 LISTENING

a In your country, if people want to do renovations to their home, do they do it themselves or do they usually have them done by an expert?

b 3.11 Listen to Antonia and Rob talk about house renovations. Do they feel the same about renovating?

c 3.11 Listen again. Answer the questions for each person, Antonia and Rob.

1 What changes has he/she made?
2 What's the result?
3 What will he/she do next?

d Do you know people like Antonia and Rob? What do you think about them?

6 SPEAKING

a Imagine you are a TV producer for a new home renovation show. Rob's wife has contacted the show to ask for help with their basement renovation. Think about:

- what makes your show interesting to watch (e.g. time and budget limits)
- what you could do with Rob's basement
- what you will get Rob / professional tradespeople to do

b Present your ideas to the rest of the class. Decide which ideas would make the most interesting show.

7C Everyday English
We could have a table here or something

Learn to imagine how things could be

P Stress in compound nouns
S Using vague language

1 LISTENING

a Look at photo a. Where are Becky and Tessa and what are they doing?

b 3.12 Watch or listen to Part 1. Were your ideas correct?

c 3.12 Watch or listen again and make notes on the topics below.

1 Tessa's photo
2 the photo competition
3 Tessa's feelings about the competition
4 Becky's meeting with Tom

2 PRONUNCIATION Stress in compound nouns

a 3.13 Listen to the compound words and answer the questions.

A	B
estate agent	first prize
photography competition	free competition

1 Which word has the main stress, the first or the second?
2 Look at the first words. Are they nouns or adjectives?

b Complete the rules.

If a compound noun is noun + noun, we usually stress the ______ word.
If a compound noun is adjective + noun, we usually stress the ______ word.

c 3.14 Underline the stressed words in these compound words. Then listen and check. Then try saying them with the correct stress.

flower garden
front garden
night club
mobile phone
cell phone
computer monitor
secret agent

3 SPEAKING and LISTENING

a Think about where you live and answer the questions.

1 Is it easy to find a flat or room to rent? Why / Why not?
2 Do you think it is better to buy a flat or to rent one? Why?
3 What kind of flat or house do you live in? What kind would you like to live in?

b 3.15 Watch or listen to Part 2. Which sentence describes what happens?

1 The estate agent is positive about the flat and Tom and Becky like parts of the flat.
2 Tom and Becky like the flat, but they think it's too small and the estate agent agrees with them.
3 The estate agent is positive about the flat, but Tom and Becky think it's awful.

c How does the estate agent describe the flat? Choose words or phrases for each room.

cosy a nice view quiet practical
good-sized perfect convenient

1 the living room 2 the bedroom 3 the kitchen

d According to Tom and Becky, what problems does the flat have?

e 3.16 Watch or listen to Part 3. How is this flat different from the one in Part 2? Do Tom and Becky take the flat?

f 3.16 Are the sentences true or false? Listen again and check.

1 The flat has been on the market for a few weeks.
2 Becky is worried it's too expensive for them.
3 Tom and Becky start thinking about how to arrange the flat.
4 Two other people have expressed interest in the flat.
5 Tom needs time to decide what to do.

4 USEFUL LANGUAGE Imagining how things could be

a 3.16 In Part 3, Tom and Becky imagine how the flat might look if they lived in it. Complete these sentences from the conversation. Use modal verbs and main verbs. Then listen and check.

1 Look, this ______ ______ a kind of sitting area by the window.
2 We ______ ______ some plants and some bookshelves, or a big lamp.
3 And this ______ ______ a great dining area.
4 I ______ ______ a big TV right here.

b What does sentence 3 in 4a mean?

1 We'd need to do some work on it.
2 It could have this function
3 It's a dining room.

c Work in small groups. Look at your classroom and try to imagine it as one of the following:

- an office
- a book shop
- a small flat for a student.

Imagine how it might look and what might be in it. Use expressions in 4a.

d Present your ideas to other groups. Who had the most interesting ideas?

5 CONVERSATION SKILLS Using vague language

a 3.17 Listen to the conversation. Where do the speakers add the phrases in brackets?

1 I thought this could be a separate living area by the window. (kind of)
2 We could have plants and bookshelves there, or a big lamp. (and things)
3 We could have a table here and some interesting lights. (or something)

b The phrases in 5a are examples of vague language. Why do the speakers use vague language?

- because they're not sure exactly how the flat should look
- because they're in a hurry and can't think of the exact words

c **Pronunciation** Is the vague language stressed or unstressed? What do you notice about the pronunciation of *and*, *of* and *or* in the phrases?

d Look at these vague phrases. Which phrases in 5a could they replace?

1 and things like that
2 sort of
3 or something like that
4 and so on

e Add vague phrases to these sentences. (Sometimes there is more than one possible answer.)

1 This could be a reading corner with a bookshelf and a lamp.
2 We could use this shelf for herbs and spices and jars of jam.
3 There's a walk-in cupboard in the bedroom. We could use it for coats or shoes.
4 I could imagine a big plant over there by the window.

(b)

6 SPEAKING

a Communication 7C Student A go to p.129. Student B go to p.133.

b Show your room plans to the rest of the class. Who has designed the most interesting room?

Unit Progress Test

CHECK YOUR PROGRESS

You can now do the Unit Progress Test.

7D Skills for Writing
There is a great deal of concern

Learn to write an email to complain

W Using formal language

1 SPEAKING and LISTENING

a Discuss the questions.

1 What changes in urban development have you noticed in your local area? Think about things like new facilities (hospitals, schools), new roads, shopping malls, etc.
2 Do you think these examples of urban development are positive or negative? Why?

b 3.18 Listen to six people talking about a shopping mall planned for their local area. Is each person in favour (*F*) of the plan, against (*A*) or do they have mixed views (*M*)?

c 3.18 Listen again. What reasons does each person give for his/her point of view? Make notes. Use the words/phrases in the box to help you.

progress   living space   convenient
safe   the price you pay   part of a chain

d How would you feel if a shopping mall was planned for your local area?

2 READING

a Read Ryan's email to his friend Rosie about the planned shopping mall. What does he say in the email that he didn't mention in 1b?

Hi Rosie,

Thanks for your message. Great to hear from you. I'm glad your trip's going well.

The big news here is a shopping mall – would you believe it? Last Monday the local government released their urban development plan and it shows that a shopping mall's going to be built just across the road. My parents think it's a great idea, but I think it's going to be a disaster. It'll just mean a whole lot of the same horrible chain stores. And there'll be so much traffic!

But the thing that really makes me angry is that they aren't going to discuss this with people who live in the area. It looks like they're planning to just go ahead with building the mall. I'm sure they're not allowed to do that. Actually, I'm going to write an email to the local government and complain. I think a few people are planning to do that – maybe we can get them to change their minds.

I'd better get on with it. Hope you keep having fun!

All the best,

Ryan

b Read Ryan's email to the local government. What is the main reason for his complaint?

1 The problems the local community will have when the mall is built.
2 The way the local government has communicated the plan for the mall.

Subject: Planned Riverway Shopping Mall
Dear Sir/Madam,
[a]I am writing regarding the intention to build a shopping mall which was outlined in the urban development plan.
[b]In my neighbourhood there is a great deal of concern about the effect the mall will have on our local community. However, what worries us most of all is the fact that there has been no discussion with local residents. We understand that before a change of this nature can become part of a plan, a proposal needs to be sent out so residents can give feedback on it.
[c]In the past few days, I have tried to contact different local councillors to find out how the plan was agreed, but no one has returned my calls. I also visited your offices and asked to see the minutes of the meeting where the plan was discussed. I was told they were not available. The person I spoke to suggested that I should write this email.
[d]I believe that what you are doing is against the law and I would formally like to request that local government withdraws the plan and puts out a proposal that can be discussed with local residents.
[e]If I do not hear from you within two days, my next step will be to get in touch with the media. This will ensure there is a discussion of the plan in local media and also online.
I look forward to a prompt reply.
Yours faithfully,
Ryan Fitzgerald

c Read the email again. Answer the questions.

1 Who has Ryan tried to speak to?
2 Who does he plan to contact next?
3 What does he want local government to do? Why?

3 WRITING SKILLS Using formal language

a Match paragraphs a–e in Ryan's email to the local government to the summaries below.

1 describes what action Ryan has taken
2 explains Ryan's reason for writing
3 indicates why Ryan is concerned
4 says what action he will take if there's no response
5 explains what action Ryan wants the local government to take

b Compare Ryan's informal email to Rosie with his formal email to the local government. What are the differences in ... ?

- greeting
- sign-off
- punctuation
- contractions

c Find more forms of these expressions in the formal email.

1 I'm just getting in touch about ...
2 Everyone's worried about what the mall will be like for us.
3 We reckon you should have sent out a proposal.
4 I think it's illegal and I want you to ...
5 Get back to me in a couple of days or ...
6 I want you to ...
7 I can't wait to hear from you.

d Rewrite this informal email to make it more formal.

Hi there,
That electric toothbrush you sold me online a couple of days ago is no good. The electric charge runs out after about five minutes! I reckon it should last an hour or so. How about sending a replacement? If not, I'll write a nasty review on your website.
Bye for now,
Peter

e Compare with other students. Are your emails the same?

4 WRITING

a Work on your own. Choose a situation below to complain about or use your own idea.

- your mobile phone company has changed your contract without letting you know
- your electricity / gas / water company has charged you too much on your last bill

b Make notes on:

- the background to the complaint
- what actions you have already taken
- your request for action
- what you will do next if no action is taken.

c Work in pairs. Tell each other about your situation. Help each other with ideas.

d Write your email of complaint. Use the structure and expressions from 3a–c.

e Work in new pairs. Read each other's email. Did your partner include all the points in 4b? Do you think the person receiving the email will respond to the complaint?

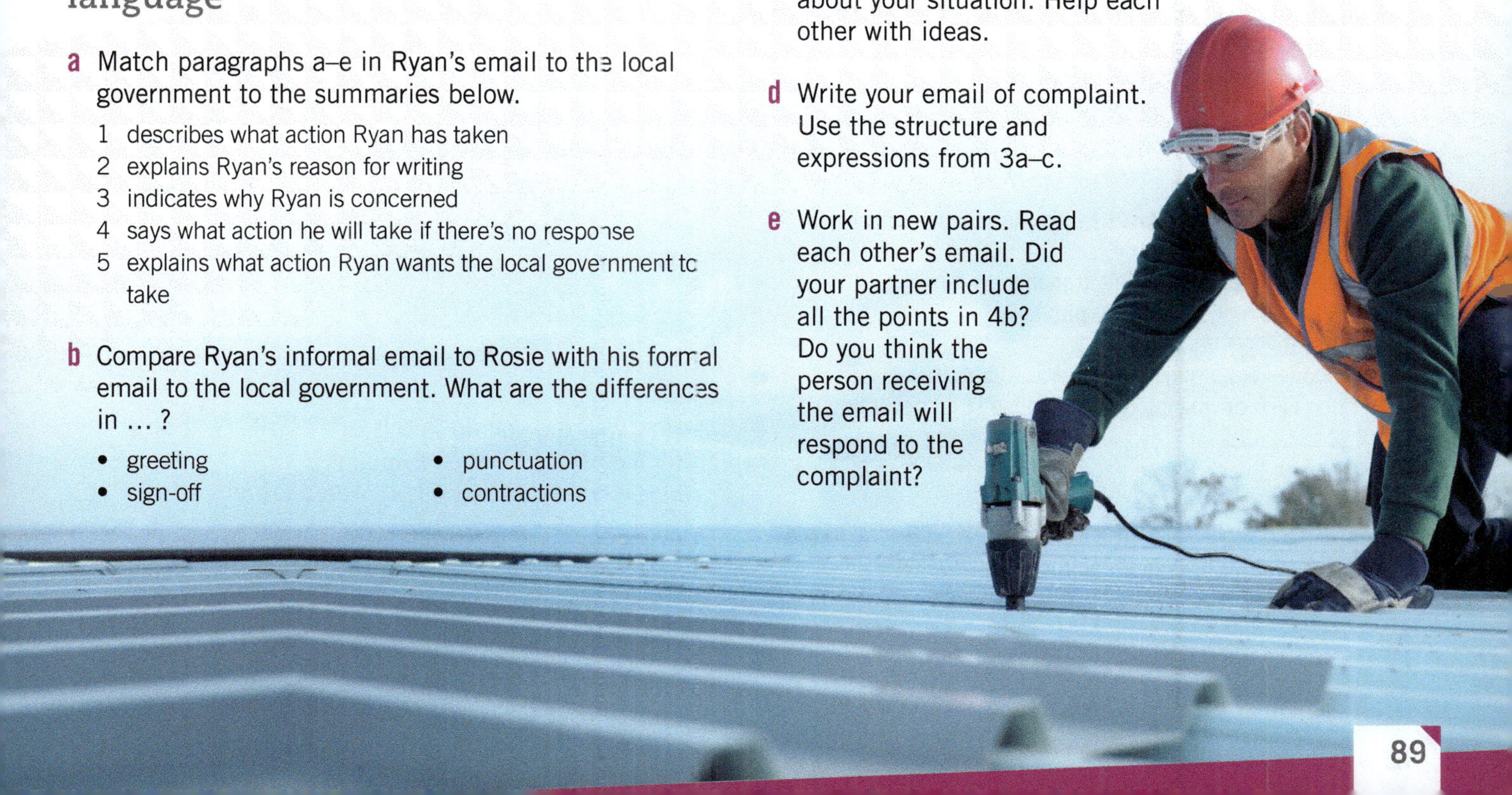

UNIT 7
Review and extension

1 GRAMMAR

a Change the sentences to *had* or *got* + past participle.

Susie stayed at the Excelsior Hotel on a business trip. Her boss told her the company would pay the hotel bill.

1 She decided not to eat in the restaurant. *She asked them to bring all her meals to her room.*
She had …
2 She called the laundry service. *They washed and ironed all her clothes.*
3 Then she went downstairs to the hairdressing salon. *They cut and dyed her hair.*
4 Then she went next door to the beauty salon. *They massaged her face and manicured her nails.*
5 The total cost was $3,500. *She asked them to add everything to her hotel bill.*

b What can you have (or get) done in these places?

1 a hairdresser's
2 a garage
3 a dental surgery
4 an optician's

c Andor is unhappy about his life. Add *too*, *too much/many* or *enough* to his sentences.

My faults …
1 I smoke.
2 I drink fizzy drinks.
3 I don't go to bed early.
4 I'm not kind to my parents.
5 I don't get exercise.
6 I download films.

d Join these sentences using *so* or *such* and *that*. You may have to change some words.

1 It was a lovely day. We decided to go to the beach.
It was such a lovely day that we decided to go to the beach.
2 There were a lot of people on the beach. We couldn't find a place to sit.
3 The water was cold. You couldn't go swimming.
4 We went to a café to eat but it was very expensive. We just ordered coffee.
5 It was very strong coffee. I couldn't drink it.

2 VOCABULARY

a Choose two words from the box for each sentence.

space traffic pollution transport
parking air congestion public

1 Factories are a major cause of ______ ______.
2 I don't like driving into town because I can never find a ______ ______.
3 We want to encourage people to leave their cars at home and use ______ ______.
4 The main problem in our city is ______ ______. It takes me two hours to drive to work in the morning.

3 WORDPOWER *down*

a Look at the pictures. What do you think is happening?

1

2

b Match the two halves of the sentences.
Which sentences go with the pictures in 3a?

1 After he got married, he decided to stop travelling and
2 I've tried, but I can't find a job anywhere. It's starting to
3 Don't get so upset. Just have a drink of water and
4 They offered me a job in Dubai, but I think I'll have to
5 OK, it's been nice chatting to you, but now I need to
6 The new PA thinks she's so important. She seems to

get down to some work.
calm down.
settle down.
look down on everyone.
turn it **down**.
get me **down**.

c Which multi-word verb means:

a stay in one place
b relax
c make (someone) feel depressed
d feel superior to
e refuse, say no
f start, concentrate on

d Complete the gaps with the correct form of a multi-word verb from 3b.

1 She works 10 hours a day in a factory and earns almost nothing. Sometimes it really ______.
2 We've considered your offer but we've decided to ______ as we've already made an agreement with another company.
3 OK, everybody, there's no danger, so please just ______ and don't panic.
4 I wanted to start my essay this evening, but I just couldn't ______ to it – I couldn't think what to write.
5 Just because they're poor and they don't have a nice car like you, there's no reason to ______.
6 You're 30. It's time to ______ and start a family.

e Work in pairs. Choose a verb and talk about it. Can your partner guess the verb?

A: I don't like our new neighbours. They always criticise people. They think they're better than everyone else …
B: They look down on other people?

REVIEW YOUR PROGRESS

How well did you do in this unit? Write 3, 2 or 1 for each objective.
3 = very well 2 = well 1 = not so well

I CAN …

discuss living in cities	☐
discuss changes to a home	☐
imagine how things would be	☐
write an email to complain	☐

CAN DO OBJECTIVES

- Discuss personal finance
- Discuss moral dilemmas and crime
- Be encouraging
- Write a review

UNIT 8
Dilemmas

GETTING STARTED

a Look at the picture and answer the questions.

1 What do you think is happening?
2 Do you think this is real money? Who put it there? Why?
3 If you had been there, would you have taken any money?

b Discuss the questions.

1 There is a common expression in English: 'Money doesn't grow on trees'. What does this mean and when do people say it?
2 If money did grow on trees, do you think most people would be happier? Why / Why not?

8A I'd like to start saving for a home

Learn to discuss personal finance

G First and second conditionals
V Money and finance

1 VOCABULARY Money and finance

a Read the money facts below. Do any of them surprise you? Do you think these statistics are similar in your country? Why / Why not?

1 The UK population has a total credit card **debt** as high as £80 billion.

2 Half of Australians don't know the **interest rate** on their credit card.

3 57% of households in the USA don't have any kind of **budget**.

4 You can make **savings** of about £69,500 over a lifetime by taking a packed lunch to work.

5 85% of students in England will never fully **pay off** their student loans.

6 A survey in the USA showed that only 53% of people understand how to make an **investment**.

7 On average, households in the UK manage to save just under 8% of their annual **income**.

8 In Australia, there has been a 46% increase in online **donations** made to charities.

b Match the definitions with the words in bold in 1a.

1 a financial plan
2 to repay money you owe in full
3 money you give to help people or organisations
4 money that you owe
5 a fixed amount you have to pay when you borrow money
6 the amount of money you have saved
7 money that you earn or receive
8 money you put into a bank or business to make a profit

c Complete the sentences with the collocations in the box. Use the correct verb form.

make / living	put aside / savings	award / grant
donate / charity	debit / account	finance / project

1 The university has decided to _____ her a _____ of £5,000 for her postgraduate study.
2 Every month, the bank _____ my _____ with about £15 in fees. It feels like robbery!
3 I don't know how he manages to _____ a _____ from his café. He never has any customers.
4 Why don't you _____ the money to a _____ like Save the Children?
5 Local businesses agreed to _____ a _____ to increase the number of trees in the city's parks.
6 Since she started work, she hasn't _____ any _____. She spends all the money she earns.

d Answer the questions and compare with other students.

- Do you or your family have a weekly or monthly budget?
- Do you know the typical interest rate on credit cards in your country?
- How often do you donate money to charity? Do you pay in cash or online?
- Do you try to put aside savings? How often?
- Do students in your country have to pay off loans after they graduate?
- Do you feel that you know how to make investments? Why / Why not?

2 LISTENING

a 3.19 Listen to a radio programme about personal finance. Tick (✓) the topics you hear.

1 ☐ saving for retirement
2 ☐ credit card debt
3 ☐ investment plans
4 ☐ paying off debt
5 ☐ personal loans
6 ☐ personal spending

b 3.19 Listen again. Complete the table.

	Jacob	Sophie
Caller's problem		
Mia's advice		

c Work in pairs. Do you agree with Mia's advice? Why / Why not?

3 GRAMMAR First and second conditionals

a Match 1–3 with a–c to make sentences from the radio programme.

1 If you transfer your card,
2 If I did that,
3 If I were you,

a I'd use the money to pay off your student loan.
b you'll probably pay as little as 3%.
c I wouldn't be able to afford things like holidays and going out for dinner.

b Match the examples in 3a with these uses:

1 to give advice to someone
2 to talk about a situation we think is a real possibility
3 to talk about a situation that we think is imaginary or less likely to happen

c What's the main difference between the examples in 3a and the examples below? Choose the correct answer.

If you transferred your card, you'd probably pay as little as 3%.
If I do that, I won't be able to afford things like holidays and going out for dinner.

1 The speaker is talking about a different period of time.
2 The speaker thinks the situations are more or less likely.

d Now go to Grammar Focus 8A on p.148

e Are these situations real possibilities for you or not? Make first conditional or second conditional sentences for each one.

1 If I (get) a loan from the bank, I (be) able to buy a new car.
2 If I (put) aside £5 a week for a year, I (have) enough money to buy a new phone.
3 If I (want) to buy a new home, I (have to) borrow a lot from the bank.
4 If I (stop) buying my lunch for a week, I (donate) the money to charity.
5 If I (download) a pay-with-your-phone app, I (have to) be careful not to over-use it.

f Discuss your sentences. Did you use the same conditionals?

4 READING

a Think of things you've bought in the past week. Tell each other why you bought it and the different ways you paid.

b Read *Is it time to give up on cash?* What is the writer's aim?

1 to promote the benefits of a cashless society
2 to question some of the benefits of a cashless society
3 to give a balanced view of the benefits and drawbacks of a cashless society

c Read the article again. Match the headings with paragraphs 2–6.

A sense of reality	The honesty of cash
Were they so wrong?	Better for everybody
Almost cashless now	

d Read the article again. Answer the questions.

1 What's the evidence we're already in a cashless society?
2 What costs do businesses and consumers have when they use cash?
3 Why might you spend more when you use a credit card?
4 What does the psychological test tell us about the relationship between digital payment and honesty?
5 What does the writer suggest the overall effect is of a cashless society?

5 SPEAKING

a Work on your own. What's your opinion of these statements? Make notes.

1 The reason people get into financial trouble is that they're not taught how to manage personal finance. This needs to be introduced as a subject in school.

2 Financial experts tend to oversell the need to save money. They forget that people need to enjoy life and that often means spending money.

3 There are too many financial experts saying too much about personal finance. This doesn't help – it just creates confusion and people feel under pressure.

4 A lot of people are so obsessed with their personal wealth that they forget about giving money to charities that can help people who are less fortunate.

b Discuss the statements in 5a with other students. Explain your opinions. Do you all agree?

c Which advice do you think is most relevant? Why?

blog | comment | media | tech | travel | finance

IS IT TIME TO GIVE UP ON CASH?

1 If I asked you to put down this article and take out your wallet or purse, what would you find inside? There would probably be quite a few plastic cards there, but how many of you have got any cash?

2 For years now, economists have predicted a gradual move to what is called a 'cashless society'. Most payments are already made by putting a plastic card into a machine and entering our pin code, or by simply waving the card in front of the machine.

3 So what's the attraction of a cashless world? Well, for one thing cash is expensive. We often pay fees when we use cash machines – people in the UK together pay almost £6 million a month in cash-machine fees. Cash also spreads disease. Dr Peter Ender, who carried out a study looking at the bacteria on one-dollar bills, claims that 'paper money is usually full of bacteria and a dollar bill could, theoretically, be the magic carpet it rides on from one host to another'. And of course, there's always a record of digital money, so it makes it harder for people to steal it. Businesses that handle large amounts of cash usually need to pay security companies to keep their cash safe, but you don't need a security guard to help you manage digital money.

4 However, do we really save? Some psychologists question this. They argue that waving your debit card in front of a machine doesn't give us a real sense of paying. Likewise, when we make one click with our mouse when shopping online, it's easy to forget that the credit card bill will arrive at the end of the month. There's plenty of psychological research to show that when we spend using physical notes and coins, we spend more sensibly. Basically, with a credit card we don't feel the 'pain of paying'. In a cashless society, we tend to buy more than we need to, because it's easier to spend and the consequences of our spending are more remote from us.

5 And it's certainly still possible to cheat and steal in a cashless society. If you manage to cheat someone and you never have to look them in the eye, then it's easier to take the payment. In a psychological test, people were twice as likely to accept a dishonest digital payment as a dishonest cash payment. Once again, psychologists suggest that the sense of being remote from payment in a cashless scenario increased the likelihood of dishonesty.

6 So, while we might laugh at the idea of our grandparents with money hidden under the mattress, maybe the joke is on us. In our bright, shiny, plastic, cashless society maybe things are not as wonderful as we think they are. Perhaps it's a society that's not quite as honest as we'd like to believe. Without doubt, it's a world where we feel distanced from the consequences of the purchases we make. Reality arrives in the form of a large credit card bill at the end of the month. So perhaps we're more efficient in our cashless society, but are we any happier?

8B I would have opened it

Learn to discuss moral dilemmas and crime

G Third conditional; *should have* + past participle
V Crime

1 READING and LISTENING

a Look at the photo of the 2012 London Olympics closing ceremony and discuss the questions.

1 What usually happens at an Olympic ceremony? Think about:
- music
- parades
- speeches
- athletes
- the Olympic flame

2 Would you buy tickets for a big event like this? Why / Why not? Would you go if someone bought you a ticket?

b Read the article *Honest London?* What did the newspaper want to find out?

1 if people wanted to go to the Closing Ceremony
2 if the Olympic Games had made people more honest
3 if people in London are friendly

c 3.21 Listen to four people saying what they would have done. Which person would have ... ?

1 opened the letter and used the tickets
2 opened the letter, then posted it
3 taken no notice of the letter
4 posted the letter without opening it

d 3.21 Listen again. What is the main point that each speaker makes? Choose a or b.

Speaker 1
a You shouldn't open letters that aren't addressed to you.
b The person who lost the letter was very careless.

Speaker 2
a It must be great to go to the Closing Ceremony at the Olympics.
b You can't enjoy an event if the tickets are stolen.

Speaker 3
a If you find a ticket, it's OK to keep it for yourself.
b You can't be sure what's in an envelope, so it's better to check.

Speaker 4
a It can be dangerous to pick up an envelope in the street.
b Someone else might want the ticket more.

e **Communication 8B** Go to p.133 and find out what people in London did. Then answer the questions.

1 How honest were Londoners during the Olympics according to this test?
2 In what way was Julia 'not only nice but also rather smart'?
3 Do you think it was a reliable test? Why / Why not?

London 2012 Olympic Games, Closing Ceremony

HONEST LONDON?

What do you think people in London are like? Do you think they're kind, friendly and helpful, or are they busy and stressed out? If you travel on the underground, do you think people will smile at you or will they stare straight ahead?

In fact, like most big cities, London doesn't have a reputation as being a very friendly place, nor a particularly honest one. If you drop your wallet in the street, you shouldn't expect someone to run after you and give it back. But when the Olympics were held in London in 2012, people said that having a major international event in their city made people not only prouder of their city, but also friendlier and more honest.

A major London newspaper wanted to see how kind and honest Londoners really were during the Olympics, so they dropped 50 stamped envelopes around the city addressed to 'Jeremy Fingham' with a London address. A note was written on the back which said 'Closing Ceremony tickets for Jeremy'. Inside were two pieces of blank card that would feel exactly like Olympic tickets. Some were left on café tables in folded newspapers, some on the Underground and some were dropped in the street near postboxes.

Would people be tempted to take the tickets for themselves, or would they put the letter in the post to Mr Fingham?

2 GRAMMAR

Third conditional; *should have* + past participle

a Look at these examples and answer the questions.

If I'd found one of the letters in the street, I would have posted it.
It would have been quite wrong to open it.

1 Are the speakers … ?
 a talking about something that really happened
 b just imagining a situation

2 Are they talking about … ?
 a the present b the future c the past

3 Complete the rules for the third conditional:

After *if*, we use the past perfect tense:
_____ + _____
In the main clause of the sentence we use:
would + _____ + _____

b Look at these examples and choose the correct answers.

Obviously the person **should have been** more careful.
Well, it wasn't my mistake. He **shouldn't have dropped** the letter.

1 The bold expressions are used:
 a to say something was possible
 b to criticise someone

2 The form of the bold expressions is:
 a *should(n't)* + present perfect
 b *should(n't)* + *have* + past participle

c 3.22 **Pronunciation** Listen to these sentences. The stressed words are bold.

He **shouldn't** have **dropped** the **letter**.
You **should** have **told** me.

What do you notice about the pronunciation of the unstressed words?
Are they … ?
1 the same length as the stressed sounds
2 shorter and said more quickly

Practise saying the sentences.

d Now go to Grammar Focus 8B on p.148

e What would you have done if you'd found an envelope? Would you have … ?

- posted the envelope to Jeremy Fingham
- kept the envelope, intending to use the tickets yourself
- opened the envelope anyway, just to check if there really were tickets inside
- ignored the envelope and walked on

3 SPEAKING

a Work in two pairs. You are going to read about two 'moral dilemmas'. Pair A: Go to 1 below. Pair B: Go to p.132.

1 Read the story and answer the questions.
 a Why was George stopped?
 b Why did they want him to sit in the police car?
 c Why did he pay them?

THE BRIBE

George Manley, his wife and two children were driving home late at night from a winter holiday. They were in a hurry to get home because their four-year-old son had a high temperature, so George was driving over the speed limit. Suddenly he saw the flashing blue lights of a police car behind him. The police car stopped them and as it was a cold night the officers asked him to bring his papers and come and sit in the police car. Then, to his surprise, they told him he would need to go to the police station to pay the fine and this would take several hours as the police station was about 50 km away. Instead, George could simply pay them in cash and he could drive on with no delay; they would fill in the forms at the police station the next day. He knew he was being asked to pay a bribe. Yet there was his young son, feeling sick and increasingly desperate to get home to bed. Quickly, he paid the money and drove on. He said nothing about it to his wife, because he knew she wouldn't agree with what he had done.

2 What do you think George should have done? Why?
3 What would you have done?

b Work with a student who read about the other dilemma. Take turns talking about your stories. Do you agree with each other's ideas?

4 VOCABULARY Crime

a Which of the words in the box could you use to discuss ... ?

1 the test described in *Honest London*?
2 the two dilemmas in 3a

burglary theft lying robbery cheating bribery murder

b Answer the questions about the words in 4a.

1 Which words describe ... ?
- crime
- dishonest behaviour which is not illegal

2 Three of the words mean 'stealing money or valuable things'. Which means ... ?
a stealing in general
b stealing from a home or a building
c stealing with violence (e.g. with a knife or a gun)

c Complete the table with the correct words in the box.

cheat kidnapping thief burglary shoplift
bribe liar rob murder kidnapper robbery
shoplifter murderer

person	behaviour/crime	verb
a burglar	______	burgle
a ______	theft	steal
a robber	______	______
a cheat	cheating	______
a ______	lying	lie
	bribery	______
a ______	murder	______
a ______	______	kidnap
a ______	shoplifting	______

d Read these news headlines and choose the correct word.

Bank *burglars / robbers* escape with $500,000 after police are forced to give up search.

Car *kidnapping / theft* is increasing, say police.

Detectives solve *murder / lying* mystery after years of investigating.

10% of University students *cheat / burgle* in exams, report claims.

Two teenagers sent to prison for *shoplifting / cheating*.

***Burglars / Kidnappers* stole items worth more than £50,000 in three months.**

e Now go to Vocabulary Focus 8B on p.161

5 SPEAKING

a Read the following situations. What would you have done?

- 'I saw my best friend stealing something in the supermarket. Of course I didn't tell anyone – she's my friend.'
- 'A colleague in my office lied about the company accounts. I was the only one who knew he was lying. I sent my manager an anonymous note.'
- 'In our final exam at university, I saw a student in our year look at answers on a small piece of paper. I didn't say anything. It wasn't anything to do with me.'

b Which of these situations do you think is most serious? Why?

c Do you think it's always important to be honest?

8C Everyday English
You'll find somewhere

Learn how to be encouraging

S Showing you have things in common

P Word groups

1 LISTENING

a Discuss the situations below.

1 If a friend or family member has a bad day, how do you try to cheer that person up?

2 When was the last time you tried to cheer someone up?

a What was the situation?

b How did they react?

b Look at the photos of Becky and Sam. Guess the problem each person has.

1 Becky has just heard they …

a can't afford the flat.

b didn't get the flat.

2 Sam's about to …

a talk to the bank manager about a loan.

b tell Becky he can't afford to employ her any more.

c 3.28 3.29 Watch or listen to Parts 1 and 2 and check your answers.

d 3.28 3.29 Watch or listen to Parts 1 and 2 again. Are the sentences true or false?

Part 1

1 Another person acted more quickly to get the flat.

2 Tom tried calling Becky earlier.

3 Becky is confident they can find another place.

Part 2

4 Sam will be away from the café for about an hour.

5 He wants to buy new furniture for the café.

6 Becky thinks the changes in the café have been good.

2 USEFUL LANGUAGE Being encouraging

a Look at these two excerpts from Part 1. Underline the expressions where Sam or Becky are being encouraging.

1 **BECKY** Flat hunting, you know …
SAM Yeah, it's never easy. Don't give up hope – you'll find somewhere.

2 **SAM** I hope the bank agrees.
BECKY I'm sure they will. Good luck.

b Look at these expressions for being encouraging for 30 seconds.

1 It might work out fine.
2 Never give up hope.
3 I'm sure it'll be fine.
4 You never know.

Now cover the expressions and complete the conversations below.

A I've got my performance review with my boss tomorrow.
B You've had a good year. I'm ____ it'll ____ fine.
A I'd like a pay rise, but I don't think I'll get it.
B Well, you ____ know.

C It's our final game of the season tomorrow and two members of our team can't play. We're bound to lose.
D It ____ work ____ ____.
C But they're our two best players.
D Never ____ up ____.

c 3.30 Listen and check.

d Work in pairs. Take turns to have short conversations like in 2b. Use expressions to be encouraging.

Student A: Tell your partner about a grammar test you've got tomorrow. You're worried that you haven't studied enough.

Student B: Tell your partner about a speaking test you've got next week. You don't think your pronunciation is good enough.

3 LISTENING

a 3.31 Watch or listen to Part 3. Sam and Tom meet by chance. How have their experiences been similar?

b 3.31 Watch or listen again and answer the questions.

1 How does Sam feel about his meeting at the bank?

2 What's Tom's reaction to his visit to the estate agent's?

3 What was Sam's experience of finding the right place for the café?

4 How do Sam and Tom respond to each other in this scene?

4 CONVERSATION SKILLS Showing you have things in common

a 3.31 In Part 3, Sam and Tom sympathise with each other by saying they have things in common. For example, Tom says:

The same thing happened to me.

Watch or listen again and find two more expressions that show they have things in common.

b Look at the expressions below. Do we use them before or after someone mentions his/her experience?

1 The same thing happened to me.
2 I've just had a similar experience.
3 I know the feeling.
4 It was just like that when …
5 It was the same with me.
6 That's just like when …

c Cover 4b and correct the mistakes.

1 It was same with me.
2 I've had the similar experience.
3 I know a feeling.
4 It was just so when …

d Tell each other about your experiences learning English. Say when you have something in common.

5 LISTENING

a 3.32 When Tom returns to his office, he finds a voicemail message. Watch or listen to Part 4 and answer the questions.

1 Who's the message from?
2 What's it about?
3 What's the telephone number?

6 PRONUNCIATION Word groups

a 3.33 Listen again to Katie's message. Add // where she pauses.

Hello, Tom. It's Katie here from Barkers Estate Agents. Thanks for coming in earlier. Something interesting's just come up. Can you call me back on 249 456?

b Why does Katie use pauses? Choose the correct description.

1 She needs to stop and think about what she's going to say next.
2 She wants to make sure the information in her message is clear.

c Work alone. Think of a message you can leave for your partner. Decide where you need to pause to make the message clear.

d Work in pairs.

Student A: Give a telephone message to Student B.
Student B: Listen and write Student A's message.
Swap roles.

7 SPEAKING

a Think of a hope you have but are worried about. For example, it could be:

- a holiday
- a job
- a study goal
- a place to live.

b Take turns talking about your hopes. Encourage your partner and show him/her you have something in common if they talk about similar experiences.

I don't know whether I can afford to go to both Rome and Florence.

Yeah, never easy. But you can stay in a hostel.

I've heard the job interviewing process is quite hard.

Yes, I know the feeling. But you're good at interviews …

Unit Progress Test

CHECK YOUR PROGRESS

You can now do the Unit Progress Test.

1 SPEAKING and LISTENING

a What TV programmes do you enjoy watching? What do you like about them? What don't you like?

b Look at the photos of three people who were on a reality TV crime programme. They are all connected by a crime that involved the credit card statement below. What do you think could have happened?

CREDIT CARD STATEMENT

ACCOUNT NUMBER 256-6658-1153

DUE DATE 15/06

TRANSACTION DATE	DESCRIPTION	AMOUNT
04/05	Groceries	69.00
04/05	Dentist	18.00
05/05	Bus pass	36.00
06/05	Jewellery	105.00
06/05	Handbag	90.00
	TOTAL:	318.00

2

1

3

c 3.34 Listen to Paul and Zoe talking about the TV programme. Were any of your ideas in 1b correct?

d 3.34 Listen again. Are the sentences true or false?

1 Paul thinks the programme shows people how to commit crime.
2 The man's niece went looking for the credit card statement.
3 Zoe isn't sure the niece did the right thing.
4 The man talked about how frightened he was by the theft.
5 Paul didn't like the attitude of the presenter.
6 Zoe thinks the programme could be seen as useful advice.
7 Paul thinks the presenter had an original point of view.

e Discuss the questions.

- Do you know of any similar crimes to this? Or any famous crimes? What happened?
- Do you think these TV programmes show people how to commit crimes? Why / Why not?

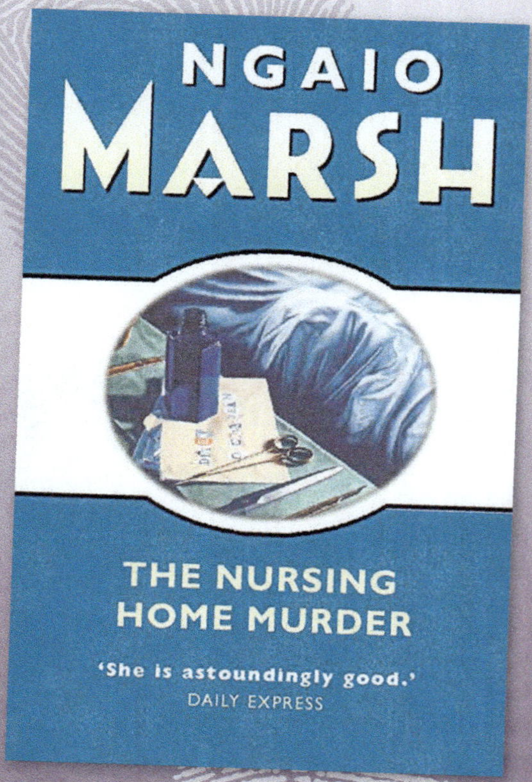

2 READING

a Read the review *Did the doctor do it?* of a crime story. Is this story fact or fiction?

b Read the review again and complete the table.

author	
characters	
setting	
kind of story	
reason for liking	
why it's recommended	

DID THE DOCTOR DO IT?

[1]If you enjoy a classic 'whodunit' and you want a great read, you can't do better than *The Nursing Home Murder*. This is my absolute favourite, old-fashioned crime story, which I read on my last summer holiday. *The Nursing Home Murder* was written by Ngaio Marsh in 1935 and one of the things I love about it is the authentic 1930s atmosphere of the story and characters.

[2]The main setting is a private hospital (these were called 'nursing homes' in the 1930s) in London. In the home, a famous politician, Sir Derek O'Callaghan dies after an operation. At first, it seems that his death is the result of complications associated with surgery. However, his wife is suspicious and we eventually discover that he was deliberately poisoned during the operation. All the doctors and the nurses in the operating team had a motive for killing Sir Derek. It's up to Chief Detective Inspector Alleyn of Scotland Yard to find the murderer.

[3]What makes this a classic whodunit is the fact that the murder takes place in an enclosed space with a limited number of suspects. Clues are gradually revealed as the story continues, and the detective's approach to solving the crime is highly original. It's an example of very imaginative crime fiction. The other thing I loved is that the characters are all very clearly described, and they're all a bit eccentric in one way or another, including the detective.

[4]*The Nursing Home Murder* is a hugely entertaining read and I really recommend it if you want to escape into a mystery story set in a completely different place and time. I couldn't put it down and it kept me guessing all the way through.

3 WRITING SKILLS

Organising a review

a Read the review in 2a again. Choose the correct endings for the descriptions of paragraphs 1–4.

1 ☐ This introduces the book and gives …
2 ☐ This outlines the plot and introduces …
3 ☐ This outlines the key strengths of the book and the reviewer's …
4 ☐ This is a summary of the review and a final …

a positive recommendation.
b personal opinion.
c information about it.
d the main characters.

b Underline phrases in the review in 2a that show the writer's positive opinion of the book.

c Notice how the words and phrases in the box are alternatives to the language used in the review. Complete the sentences below with the words and phrases in the box. Sometimes more than one answer is possible.

enormously   really liked   beat
enjoy   highly   number one

1 … you can't ____ *The Nursing Home Murder.*
2 This is my ____ old-fashioned crime story.
3 … one of the things I ____ about it is the authentic 1930s atmosphere.
4 The other thing I ____ was that the characters are all very clearly described.
5 *The Nursing Home Murder* is a(n) ____ entertaining read and I ____ recommend it.

4 WRITING

a Think of a book, film or TV programme that you like and would recommend. Make notes using the table in 2b.

b Work on your own. Write your review. Organise the review clearly, using the advice in 3a. Include your positive opinions, using language in 3b and 3c.

c Work in pairs. Read each other's reviews and check that each paragraph has a clear purpose and the paragraphs are in the right order. Check the correct use of positive expressions.

d Swap your review with other students. Would you like to read the book or watch the film or TV programme you read about?

UNIT 8
Review and extension

1 GRAMMAR

a Complete the sentences with your own ideas.

1 If I go out tonight …
2 If I went to a very expensive restaurant …
3 If I buy some new clothes this weekend …
4 If I bought a new IT product …
5 If I download some new music …

b Discuss your sentences.

c Read about Sam's disastrous night out.

As he went out, he forgot to lock the front door so some burglars stole all his electronic equipment. He didn't put any petrol in his car so he ran out and had to pay for a taxi home. He didn't check the name of the club he was going to so he couldn't meet his friends. He put his phone in his back pocket so it got stolen.

Imagine a different night out for Sam with sentences beginning with *if*. For example:

If he'd remembered to lock his front door, he wouldn't have been burgled.

d Make sentences criticising Sam. Begin each sentence with *He should/shouldn't have …*

2 VOCABULARY

a Put the letters of the underlined words in the correct order.

1 Every month I work out the dteugb for household expenses.
2 My weekly ceinmo is just over £500 and I don't think it's nearly enough.
3 They borrowed money from the bank and have a bdte of £8,000.
4 I've got a new credit card which has a very low eernitts eatr on repayments.
5 Last year I made a total of 12 oonndasti to different charities.
6 We've just daip fof a loan from my parents so we can start saving for a home.

b Put the correct noun form of the verb in brackets in the gaps below.

1 There have been a lot of _____ (burgle) in our neighbourhood of late.
2 Police charged the man with _____ (steal) and sent him to prison to wait for a trial.
3 She's a _____ (cheat) and is always copying my ideas and work.
4 There was a real problem with _____ (bribe) and corruption in local government.

3 WORDPOWER *take*

a Join a sentence from 1–6 to another from a–f.

1 ☐ There seems to be no one who's responsible for the project.
2 ☐ You may not believe what the adverts say, but this chocolate tastes great.
3 ☐ My friends tell me not to worry about the exam.
4 ☐ I love the food she makes because she's such an enthusiastic cook.
5 ☐ It's done nothing but rain since we arrived. It's making me feel so depressed.
6 ☐ I didn't read the conditions on the ticket carefully.

a You can tell she takes pleasure in what she makes.
b I took it for granted that we could get a refund easily.
c But I take all assessment seriously and make sure I study hard.
d Take my word for it.
e I can't take it for much longer.
f I'm more than happy to take charge.

b Answer the questions about the *take* expressions.

1 Which word can be replaced with the word *control*?
2 What preposition follows these expressions: *take interest, take pride, take pleasure*?
3 What's the problem with this example? *We take seriously all security matters.*
4 What's the problem with this example? *Please believe me – take the word for it.*
5 Which expression is followed by *that* + clause?

c Add a *take* expression where you see ^. Think about the verb form and word order.

I always ^ that my friends ^ in the hiking trips I used to organise. I was happy to ^ of all the preparation. However, one of my friends, Julia, admitted that no one was really that interested in going hiking apart from me. Julia was quite diplomatic when she said that it was important to ^ people's different interests. However, another friend, Shelley, was far more direct. She said, "I'm sorry, but I ^ it any longer – I've had enough of hiking!" Well, we won't be going hiking ever again ^ !

d Discuss your answers to the questions.

1 What do you take pleasure in?
2 Are you someone who likes to take charge? Why / Why not?
3 What's something you take seriously?

REVIEW YOUR PROGRESS

How well did you do in this unit? Write 3, 2 or 1 for each objective.
3 = very well 2 = well 1 = not so well

I CAN …

discuss personal finance	☐
discuss moral dilemmas and crime	☐
be encouraging	☐
write a review	☐

CAN DO OBJECTIVES

- Discuss new inventions
- Discuss people's lives and achievements
- Express uncertainty
- Write an essay expressing a point of view

UNIT 9
Discoveries

GETTING STARTED

a Look at the picture and answer the questions.

1 Who do you think the man is and how is he feeling?
2 What do you think this robot is capable of?

b Discuss the questions.

1 Imagine you could have a robot built for you. What would you want it to do? Why?
2 Do you think new inventions and discoveries always lead to an improved quality of life? Why / Why not? Think of examples.
3 Do you think there are some things people will always want to do themselves and not get machines to do? Which ones? Why?

9A What really shocks me is that it costs €250,000

Learn to discuss new inventions

G Relative clauses
V Health

1 READING

a Read about inventions in medical science. Do you think they are fact or fiction?

b Read the article *Too good to be true?* Which of the inventions in 1a are facts?

MEDICAL SCIENCE OR SCIENCE FICTION?

1 Blind people can see with a video camera that transmits images to the back of their eyes.

2 A person's genes can be changed, so they stop eating food that makes them overweight.

3 Hospital patients can wear electronic skin to send radio waves from their body to machines.

4 During an operation, it's likely that a computer tablet will care for you.

5 Medical scientists are close to finding a vaccine against the common cold.

6 It'll soon be possible to prevent people from suffering from food allergies.

7 Electronic devices placed in the chests of asthma sufferers can permanently cure the illness.

8 A small electronic device put in the brain of an epilepsy sufferer can stop them from having seizures.

Too good to be true?

We're always hoping for the next medical miracle – like a simple pill that can cure cancer. Often we hear of breakthroughs in medical science that sound almost too good to be true. However, sometimes they really are as good as they say they are. Here are five inventions from the world of medical science. If they sound like science fiction, that just means that the future is here – now.

1 Black and white

Wouldn't it be great if people who had lost their sight could see again? This is already happening for some blind people. A small device is put in the back part of a blind person's eye. They then wear special sunglasses with a camera, which transmits images to the device. It isn't a perfect system, but it's enough for them to be able to walk down a footpath or to know the difference between black and white socks.

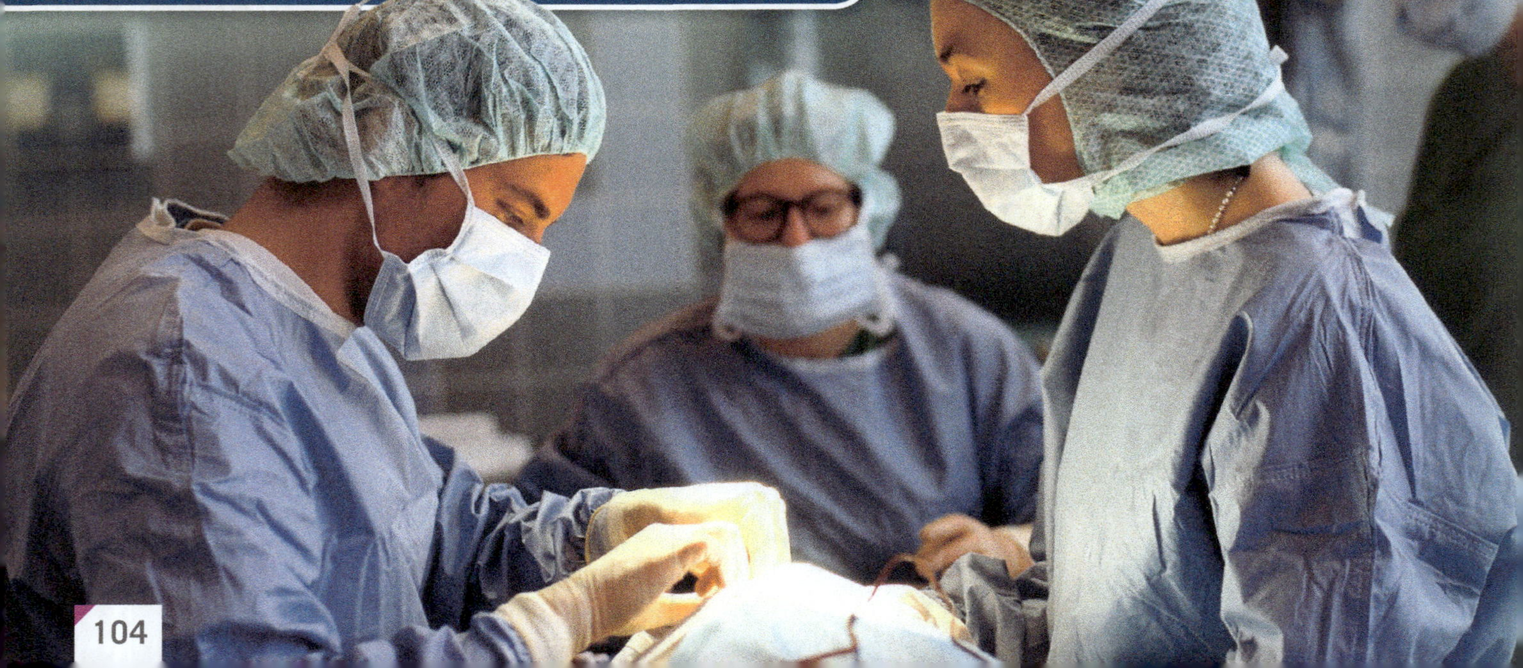

c Read the article again. Are the sentences true or false?

1 Anyone who's blind is able to get some sight back with the new glasses and almost see perfectly.
2 Electronic skin can be used to monitor patients and speed up the healing process.
3 The tablet now means that the anaesthetist can leave the patient once the operation begins.
4 Scientists hope that it will be possible to turn off other allergies in the future.
5 The epilepsy device has two functions: prediction and prevention.

2 It's all about comfort

In hospital, patients often complain about all the uncomfortable cables and wires that connect them to monitors. It's now possible to get rid of all this wiring simply by putting on electronic skin. This piece of 'skin' is very small and very thin. It's about the size of a postage stamp and as thick as a piece of human hair. It's made of silicon and is attached using water in the same way that a fake tattoo is. Despite being extremely small and thin, the skin contains electronic circuits that can receive and send radio waves to and from monitors. It can also be used to help heal wounds by sending out heat that speeds up the repair process.

3 Under the care of three

During an operation, there's always a surgeon in the operating theatre and an anaesthetist, whose job is to check the patient constantly. In the past, the anaesthetist had to watch the patient carefully, but these days they are also likely to use a touchscreen computer like a tablet. This tablet monitors key functions like breathing and heart rate, but more importantly, it can send the anaesthetist warnings and suggest how medication should be altered during the operation. It also keeps a record of everything the surgeon does. So these days, when you have an operation, you're under the care of three 'professionals': the surgeon, the anaesthetist and the tablet.

4 Sometimes a matter of life and death

It's surprising how many people are allergic to different kinds of food. Sometimes this can be life-threatening, for example for people who are allergic to peanuts. Scientists at Northwestern University in Chicago have found a way to turn off an allergy to peanuts. They attached some peanut protein to blood cells and reintroduced them into the body of someone suffering from the allergy. This makes the body think that peanuts are no longer a threat and there's no allergic response. Scientists think this approach could be used with a wide range of food allergies.

5 Warning signs

People who suffer from epilepsy never know when they are going to have an attack. This lack of certainty can be very stressful. Researchers have now created a device that makes an epileptic seizure predictable. These very small devices are planted in the brain. They're able to tell if an attack is about to happen and they can then send out electrical signals to other parts of the brain that can stop the seizure.

d Discuss the questions.

1 Which of the inventions do you think is the biggest breakthrough in medical science? Why?
2 Imagine a medical invention you would like to exist. What would it do? Why would you like it to be real?

2 VOCABULARY Health

a Underline the medical verb in each example. Then match the verbs with definitions 1–3.

... simple pill that can cure cancer.
It can also be used to help heal wounds ...
... a computer tablet will care for you.

1 treat a disease and make healthy again
2 look after
3 treat an injury and make healthy again

b Complete the sentences with the correct form of the verbs in the box.

get	develop	strain	come	treat

1 I feel terrible. I've _____ down with the flu.
2 His doctor _____ his throat infection with antibiotics and that helped.
3 I can't stand up for very long, because I've _____ my back.
4 I don't want to go out yet. I'm still _____ over a heavy cold.
5 People who eat too much fatty food are likely to _____ heart disease.

c Match verbs 1–5 with the pictures. Two verbs describe one picture.

1 cough	2 faint	3 sneeze
4 pass out	5 shiver	

d Discuss the questions.

- When did you last come down with the flu?
- What do you think is the best way to treat a sore throat?
- Have you ever fainted? What happened?
- Have you ever strained a muscle? Which muscle? How did it happen?
- What serious disease or illness are people in your country most likely to develop?

e Now go to Vocabulary Focus 9A on p.162

3 LISTENING

a 3.37 Listen to Toby and Rosie talk about inventions. Which medical invention and which food invention do they talk about?

b 3.37 Listen again and answer the questions.

1 What did the scientist do with the meat?
2 Why's this meat better for the environment?
3 What does Rosie suggest that Toby does to reduce crop production?
4 What does Rosie say about the taste of the meat?
5 Why does Rosie think it's strange that Toby's worried about global warming?

c Whose point of view do you agree with more, Toby's or Rosie's?

4 GRAMMAR Relative clauses

a Look at these examples from the conversation. Underline the relative clause. Decide if it adds information about a thing (T), a person (P) or a place (PL).

1 Yeah, there's this laboratory where they're growing meat.
2 There was that scientist who made his own hamburger and ate it online.
3 But all these tiny pieces of meat that they have to push together just to make one burger
4 And the end result is something which costs €250,000.
5 There's no fat or blood in it, which means no flavour.
6 I mean, these scientists, who are sort of like Dr Frankenstein, how can they justify that?

b Answer the questions about the clauses you underlined in 4a. Which clauses ... ?

1 add extra information that is not necessary to the overall meaning of the sentence
2 are necessary for the sentence to make sense

c Now go to Grammar Focus 9A on p.150

d Discuss what you think about the following inventions. Do you think they have been useful for people in general? When do you use them? Could people manage without them now?

- cameras
- light bulbs
- penicillin

5 SPEAKING

a **Communication 9A** Student A: Go to p.129. Student B: Go to p.133.

b Put the inventions in order of usefulness 1–4 (1 = very useful, 4 = completely useless). Discuss your ideas with the class.

9B No one knew who he was

Learn to discuss people's lives and achievements

G Reported speech; reporting verbs

V Verbs describing thought and knowledge

1 READING

a Discuss the questions.

1 What kind of music do you like?
2 Who are your favourite singers?
3 Do you know any music from before the 1990s?

b Look at the picture of Sixto Rodriguez. What kind of music do you think he played? What do you think his life was like?

c Read the article *The rockstar who wasn't* about the first part of Rodriguez's music career. Which of these sentences describes Rodriguez when the two producers first met him?

1 He was well known as a brilliant musician.
2 He was almost completely unknown and playing in small nightclubs.
3 He was quite well known in Detroit, but not very successful.

d Read the article again. Are the statements true, false or we don't know?

1 The Sewer was a luxurious nightclub in Detroit.
2 It took them some time to see who Rodriguez was.
3 They were surprised by the way Rodriguez played.
4 Rodriguez made two successful albums.
5 Rodriguez wasn't talented enough to become famous.
6 Rodriguez carried on recording music after he left the record company.

e Does the article give us any idea why Rodriguez wasn't successful? What do you think could be the reasons? Why do you think he was becoming famous in South Africa?

THE ROCK STAR WHO WASN'T

Sixto Rodriguez was a Detroit singer-songwriter, an "inner city poet" who looked like he would become a star. But his breakthrough album failed to sell, his second album didn't do any better and his record label dropped him. That's when his story became very strange indeed; a story of talent, bad luck and a happy ending many years later.

In 1968, two record producers, Dennis Coffey and Mike Theodore, heard that a singer called Sixto Rodriguez was playing in *The Sewer*, a rundown nightclub on the edge of Detroit. They were told that he was 'as great as Bob Dylan', but no one knew who he was. So, one evening, they decided to drive down to the nightclub and have a look for themselves.

The nightclub was so dark and smoky that at first they couldn't see anything. For a moment they weren't sure if they had come to the right place, but then they spotted him. He was playing the guitar in a corner with his back to the audience singing quietly, almost to himself. His music was amazing and they knew immediately that they wanted to record him.

A few days later they asked him if he wanted to sign a contract and he agreed. Over the next two years he made two brilliant albums, but hardly any copies were sold. Steve Rowland, producer of the second album, often wondered why Rodriguez didn't succeed. 'This guy was like a wise man, a prophet, I've never worked with anyone as talented.' Two months after his second record came out, the record company told Rodriguez that they had dropped him from their label. Rodriguez vanished from the music scene. He went back to his life in Detroit and to his old job, doing building work and renovating old houses to make ends meet and raise his three daughters. He never recorded another album.

Meanwhile, on the other side of the world, in South Africa, Rodriguez was becoming a star.

2 GRAMMAR

Reported speech; reporting verbs

a Look at these examples of things people said or thought.

Sixto Rodriguez **is playing** in The Sewer tonight.

We definitely **want** to record this guy.

Sorry, we**'ve dropped** you from our label.

These statements or thoughts are reported in the sentences below using reporting verbs. Complete the sentences with the correct form of the verbs above. Then check your answers in the text.

1 They heard that a singer called Sixto Rodriguez _____ (play) in *The Sewer*.
2 They knew immediately that they _____ (want) to record him.
3 The record company told Rodriquez that they _____ (drop) him from their label.

b Complete the rule with the correct answers.

Because the reporting verbs (*heard, told, knew*) are in the *present / past*, what the people said moves 'one tense back' into the *present / past*.

c Look at these examples of questions people asked or thought.

Do you want to sign a contract?

Who **is** he?

Have we **come** to the right place?

Complete the reported questions with the correct form of the verbs above. Check your answers in the article.

1 No one knew who he _____.
2 For a moment they weren't sure if they _____ to the right place.
3 A few days later they asked him if he _____ to sign a contract.

Choose the correct word to complete the rule:
In reported questions *use / don't use* question word order.

d Now go to Grammar Focus 9B on p.150

e Correct the mistakes in these sentences.

1 They weren't quite sure if they came to the right place.
2 They asked him if he can meet them the next day.
3 They didn't understand why does no one want to buy the album.
4 They wondered will the second record be successful.

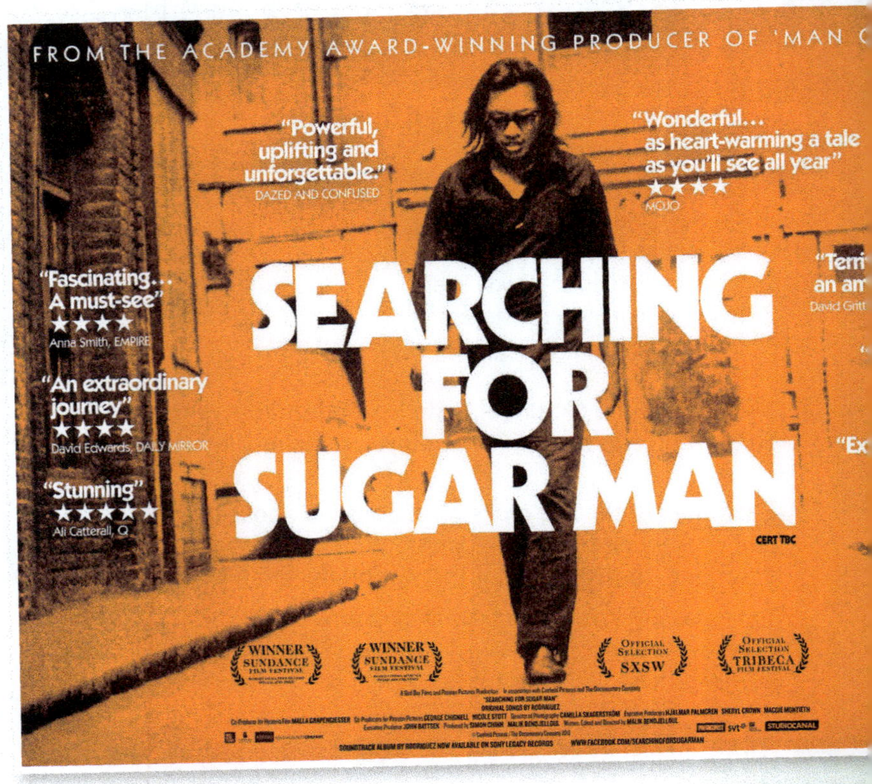

3 READING

a Look at these key phrases from the final part of the story of Rodriguez. What do you think happened? Try to make up a story using as many phrases as possible.

South Africa   committed suicide   a South African reporter
Rodriguez's producer   living in Detroit   a huge success

b Communication 9B Now go to p.131. How much did you guess correctly? How are the phrases in 3a important to the story?

4 LISTENING

a 3.41 In 2012, Swedish director Malik Bendjelloul made a documentary about Rodriguez's life. Listen to two friends talking about the documentary. Which of the sentences are true?

1 The two South African reporters decided to make a film.
2 No one in South Africa really knew Rodriguez.
3 The Swedish director went to talk to Rodriguez.
4 The director did the last bit of filming himself.

b 3.41 Listen again. What reasons does the speaker give for these things?

1 The director was travelling to different countries.
2 The director wanted to tell Rodriguez's story.
3 Rodriguez didn't say much in the interviews.
4 Parts of the film weren't filmed with a camera.
5 A lot of people now know about Rodriguez.

c Would you like to watch the documentary? Why / Why not?

5 VOCABULARY

Verbs describing thought and knowledge

a Look at the sentences from the recording. Which verbs from the box can you use instead of *thought* or *knew* to make the meaning more precise? Put them into the correct form.

realise	be aware	doubt	assume	wonder	estimate
make sure	come to the conclusion	not have any idea			

1 He *thought* that Rodriguez would be dying to tell his story.
2 He wanted to *know* that Rodriguez really was that popular in South Africa.
3 The director *knew* by now this really was a story worth telling.
4 He *didn't know* who they were.
5 He *didn't know* why they'd come to see him.
6 People *thought* he'd sold about 1.5 million records in South Africa.
7 He *thought* that Rodriguez's story was the one to tell.
8 Most people *didn't really think* that he could be a superstar in one country when no one else had heard of him.
9 He *knew* that he might not be able to finish the film.

b 3.42 Listen and check your answers.

c Write possible continuations to these sentences. Be careful what verb tense you use!

1 After getting to know her better, I came to the conclusion …
2 Before she went to Japan she started a Japanese language course, but she doubted …
3 It was already 5.30. She realised …
4 We never saw our new neighbour go out. We wondered …
5 After working for the company for five years, she estimated …
6 Before she left the house she looked out of the window. She wanted to make sure …

6 SPEAKING

a Choose someone you know about (present or past) who is not widely known but you think should be. It could be an artist, someone who has done something amazing or simply someone you think is an incredible person.

b Think of what you know about them and make notes on:

- their life and background
- what they achieved or have achieved
- your opinion about them.

c Work with another student. Imagine you had to make a documentary about your partner's person. Ask questions about the topics in 6b.

d Tell the class about the person your partner chose. Were you convinced that they deserve to be better known?

9C Everyday English
What's the big secret?

Learn how to express uncertainty

P Linking and intrusion

S Clarifying a misunderstanding

a

1 LISTENING

a Discuss the questions.

1 When was the last time you had a surprise?
2 Was it a good or bad surprise? What happened?
3 Do you usually like surprises?

b Look at photo a and answer the questions.

1 Who has organised a surprise?
2 How does Becky feel about it?
3 Do you think Becky knows where she is?

c 3.43 Watch or listen to Part 1. Check your ideas in 1b.

d What do you think the surprise is? Discuss your ideas.

2 USEFUL LANGUAGE
Expressing uncertainty

a 3.44 Read the conversation below. Is it what Becky and Tom said? Listen and check.

BECKY I don't know where we are.
TOM Just wait and see.
BECKY Where are we going?
TOM Wait and see.

b In which version does Becky express herself more strongly? Why does she do this?

c Becky talks about a place: 'I've no idea where we are.'

Look at these expressions for talking about a thing.

1 I've (really) (got) no idea what that is.
2 I haven't got a clue what that is.
3 What on earth is that?

Change expressions 1–3 to talk about a person.

d **Communication 9C** Student A: Go to p.127. Student B: Go to p.132.

3 LISTENING

a Look at photo b and answer the questions.

1 What has Tom done?
2 How does Becky feel about it?

b 3.45 Watch or listen to Part 2 and check your ideas in 3a.

c 3.45 Watch or listen again. Answer the questions.

1 How did Tom manage to get the flat?
2 What did Tom do earlier in the afternoon?
3 Why's Becky a little annoyed?
4 What things does Becky like about the flat?
5 Why didn't Becky guess?
6 What two documents do Tom and Becky have to sign?

b

4 PRONUNCIATION Linking and intrusion

a 3.46 Listen to an excerpt from the conversation. Pay attention to the underlined phrases. Do they sound like separate words or one word?

TOM You're not too annoyed?
BECKY No. In fact, <u>not at all</u>.
TOM You did say it was the perfect flat.
BECKY <u>And it is</u>.

b Why do the sounds join together? Choose the correct description.

1 All the vowel sounds in these words are short sounds.
2 Final consonant sounds are followed by vowel sounds.
3 There is no stress in any of these phrases

c 3.47 Listen to the excerpt. Notice the phrases with ^. Where are the sounds in the box added?

/j/ /r/ /w/

BECKY I've no ^ idea where we ^ are. I've never seen this street before.
TOM Just wait and see.
BECKY Where ^ on earth are we going?
TOM Wait and see.

d Why do we add the sounds in 4c? Choose the correct explanation.

1 The main stress is on the word that comes after each added sound.
2 The consonants in the two words are voiced.
3 The last sound in the first word and the first sound in the following word are both vowels.

e 3.48 Using the rules from 4b and d, predict where the speaker is going to use linking and intrusion. Then listen and check.

Here at work, I've just received a gift from my aunt. I've got no idea what it is. I'm going to open it when I get home this evening.

5 CONVERSATION SKILLS Clarifying a misunderstanding

a 3.49 Listen to part of Tom and Becky's conversation. Which two expressions does Becky use to clarify a misunderstanding? (Both expressions begin with *but*.)

b Look at the exchanges. Which are social situations? Which are work situations? Underline the expressions in B's replies used to clarify misunderstandings.

1 **A** I'm off to the movies now.
B I thought that you were going to go to a football game.
2 **A** Our next meeting's in two weeks.
B I understood that we were going to meet once a week.
3 **A** Here's your ticket. It's £50.
B Did I get this wrong? I thought it was free.
4 **A** By the end of this month, you'll be able to take a week's holiday.
B Have I misunderstood something? I thought I could take two weeks' holiday.
5 **A** How about if I make the starter and you make the dessert?
B Didn't we say that I'd make the starter?

c What could you say in the situations below? Write your ideas and compare with your partner.

1 You're in a restaurant. Your friend told you he/she wasn't hungry, but has ordered a starter, a main and dessert.
2 You stay in a hotel. When you pay the bill, you're surprised to find breakfast is extra.
3 A friend offers you a lift to the station. When you get in, he/she starts driving in the opposite direction.

6 SPEAKING

a Communication 9C Student A: Go to p.129. Student B: Go to p.130.

Unit Progress Test

CHECK YOUR PROGRESS

You can now do the Unit Progress Test.

9D Skills for Writing
People argue that it is no use at all

Learn to write an essay expressing a point of view

W Presenting a series of arguments

1 SPEAKING and LISTENING

a Discuss the questions.

1 Do you think alternative treatments really work or do you think people just imagine that they work?
2 What kinds of alternative medicine are common in your country?
3 If you were ill, would you try alternative medicine? Why / Why not?

Alternative medicine Kinds of medical treatment that use different methods from standard Western medicine (also called *conventional medicine*). Examples of alternative medicine are homeopathy, herbal medicine and acupuncture.

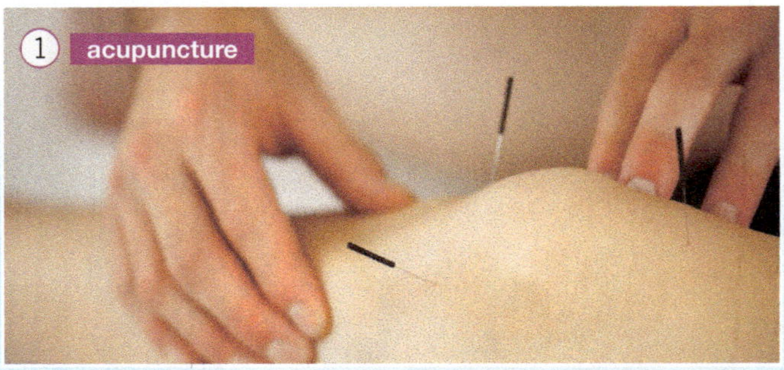

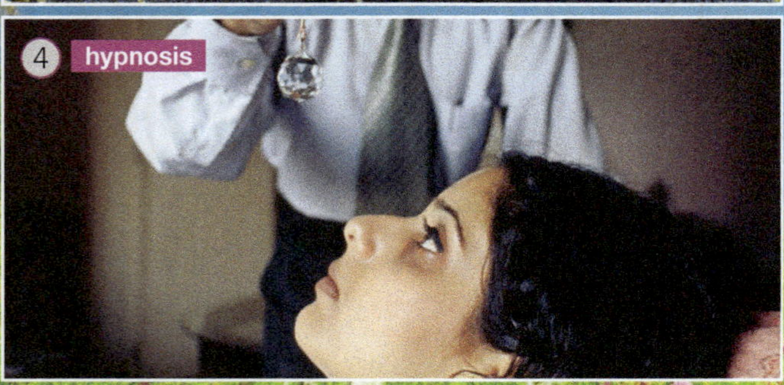

b 3.50 Listen to people talking about four alternative treatments. What treatment does each person talk about? Match them with the photos.

c 3.50 Listen again and answer the questions for all the speakers.

1 Why did the person try this treatment?
2 What did the doctor/therapist do?
3 Does the speaker feel positive or negative about it?
4 Do we know if the treatment worked?

2 READING

a Read Aisha's essay *The value of alternative medicine*. Which sentence best summarises her argument?

1 Conventional medicine is more effective but alternative medicine may be useful sometimes.
2 Alternative medicine is often more effective than conventional medicine, so it should be used more widely.
3 Conventional and alternative medicine work in different ways and both of them are important.

The value of

People often have extreme points of view about alternative medicine. People who believe in conventional medicine often argue that alternative medicine is of no use at all and supporters of alternative medicine sometimes claim that it can replace conventional medicine completely.

There are several good reasons for taking alternative medicine seriously. Firstly, many forms of alternative medicine, such as acupuncture and herbal medicine, have a very long tradition and are widely used in many parts of the world. It's important not to ignore traditional knowledge that has been developed over centuries.

b Look at the points that Aisha makes in her essay. Which are about conventional medicine and which are about alternative medicine? Write *C* or *A*.

1 It has been used for a very long time and in many different countries.
2 It is usually cheaper.
3 It may have harmful side effects.
4 We can't show scientifically that it works.
5 People who use it often say it works.

3 WRITING SKILLS

Presenting a series of arguments

a Aisha's essay in 2a has five paragraphs. What is the purpose of each one? Complete the sentences.

1 In the first paragraph, she outlines …
2 In the next three paragraphs, she presents …
3 In the final paragraph, she summarises …

b Find six expressions in Aisha's essay which introduce arguments and points of view.

People often argue that …

c Aisha uses linking words and phrases to show how her ideas join together. Find words and phrases that mean:

1 also (x2) 2 but 3 so 4 although
5 finally

d Choose one of the topics below and think about your point of view. Write three sentences about the topic, using expressions from 3b and 3c.

- Are zoos cruel to animals?
- Does dieting make people fat?
- Is democracy the best system for all countries?
- Is love a good basis for marriage?
- Should smoking be made illegal?

4 WRITING

a Think again about the topic you chose in 3d. Plan an essay using the structure in 3a. Think about:

- how you will introduce the topic
- what arguments you will present and what examples you will give to support them
- what conclusion you will give.

b Write the essay in around 200 words.

c Swap essays with your partner. Read the essay. Does it … ?

- have a clear introduction and conclusion
- present the arguments clearly, with a separate paragraph for each main idea
- include examples to support the arguments
- use appropriate expressions to introduce the arguments

d Work in new pairs. Read another student's essay. Then say if you agree with his/her viewpoint and why.

alternative medicine

One argument against alternative medicine is that there is very little scientific evidence to prove that it is effective. Yet, in spite of the lack of scientific evidence, people who use alternative therapies generally say that they work. This suggests that alternative therapies may perhaps work in ways that we do not yet fully understand. Furthermore, people are often prepared to spend a large amount of money on alternative treatment,despite the fact that conventional medicine is usually much cheaper.

In addition, unlike the drugs and antibiotics used in conventional medicine that can be harmful to the human body, most alternative therapies are completely harmless. Homeopathic treatments, for example, have few or no side effects and consequently the worst that can happen is that they have no effect at all.

In conclusion, I believe that conventional medicine and alternative therapies should exist side by side. They work in completely different ways and are often effective for different kinds of illness, so they should both be seen as a useful way to keep us healthy.

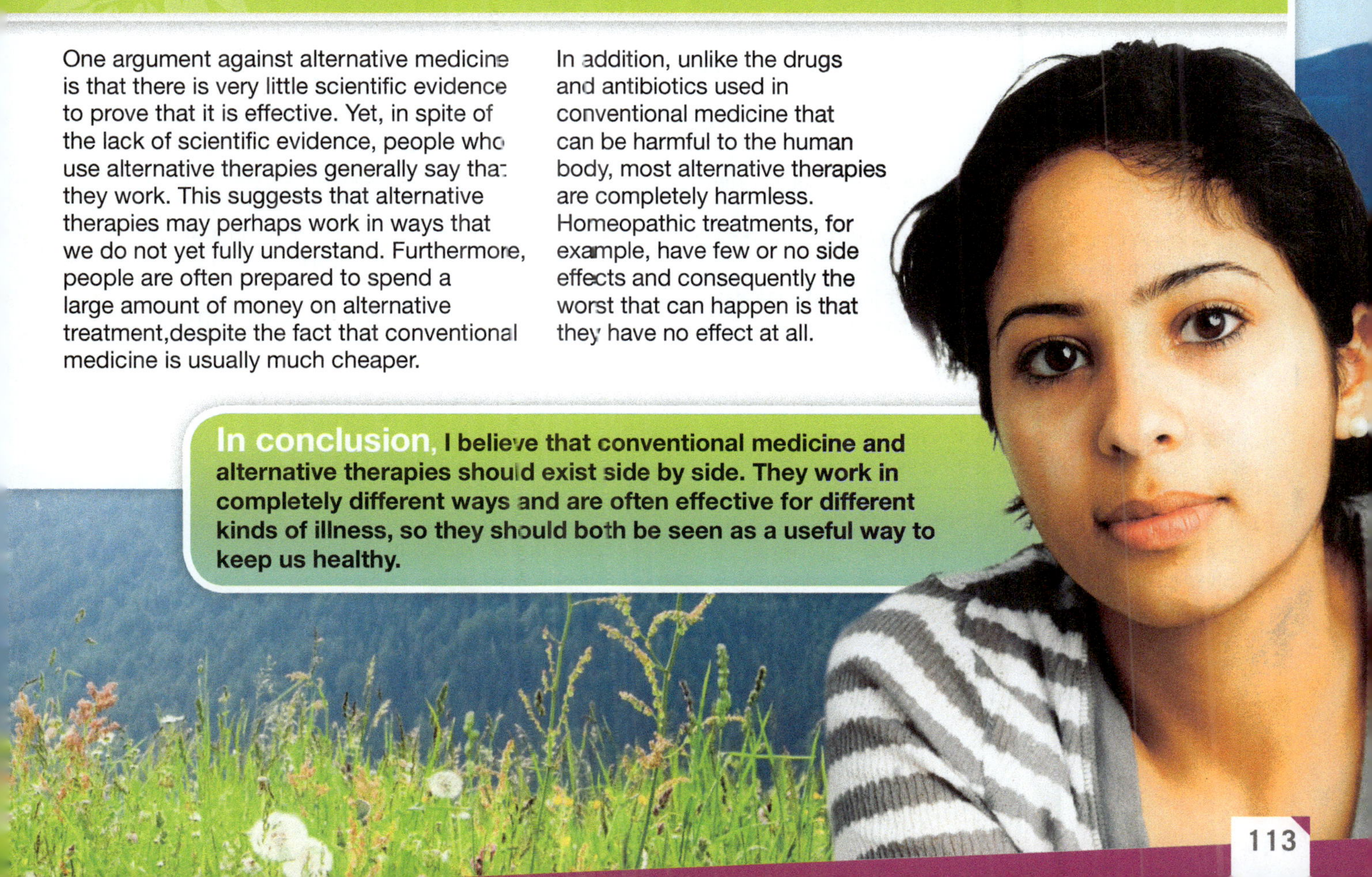

UNIT 9
Review and extension

1 GRAMMAR

a Join the sentences together using a relative clause. Use a relative pronoun if it's necessary. Cut any unnecessary words.

1 The plaster is like a piece of skin. The plaster is very small and thin.
2 The skin contains electronic circuits. The circuits can communicate with monitors.
3 An operating theatre is a sophisticated environment. Patients require extra care in an operating theatre.
4 Some people have to check everything they eat. Some people are allergic to peanuts.

b Tell the story, changing the parts in italics into indirect speech, using reporting verbs.

I was on a business trip and I had a terrible journey back home. My flight was at 12.30. But when I arrived at the airport they announced:
[1]*'There has been a delay to the incoming flight, so the flight will be delayed by about an hour.'* After an hour we still hadn't heard anything and I started to wonder: [2]*'What's happening?'* I asked one of the ground staff: [3]*'Do you know when the flight will leave?'* She told me: [4]*'I haven't heard anything.'* I waited for two more hours. At about 5.00 they told us: [5]*'The flight has been cancelled.'* I realised: [6]*'I'll have to spend the night in an airport hotel and I probably won't be home for another 18 hours.'*

2 VOCABULARY

a Choose the best word in these sentences.

1 Some scientists *estimate / realise* that there are 100 billion stars just in our galaxy.
2 I'm sorry I didn't say anything. I didn't *assume / realise* it was your birthday.
3 I followed you because I *doubted / assumed* that you knew the way.
4 I *wonder / come to the conclusion* how much she earns in a month. It must be at least €10,000.
5 As I left the flat, I *doubted / was aware* that someone was following me, and I was fairly sure I knew who it was.

b Add words from the box to each gap.

patients strained feel back lost dizzy scar cares for consciousness heals

1 I ____ quite ____. I think I'm going to faint.
2 It hurts when I try to stand up. I think I've ____ my ____.
3 She's a student nurse. She ________ ____ in the hospital and she also has to study for exams.
4 They hit me on the head and I ____ ____.
5 When the wound ____, it will probably leave a ____.

3 WORDPOWER *come*

a Match the sentence beginnings and endings.

1 Her dream was to see the sea, and last month her dream **came**
2 I think we should go to the cinema, unless you can **come**
3 Look, there's a photo of you in the paper. I **came**
4 The restaurant was rather expensive – the bill **came**
5 I thought for ages about buying the car, but I **came**
6 We were talking about who to ask, and your name **came**

a **across** it this morning.
b **true**.
c **to** more than €250.
d **up** as a possible person.
e **to the conclusion** that I couldn't afford it.
f **up with** a better idea.

b Match the expressions in 3a with the definitions.

a see something by chance
b think of
c be mentioned
d add up to
e reach a decision
f really happen

c Choose the correct words or phrases.

1 'OK – two coffees – that comes *to / up* £9.50.'
2 At the meeting we came up *to / with* lots of new ideas.
3 Nuclear power is a topic that often comes *true / up* in students' essays.
4 We thought about going to Paris but we came *to / across* the conclusion that Rome would be nicer.
5 I came *across / to* an interesting article in this magazine. It might interest you.
6 I always wanted to own a BMW, and now my dream has finally come *true / across*.

d Complete each question with one word.

1 Do you know anyone whose dream came ____?
2 Have you ever been given a bill that came ____ more than you could afford?
3 Have you ever come to the ____ that something you bought was a waste of money?
4 How do you feel if someone says: 'Your name came ____ in our conversation'?
5 Many people come ____ with new ideas when they're asleep or going for a walk. Is that true of you?
6 Have you ever come ____ a bargain in a shop or a market that you couldn't resist?

e Ask and answer the questions in 3d.

REVIEW YOUR PROGRESS

How well did you do in this unit? Write 3, 2 or 1 for each objective.
3 = very well 2 = well 1 = not so well

I CAN ...

discuss new inventions	☐
discuss people's lives and achievements	☐
express uncertainty	☐
write an essay expressing a point of view	☐

CAN DO OBJECTIVES

- Speculate about the past
- Discuss life achievements
- Describe how you felt
- Write a narrative

UNIT 10
Possibilities

GETTING STARTED

a Look at the picture and answer the questions.

1 What has just happened to this man?
2 What is he thinking? What are his feelings?

b Discuss the questions.

1 When people have high ambitions, what kinds of expectations do they have of themselves?
2 Do you think people are sometimes unrealistic in setting goals for themselves? Why?
3 What are the positive and negative consequences of having high expectations of yourself?

10A It might not have been his real name

Learn to speculate about the past

G Past modals of deduction

V Adjectives with prefixes

1 READING

a You are going to read a story about Dan Cooper, who mysteriously disappeared in 1971. Look at the pictures of people and events in the story. Can you guess what happened?

b Read *The man who disappeared* quickly. How similar is it to your ideas?

c Find sentences in the story which show that:

1 the flight from Portland to Seattle was a short one
2 we're not sure if Dan Cooper was the man's real name
3 the passengers didn't know about the note or the bomb
4 Cooper told the pilots to fly towards Mexico as slowly and as low as possible
5 the pilots didn't want to leave the rear door open
6 the pilots knew when the rear door was opened.

d Discuss the questions.

- What questions would you like answered that are not explained in the text?
- Do you think Cooper survived? What would you prefer to believe, that he survived or that he didn't survive? Why?

DAN COOPER

The man who DISAPPEARED

Flight attendant Florence Schaffner was sitting in her seat during take-off. A man in a seat near her passed her a note. It read: 'I have a bomb in my briefcase. I will use it if necessary. Sit next to me.'

It was 2.50 pm on 24 November 1971 on flight 305, a 30-minute flight from Portland to Seattle in the north-west of the USA. And it was the beginning of one of the strangest stories in the history of plane travel – a mystery that remains unsolved to this day. The man's name – or at least, the name he gave when he bought the ticket – was Dan Cooper. Of course, this might not have been his real name; no one really knows for sure.

Schaffner quietly got up and sat next to the man. He opened his briefcase slightly and she glimpsed eight red sticks inside before he closed it again. Then Cooper made his demands: $200,000 (a huge amount of money in 1971), four parachutes and a fuel truck ready at Seattle Airport to refuel the plane. The attendant told the pilot, who passed the demands to the airline company and they agreed to them. The other passengers were told there was a 'technical difficulty' and the plane circled for almost two hours over the sea to give the airline time to get the money and parachutes ready.

Cooper was told that his demands had been met and the plane landed at Seattle-Tacoma airport at 5.45 pm. The money (in $20 notes) and the parachutes were delivered and the passengers and Schaffner left the plane. Cooper talked to the pilots and ordered them to fly towards Mexico at minimum speed and altitude, with a refuelling stop in Reno. The plane, a Boeing 727, had a door at the back which opened downwards – Cooper ordered the pilots to leave it open all the time. They objected, so Cooper said that he himself would open it when they were in the air.

After refuelling, the plane took off at approximately 7.40, with Cooper and four crew members on board. After take-off, Cooper told the lone flight attendant to go to the cockpit. As she went, she saw him tie something around his waist, which may have been the bags of money. At eight o'clock, a warning light went on in the cockpit, so they knew that he must have opened the rear door. The plane landed in Reno at 10.15, with the rear door still open. Police searched the plane immediately, but they quickly confirmed that Cooper was gone.

Cooper was never seen again, dead or alive. No one has even found out if he really was Dan Cooper. And many people say that he can't have survived the jump (if indeed he jumped – he could have hidden on the plane and then escaped later) but no body, or parachute, was ever found. A bag with almost $6,000 of the money was found in a river, but the rest never showed up. The money might have belonged to Cooper, but even that wasn't certain.

Over 40 years later, the crime remains unsolved – and it will probably remain that way for ever.

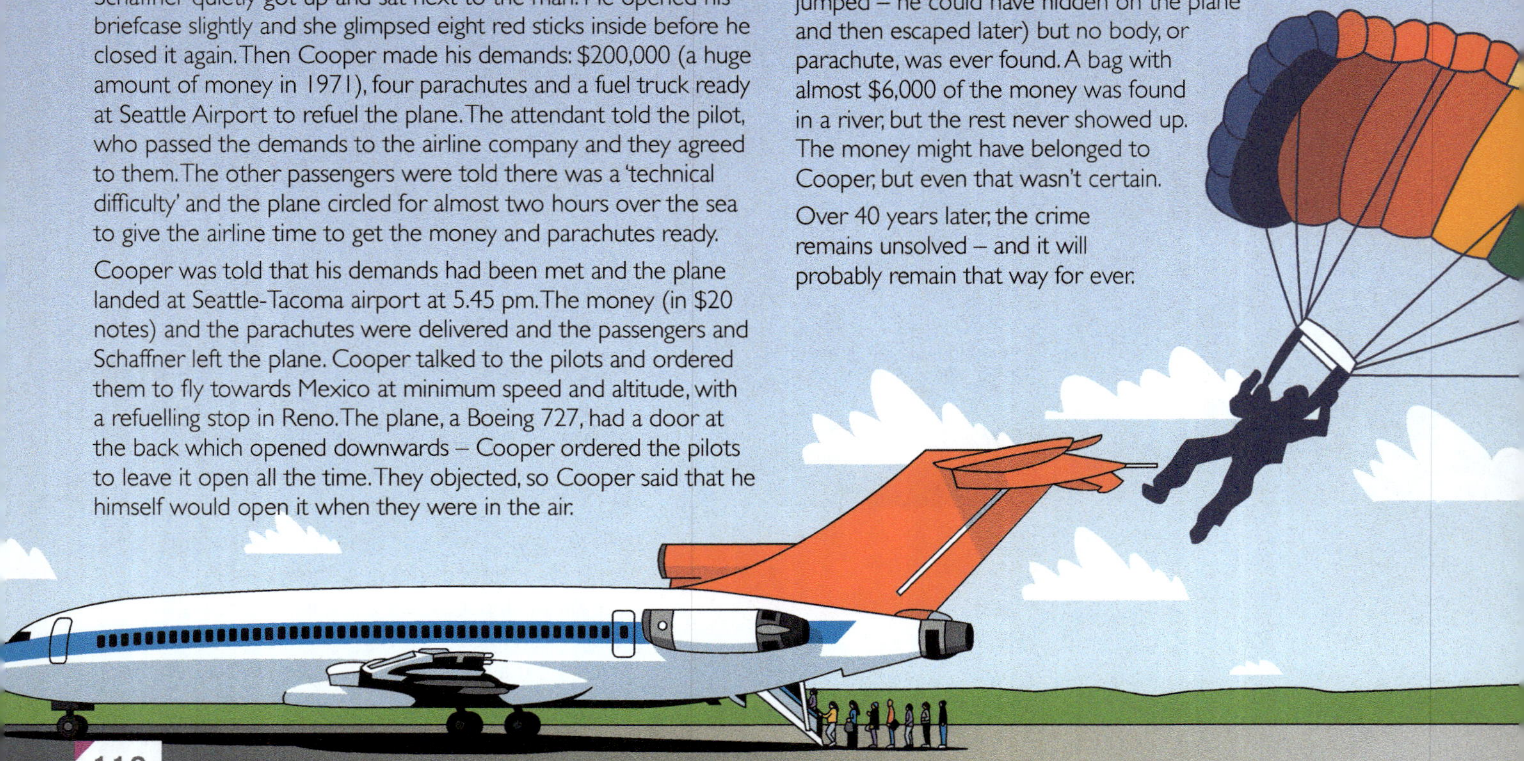

2 GRAMMAR Past modals of deduction

a Match sentences 1–5 with meanings a–d.

1 He tied something round his waist, which **may have been** the bags of money.
2 Many people say that he **can't have survived** the jump.
3 It **might not have been** his real name.
4 He **could have hidden** on the plane.
5 A warning light went on in the cockpit, so they knew that he **must have opened** the door.

a It seems certain that this was the case.
b It seems certain that this was not the case.
c It's possible that this was the case. (x2)
d It's possible that this was not the case.

b Look at the examples in 2a again.

1 Complete the rule with the modal verbs in the box.

must may might can't could

To speculate about things in the past:
- we use ____ or ____ + *have* + past participle to talk about things we think are certain
- we use ____, ____ or ____ + *have* + past participle to talk about things we think are possible.

2 Choose the correct answer, a or b.
- *must* and *can't* mean a) the same b) the opposite
- *may*, *might* and *could* mean a) the same b) the opposite

3 In the examples *have* is:
a part of the present perfect tense
b an infinitive form which always stays the same.

c 3.51 **Pronunciation** Listen to the sentences. Underline the stressed syllables in each sentence.

1 He can't have survived the jump.
2 It might not have been his real name.
3 He must have opened the door.

Practise saying the sentences.

d Now go to Grammar Focus 10A on p.152

e Read these situations. What do you think happened? Use past modals of deduction to discuss each one.

1 Renato Nicolai was in his garden in the south of France when he heard a whistling sound and saw what he thought was an experimental aircraft. He watched as it dropped out of the sky, hovered about two metres off the ground, then rose into the sky and disappeared. When experts studied the place where it had come down, they found a 'black material' on the ground that was not oil.

2 A ship called *The Joyita* disappeared in the Pacific without sending a call for help. It was found a month later floating in the ocean with no one on board. The lifeboats and the food were missing. There was a hole in the side, but it wasn't serious and the engines weren't damaged. The crew was never found.

3 LISTENING

a 3.53 Listen to an interview about Dan Cooper's disappearance. Number the topics in the order you hear them. There is one extra topic that you do not need.

the river ___
Dan Cooper's 'wife' ___
airport security ___
the pilot of the Boeing 727 ___
the parachute ___
the money ___

b 3.53 What evidence is there for the opinions below? Listen again and check.

1 Dan Cooper wasn't his real name.
2 He worked in the aircraft industry.
3 He survived the jump.
4 He didn't survive the jump.
5 Someone helped him.

c What do you think might have happened?

4 READING

a What famous event is shown here? What's happening in the picture?

b Read the blog *Ten amazing coincidences* about strange coincidences and answer the questions.

1 Which came first, the *Titanic* disaster or the book *The Wreck of the Titan*?
2 What is unusual about the book?

c Read the blog again. Which of these features of the book were similar to the *Titanic* disaster? Write Yes, No or Don't know.

1 the name of the ship ___
2 the cover picture ___
3 the number of passengers ___
4 the description of the ship ___
5 where and when it sank ___
6 the reason it sank ___
7 how many people were rescued ___

d Discuss these three opinions about the blog. Which do you agree with most? Why?

It's amazing. Morgan Robertson must have been able to see into the future in some way.

It might have been just a coincidence, but it's very difficult to explain it.

It's not so extraordinary. Morgan Robertson must have known that large ships were being built and that icebergs were a danger.

BLOG | REVIEWS | GIVEAWAYS | ABOUT

Ten amazing coincidences

The Wreck of the Titan by Morgan Robertson

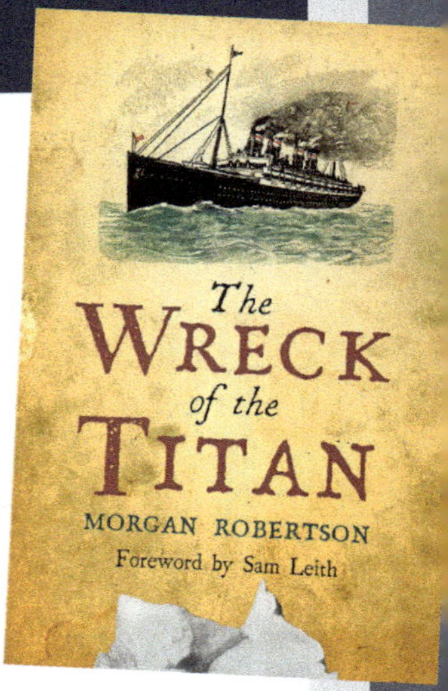

Morgan Robertson writes about the *Titanic* … 14 years early!

A hundred years before James Cameron made the film *Titanic*, American author Morgan Robertson wrote a rather unsuccessful book called *The Wreck of the Titan* about the sinking of an ocean liner. It's a story that's been told lots of times and 13 films have been made about it.

The incredible thing is …

Robertson's *The Wreck of the Titan* was published in 1898, that's 14 years before the *Titanic* was even built.

The similarities between Robertson's work and the *Titanic* disaster are really improbable. The *Titan*, like the *Titanic*, was described as "the largest craft afloat", "like a first class hotel", and "unsinkable". Both ships were British-owned steel vessels, they were both around 800 feet long and they both sank after hitting an iceberg in the North Atlantic, in April, "around midnight".

What's even more unbelievable

In the novel, the *Titan* crashed into an iceberg 400 miles from the coast of Canada at 25 knots. The real-life *Titanic* crashed into an iceberg 400 miles from the coast of Canada at 22.5 knots. If you think of the size of the Atlantic, about 40 million square miles, that's such a close guess it seems impossible that Robertson didn't know in advance what was going to happen.

The weirdest thing of all

But maybe the weirdest thing about the *Titan* were details that were irrelevant to the story, but match what happened to the *Titanic*. For example, both the *Titan* and the *Titanic* had too few lifeboats to take every passenger on board. But it's an odd point to mention in the book when you consider that lifeboats had nothing to do with the story. In the book, when the *Titan* hit the iceberg the ship sank immediately – so why did Robertson mention the lifeboats? Was it just coincidence or did he somehow know what was going to happen?

5 VOCABULARY Adjectives with prefixes

a Find adjectives in the blog in 4b which mean:

1 you can't believe it (x2)
2 it's not likely
3 it's not possible
4 it didn't sell many copies
5 it's not part of the main point.

What do all these adjectives have in common?

b Now go to Vocabulary Focus 10A on p.163

6 SPEAKING

a **Communication 10A** You are going to read two more stories from the series 'Ten amazing coincidences'. Student A: Go to p.129. Student B: Go to p.127.

b Tell each other your story. Do you think the events are coincidences or is there some other explanation for what happened? Do you know any other stories like these?

10B I've managed to make a dream come true

Learn to discuss life achievements

G Wishes and regrets
V Verbs of effort

1 LISTENING

a Read quotes a–c about believing in your dreams. Which one do you like most? Why?

(a) Work hard and dream the biggest dream you can – you'll see amazing things happen!"

(b) "Dreams are all about what's going to happen tomorrow. Don't let your dreams get in the way of being the best person you can be – right here, right now."

(c) "You need dreams when life gets boring or difficult – they're what gets you out of bed in the morning and keeps a smile on your face."

b What do you think is the most important ingredient in realising your dreams? Why?

believing in yourself   hard work   knowing the right people   luck   money

c 3.55 Listen to Louise and Terry. They both decided to pursue their dreams. Match the speakers with the pictures. They both made one change that was the same. What was it?

d 3.55 Listen again. What reasons do Louise and Terry give for making their change?

e What do you think happened next to Louise and Terry?

f 3.56 Listen to the second parts of their stories. Were your predictions correct?

g 3.56 Listen again. Complete the table.

	What problems did he/she experience?	What regrets does he/she have?
Louise		
Terry		

h Would you do what Louise and Terry did? Why / Why not?

2 GRAMMAR Wishes and regrets

a Look at these examples. Who says them, Louise or Terry?

1 If only I'd applied for his job when it came free.
2 I found it a bit crowded. I wish I'd checked this before leaving.
3 I should have checked out other companies.

b What are the speakers doing in the examples in 2a? Are they … ?

1 wishing for a change in their life
2 expressing regrets for things they have done
3 expressing regrets for things they didn't do

c Complete the rule.

To express regret about the past we use:
1 *I wish* or *if only* + *I* + ___
2 *I should have* + _____

d 3.57 **Pronunciation** Listen to the examples in 2a. Notice the linking sounds. Which two words in each example are stressed?

1 If_only I'd applied for his job
2 I wish_I'd checked this
3 I should_have checked out other companies

e Now go to Grammar Focus 10B on p.152

f Think of something you did in the past with mixed results (some parts were good, but others weren't). What would you do differently now? Make notes.

g Tell each other about your past experiences and regrets.

3 READING

a Do you agree with the statement below? Why / Why not?

If you're going to succeed in something, you need to get started before you're too old. If you leave things too late, you lose the ability to change and learn.

GOLDEN DREAMS AND GOLDEN GIRLS!

Too many people never realise their dreams, listing instead all the reasons why they cannot achieve them. Not so for three remarkable American women who never gave up on their dreams. Their stories tell us that you should never give up and you're never too old to make your dream come true.

DIANA NYAD – DON'T STOP SWIMMING!

On September 1, 2013, Diana Nyad became the first person to swim successfully the treacherous Florida Straits, a 177 km passage from Cuba to Florida, without the protection of a shark cage. She was 64 years old.

When she was in her twenties, Diana was already a famous long-distance swimmer, but she retired in 1979. During her early career, Diana had one unsuccessful swim: her attempt to swim from Cuba to Florida in 1978 ended after 42 hours in the water. Although she got on with her life, this unrealised dream remained in the back of her mind.

In early 2010, she turned 60 and decided it was time to pursue her dream again. She began training and, in August 2011, she entered the water to try again 33 years after she first tackled this challenging swim. However, she faced strong winds and sea currents and had to give up after 29 hours in the water.

She tried again a month later, but still wasn't successful. She waited until the following year for her fourth attempt, but pain from jellyfish stings forced her to give up. Her fifth attempt began on 31st August 2013. After 53 hours in the water, she reached Florida and set a new world record.

It was an incredible achievement, not only physically, but emotionally and mentally as well, but in the words of Diana, 'Find a way. Never, ever give up.'

BARBARA JOE – PEACE GAVE HER A CHANCE

At 73, Barbara Joe still remembers hearing President Kennedy announcing the creation of the Peace Corps, a volunteer programme to provide economic and social aid to people in developing countries. Barbara Joe was 23 years old and the idea immediately appealed to her. But she was already married, completing a degree, and she would soon have her own family.

Over the years, Barbara did occasional volunteer work and visited many developing countries in South America. However, it wasn't until 1998 that she told herself it was now or never. She finally became a full-time volunteer and joined the Peace Corps. She was 60.

The Peace Corps has no upper age limit, but volunteers are often young. The selection process is rigorous and only one applicant in ten is accepted. Barbara was by far the oldest person on her training course.

Barbara was a Peace Corps volunteer in Honduras for three and a half years and in that time she taught locals about Aids prevention, handed out medications and even helped deliver a few babies. Her daughter went to visit her during her stay. She was surprised to see how happy her mother was and how well she coped with the primitive living conditions.

Barbara has since written a book about her experience. She thinks you're never too old to volunteer. 'You are never too old to follow your dreams,' she says. 'It's never too late to reinvent yourself.'

b Read the introduction to *Golden dreams and golden girls!*, about three American women. Do you think the writer agrees with the statement in 3a?

c Work in groups of three. Each read about one woman and make notes.

d Tell each other about your famous woman. Decide together which woman you admire most and give a reason.

e The three people in this article all changed their lives to follow their passion. How important do you think it is to do that? What kind of person does it take?

JULIA CHILD – FRENCH FOOD AFFAIR

During World War 2, Julia Child met her husband, Paul, in Sri Lanka, where he worked for the US government. After the war, Paul became a diplomat, and he and Julia were sent to Paris, France. Julia was in her thirties, and it was then she discovered her real passion in life.

She described one of her first meals in France as a 'revelation', and so her love affair with French cooking began. She attended the Cordon Bleu cooking school and had to overcome the negative attitude of her all-male class. She then joined a cooking club and met two French women who were working on a French cookery book for Americans. They asked Julia to help them write the book.

It took ten more years to work on the book. Julia left France and moved around Europe with her husband. When Julia was 49 years old, the English edition of *Mastering the Art of French Cooking* was finally published and became a bestseller. The book led to a career as a TV chef on American television. This was in the 1960s, and Julia Child was one of the first celebrity TV chefs. By then, she was in her fifties.

Julia died in 2004, but lived again in the 2009 film *Julie & Julia*, where she was portrayed by Meryl Streep. Julia's advice to others was to work hard, be creative and enjoy what you're doing.

4 VOCABULARY Verbs of effort

a Notice the bold verbs in these examples from *Golden dreams and golden girls!*. They are connected with the idea of making an effort to do something. Match the verbs with their meanings.

1 … she felt the time was right to **go ahead with** an application …
2 … and was surprised to see how well her mother **coped with** the primitive living conditions …
3 … and had to **overcome** the negative attitude of her all-male classmates.
4 It took ten more years to **work on** the book.
5 Although she **got on with** her life, this unrealised dream remained in the back of her mind.
6 … 33 years after she first **tackled** this challenging swim
7 … she faced strong winds and sea currents and had to **give up** after 29 hours …

a to succeed in controlling difficult circumstances
b continue doing something and not worry about the past
c start doing something
d spend time doing something to improve it
e try to do a difficult task
f stop doing something
g manage to live with something quite well although it's difficult

b Replace the verbs/phrases in italics with the bold verbs/phrases in 4a.

1 When was the last time you had to *succeed in controlling* a difficult work or study problem?
2 What's something that you do regularly and wouldn't want to *stop doing*?
3 In your free time, is there something you're *spending time to improve*?
4 If you decide to do something, do you like to *start* it immediately or do you prefer to think about it first?
5 How well do you *manage* in emergency situations?
6 How easy do you find it to *continue doing* tasks when you're worried about something else?
7 Do you have a difficult task you're *trying to do* at the moment?

c Ask and answer the questions in 4b.

5 SPEAKING

a Think of someone you know who is older than you and has done something you think is brave or amazing. He/She could be:

- a relative
- a family friend
- a colleague
- someone well known in your country.

Make notes on this person's background and his/her achievement.

b Tell each other about your person. What similarities are there between your two people?

10C Everyday English
Two things to celebrate today

Learn to describe how you felt

P Consonant groups

S Interrupting and announcing news

1 LISTENING

a Discuss the questions.

1. When was the last time you celebrated something?
2. Was the celebration for yourself or for someone else?
3. How did you celebrate?

b Look at the photo. The tutor wants to speak to Tessa in his office. Why do you think he wants to see her?

c 3.60 Watch or listen to Part 1. Check your ideas.

d Answer the questions with the adjectives in the box.

delighted pleased surprised worried

1. How does Tessa feel at first?
2. How does she feel after she hears the news?
3. How does the tutor feel? Why?

e 3.61 Watch or listen to Part 2. Which of these things are they celebrating?

1. It's Sam's birthday.
2. Tom and Becky have got married.
3. Tom and Becky have found a flat.
4. The café is making more money.
5. Emma has got a job.

f 3.61 Answer these questions. Watch or listen again if necessary.

1. What was Tom's 'quick decision'?
2. Why does Sam thank Emma and Phil?

2 PRONUNCIATION
Consonant groups

a 3.62 Look at the words below. The underlined consonant sounds are pronounced together. We call these 'consonant groups'. Listen and repeat.

prize pleased celebrate

b 3.63 Underline the consonant groups in the words below. Then practise saying the words. Listen and check.

flat dreams brilliant crazy frightened flight agree Africa glasses asleep climate

c 3.64 Look at the words with three consonant sounds together (three sounds, but not always three letters). Listen and underline them.

asked balanced scream sixth text strength lamps hands watched spread

d Practise saying the words in 2b and 2c that are difficult for you.

3 LISTENING

a In Part 2, Becky said 'There's something else we have to celebrate.' What do you think she'll say next?

b 3.65 Watch or listen to Part 3 and check. They celebrate three more things. What are they?

c Which person ... ?

1. invites everyone to a celebration
2. cuts the cake
3. offers to buy everyone coffee
4. admires Phil's novel
5. admires Tessa's photos

4 USEFUL LANGUAGE
Describing how you felt

a 3.66 Complete what Tessa says with the words in the box. Then listen and check.

get	believe	can't	surprised	so	over	couldn't

I ______ ______ it. I was ______ ______. First prize! I still ______ ______ ______ it.

b Discuss the questions.

1 How does Tessa say she felt?
 a) happy b) disappointed c) surprised
2 Which word has the main stress in each sentence? Practise saying the sentences.

c Here are some more ways to describe how you felt.

1 I wasn't expecting it.
2 It was quite a blow.
3 I was really pleased.
4 I was expecting it.

Which mean … ?

- I was surprised.
- I wasn't surprised.
- I was happy.
- I was shocked or disappointed.

d Choose one of the situations below. Make notes to describe how you felt and why, but don't mention what happened! Use expressions in 4a and 4c.

1 Your boss called you into his office and said that you were fired.
2 You have won £10,000 on the lottery.
3 You didn't prepare for the exam and you failed it.
4 Your best friend told you he/she is getting married
5 Someone stole your wallet.
6 You were promoted.

e Read out your sentences. Can other students guess the situation?

- I really wasn't expecting it.
- I was so surprised because I only bought one ticket.
- I still can't believe it.

5 CONVERSATION SKILLS
Interrupting and announcing news

a 3.65 Watch or listen to Part 3 again. Complete the remarks.

1 Hold ______.
2 There's something ______ we have to celebrate.
3 Hang ______ a minute.
4 I know you won't ______ this …
5 Just a ______.
6 One more ______.

b Which remarks … ?

1 are ways to stop people ending a conversation
2 are ways to show you are about to say something important

c Answer these questions.

1 At the end of each remark, does the voice … ?
 a stay high
 b go down
2 Does this show the other person … ?
 a that you've finished speaking
 b that you haven't finished speaking

d Practise saying the remarks.

6 SPEAKING

a Work in groups of four (A, B, C and D). You're in a restaurant. You each have an important piece of news to tell your group.

Student A: You've just been offered a new job.
Student B: You've won a free trip to Paris for two weeks.
Student C: You're getting married.
Student D: You've won a prize in a poetry competition.

Work alone and decide:

- what details you will give
- which expressions you will use in 4a, 4c and 5a.

b Have a conversation. Take it in turns to announce your news. Then continue talking until the next person interrupts.

Unit Progress Test

CHECK YOUR PROGRESS

You can now do the Unit Progress Test.

10D Skills for Writing
I forced myself to be calm

Learn to write a narrative

W Making a story interesting

1 SPEAKING and LISTENING

a Look at picture a from a story. How would you use these words to describe the picture?

valley flows steep wooded shining flat sticks out still bends fish

a

b The picture is a scene from a thriller. What do you think will happen next? What do you think the man will do?

c 3.67 Listen as the scene is set for the story. Was the description similar to your description in 1a? What happened to the man?

d What do you think will happen next?

A tangled web

... The pain exploded in my ear, sending shockwaves through my body. When I saw the blood on my hand, I knew it was a bullet. Someone had shot at me from the hillside. I immediately fell forward and swam underwater further up the river. Far above me, the green and yellow light of the surface seemed out of reach. But I had to swim as far up river as I could. They might fire at me again if I showed my head above the surface. When I felt as if I could swim no further, I came up under some trees by the riverbank. Here I was safe. No one could see me from the hillside.

My heart was racing. Someone had tried to kill me. Why would anyone want to kill me? Where were they now? What would they do next?

I forced myself to be calm. All the old spy training came back to me – stop before you act, decide on the most important thing to do, take one thing at a time. Above all, don't panic, never lose your cool and always stay calm.

Whoever had shot me would probably come to check that I was dead. I decided to find a place to hide and wait there. Slowly and carefully, I crept on hands and knees along the riverbank, keeping my head as low as possible, until I could see the rock clearly again. I sat down behind some bushes and waited, trying not to move. I pressed my wet shirt against my ear to try and stop the bleeding. Only five minutes later, I heard the sound of someone coming down the path from the hillside.

He was a tall man about my age. He had his back to me, so I could not see his face. But when he looked in my direction, I saw that it was ... Heid! He turned and walked down the path.

Jurgen Heid – a friend. Why had he tried to kill me? I didn't understand. We had been on the San Cristobal operation together: Heid, Nina, Cas and me. We were a team until the operation failed. We had all been sent to 'safe' houses after that. We were all told to disappear – to start new lives, to become other people. Above all, we were told never to meet each other again. That was five years ago. So how had Heid found me? Someone must have sent him. But who? And why? What had happened to bring him here?

As I watched, Heid came back to the riverbank. He put his rifle against a tree and took out a pair of binoculars. Slowly he looked along the other bank of the river. He was obviously looking for my body. I suddenly felt angry. He had been my friend and he had tried to kill me. And now he was looking for my body. I had to find out why he had tried to kill me and who had sent him.

2 READING

a Read the first paragraph of *A tangled web*. Were your ideas in 1d correct?

b Read the whole story. Tick (✓) the things the man did and put them in the correct order.

1 ☐ ☐ He swam up the river under water.
2 ☐ ☐ He swam back to the rock.
3 ☑ 1 He fell into the water.
4 ☐ ☐ He hid on the riverbank under some trees.
5 ☐ ☐ He walked carefully back to the rock.
6 ☐ ☐ He swam down the river.
7 ☐ ☐ He came out onto the bank further up the river.
8 ☐ ☐ He went back along the bank to a place where he could see the rock.

c Think about the story so far. What do we know about … ?

1 the man's past life
2 the people he worked with
3 how he has spent the last five years

3 WRITING SKILLS Making a story interesting

a The writer uses various ways to make the story interesting. Find one more example of these in the story.

1 short sentences to describe what the man saw, thought and felt
Here I was safe. No one could see me from the hillside.
2 questions to describe the man's thoughts
Why would anyone want to kill me?
3 phrases with verb + *-ing* to describe actions and events
The pain exploded in my ear, sending shockwaves through my body.

b Look at these sentences from other stories. Complete the beginnings in A with endings in B. Are some endings more likely than others?

A
1 ☐ She sat in a corner of the café,
2 ☐ She ran up the stairs,
3 ☐ She drove at top speed down the motorway,
4 ☐ He stood on the bridge,
5 ☐ A man stood in the doorway,

B
a singing at the top of her voice.
b staring thoughtfully into the water.
c blocking my way out of the room.
d reading a book.
e gasping for breath.

c Choose one of the beginnings in A. Continue the story, using a new phrase with verb + *-ing*.

d Read out the phrase you added. Can other students guess which beginning in 3b you chose?

e Look at these examples. What verb tenses does the writer use?

When I saw the blood on my hand, I knew it was a bullet. Someone had shot at me from the hillside.
My heart was racing. Someone had tried to kill me.

Which tense does the writer use … ?
1 to tell the main events of the story
2 to refer to an earlier event that explains what happened

f Continue these sentences with your own ideas, using the past perfect tense.

1 When I looked in my wallet, I saw that it was empty.
2 I jumped to the side of the road as the car flashed past me.
3 When I saw Nina again, I hardly recognised her.
4 I put my hand in my coat pocket. The letter was still there.

4 WRITING

a Look at the sentence below, which continues the story *A tangled web*.

I picked up a piece of wood lying near my hiding place …

In pairs, imagine how the story could continue. Write two or three more paragraphs. Use the techniques in 3a–f to make your story interesting.

b Read another pair's story. Did they use … ?

- short sentences
- direct questions
- verb + *-ing*

Did they use different narrative tenses to explain the background to actions?

c Compare your story with other students. Which was … ?

- the most exciting
- the most unusual

d 3.68 Now listen to the rest of the story. Whose ending was most similar to the real story?

UNIT 10
Review and extension

1 GRAMMAR

a Complete the dialogue using the verb in brackets with a past modal of deduction.

A: Who left those flowers for us?
B: It [1]_____ (be) Rachel – she's away at the moment.
A: Janet [2]_____ (leave) them – she occasionally does surprise things like that.
B: Actually, it [3]_____ (be) Elaine. She rang this morning and said something about a surprise for us.
A: Well, whoever left them – they're beautiful.

b Imagine different past possibilities for the following situations. Make notes.

1 You check your online bank account and find someone has deposited £100 into the account.
2 You arrive home and find the front door wide open.
3 You receive a parcel addressed to you containing a brand-new tablet and an anonymous card saying "Enjoy!"

c Discuss your different ideas.

d Put the verbs in brackets in the correct form.

1 My business degree wasn't very interesting or useful when it came to finding a job. I wish I _____ (study) history at university instead.
2 She didn't start studying Mandarin until she went to China. She should _____ (do) a course about six months before going there.
3 In his new job, he has to interpret a lot of statistics. If only he _____ (pay) more attention in maths classes at high school.

2 VOCABULARY

a Correct the adjective prefixes.

1 She's very good with young children, but she can get a bit inpatient with teenagers.
2 He left without saying goodbye – that's very unpolite.
3 They made an inexpected visit to the children's hospital. It was a lovely surprise for the patients.
4 We were extremely missatisfied with the level of service we experienced during our stay.

b Complete the sentences using the correct verb from the box.

work	overcome	cope	tackle

1 When I lived in Northern Australia, I found it easy to _____ with the heat.
2 On Sunday I like nothing more than to _____ a really difficult crossword in the Sunday paper.
3 He managed to _____ his shyness and make friends at university.
4 My grammar's quite good – I just need to _____ on my pronunciation.

3 WORDPOWER *way*

a Match the *way* expression in 1–6 with the correct meanings in a–f.

1 ☐ I'm sorry but there's *no way* I can sign that contract – the conditions aren't clearly described.
2 ☐ *One way or another* we have to know all that vocabulary for the test.
3 ☐ I thought it would be cheaper to go by bus than train, but it was *the other way round*.
4 ☐ After a quick supper, we *made our way* to the concert.
5 ☐ I ran *all the way* around the park and I'm exhausted.
6 ☐ *In some ways* it would be easier to not go abroad on holiday this year.

a We can't avoid it.
b I can't do it.
c We went there.
d It's partly true.
e I went the complete distance.
f It was the opposite.

b Replace the incorrect *way* expressions. Tick (✓) the ones that are correct.

1 We travelled in some ways to the end of the island.
2 I thought she'd be nicer than her brother, but it was one way or another.
3 I don't feel well and there's no way I can go out.
4 It might all the way be more straightforward to talk to him rather than send an email.
5 If you hear an alarm, please make your way towards the exit as quickly as possible.

c Answer the questions. Make notes.

1 What's something that you would just never do?
2 When did you last go the whole distance somewhere?
3 What's something you think is partly true?
4 What's a situation where you found that the opposite was true?

d Discuss the situations in 3c. Use a *way* expression with each example.

REVIEW YOUR PROGRESS

How well did you do in this unit? Write 3, 2 or 1 for each objective.
3 = very well 2 = well 1 = not so well

I CAN ...

speculate about the past	☐
discuss life achievements	☐
describe how I felt	☐
write a narrative	☐

10A Student B

a Read the story.

A falling baby caught twice by the same man

In Detroit, sometime in the 1930s, a baby fell from a window. But it fell onto a passerby, a man named Joseph Figlock. He broke the baby's fall and it survived unharmed.

A year later, the same baby fell from the same window again. Once again, Joseph Figlock happened to be passing by. The baby fell on him again and the same thing happened!

b ▶ Now go back to p.118

9C Student A

a Have two conversations.

Conversation 1

Look at the guide to drawing a panda. Follow the steps to draw your own panda. Student B will try and guess what you are drawing. Be prepared to explain or add more detail.

Conversation 2

Student B is going to draw a picture in four steps. After each step use expressions from 2c (p.110) to show that you're unsure what the picture is. Get Student B to explain or add more detail to the picture until you can guess what it is.

What on earth is that?

I haven't got a clue what that is.

b ▶ Now go back to p.110

2B

a Read the texts and check your answers to 1f on p.24.

Wolf

If you see a wolf before it sees you, walk away silently. If the wolf sees you, back away slowly and avoid eye contact. Wolves see eye contact as a challenge. If the wolf runs towards you, don't run away, as wolves are faster than you. Instead, turn to face the wolf. If the wolf attacks you, curl up in a ball, or defend yourself with a stick. A wolf's nose is very sensitive, so if you hit it on the nose it will probably run away. Wolves are also easy to distract with food, so if you have some food, throw it to the wolf, then move slowly away, still facing the wolf.

Shark

Don't lie on the surface of the water in areas where there are sharks, as this makes you look like a seal. Instead try to keep vertical in the water. Sharks normally won't attack unless they smell your blood or they think you're food. So if a shark comes towards you, keep still or swim slowly towards the shark. As long as you don't panic, it will probably swim away. If the shark bites you, hit it in the eye.

Bear

In bear country, always wear a bell or hit trees with a stick to make a noise. This will make any bears that are near go away. If a bear comes towards you, lie on the ground and 'play dead'. Provided you stay absolutely still, the bear will lose interest. If you are on a hill, run away downhill, going from side to side. Bears find it hard to run fast downhill because they are so heavy and they can't turn quickly.

b Imagine that you had to encounter one of these three animals. Which would you prefer? Why?

c ▶ Now go back to p.24

4C Student A

a Look at the photos of Cambridge, England. Imagine you visited this place. Prepare to present your photos to other students. Decide:

- what the photos show
- what you will say about them
- which expressions in 2a on p. 50 you can use.
  Notes: The photos show a row of buildings in the city centre. Photos A and C also show bicycles (everyone uses them in Cambridge). Photo A: your favourite café.

b ▶ Now go back to p.50

6A Student B

a Read about the two tourist destinations. Make notes about them. Think about which you prefer and why.

b Tell Student A about the destination you prefer. Try to agree on which of your two destinations to visit. Use your notes from **a** to persuade your partner to visit your place.

Hampi

This small village in South West India is the chance to discover a whole new culture. Until 500 years ago, it was the capital of the Vijayanagara Empire. There's an astonishing number of monuments and ruins that belonged to this ancient civilisation. Perhaps the most impressive is the Virupaksha Temple. Hampi is a unique cultural experience like no other.

Rotorua

This small city in New Zealand is surrounded by a series of stunningly beautiful lakes and forests. But what makes it special is all its geothermal activity. You can see hot steam shoot from the ground in the form of a geyser while nearby a pool of mud boils away. Rotorua is dramatic and unique – it's well worth a visit.

c ▶ Now go back to p.70

4A Student A

a Read about Sharon Tirabassi. Use these questions and keywords to help you focus on the main points.

1. What was Sharon's life like before she won the lottery? (job, apartment)
2. How much did she win?
3. What did she do then? (trips, shopping, house, cars)
4. Who did she give money to? (family, rent, friends)
5. What's her life like now? (house, bike, work)
6. Why is she happier now? (lifestyle, kids)

Sharon Tirabassi

Nine years after her huge lottery win, Sharon Tirabassi is catching the bus to her part-time job. Tirabassi, one of this city's biggest lottery winners, has gone from being very rich to living from pay day to pay day with just enough money.

Before her win, Tirabassi used to live in a small apartment with her three children and couldn't afford a car. But in April 2004, she won $10.5 million from a Lotto Super Seven ticket. She was unprepared for the change to her lifestyle. She would take friends on wild shopping trips and pay for everything herself. She and her husband bought a huge house in the wealthiest part of town and owned four cars. Besides the house and the cars, a lot of the cash went to family and friends – too much, as she admits now. She bought several houses in the city, renting them out at affordable rates to her family. A lot of friends suddenly appeared when news broke of her win – and a lot of them she never heard from again.

But all that has changed. Today, Tirabassi is living in a rented house on a quiet industrial street – not far from where she started. She no longer has the expensive cars. These days, she rides an electric bike when she's not taking the bus.

But she says she's happier now than she used to be and she lives life more fully than she did before. 'When I had lots of money, I used to spend all my time shopping, but now other things are more important to me.' Tirabassi's now concentrating on raising her children with good family values. 'I'm trying to get them to learn that they have to work for money,' she says.

b ▶ Now go back to p.45

5C

a You're opening a café in your town. You want it to be different from other cafés. Make notes about:

- furniture
- food and drinks
- music and entertainment
- special things you could offer.

b Explain your ideas and respond to other students' ideas. Use language from 6a and 6c on p. 63.

c ▶ Now go back to p.63

3C Student B

a You'd like to go somewhere fun with Student A after class. You're not very keen on shopping unless it means going to a shop or department store that sells video games. It might be fun to go to a new juice bar that opened last week. You could also go to the movies. Make careful suggestions and try to agree on what you can do after class.

b Now go back to p.39

9C Student A

a Have two conversations.

Conversation 1

Tell your partner you have a surprise for them to do with entertainment. Make them try and guess. Eventually tell them it's free tickets for them to go and see *Hamlet*. If your partner looks a little disappointed, check that they like the theatre – you're sure they told you they did.

Conversation 2

Your partner has got a surprise for you to do with a sports game. Try to find out what it is. You like going to tennis matches and football games, but you're not very keen on basketball. Try to be polite and grateful.

b Now go back to p.111

10A Student A

a Read the story.

Separated twin boys with almost identical lives

Stories of identical twins are often incredible, but perhaps none more so than those of identical twin boys born in Ohio. They were separated at birth and grew up in different families. Unknown to each other, both families named them James. Both boys grew up not even knowing each other, but they both became police officers and both married a woman named Linda. They both had sons who one named James Alan and the other named James Allan. They both got divorced and then married again to women named Betty. They both owned dogs which they named Toy. They met for the first time after 45 years.

b Now go back to p.118

7C Student A

a Imagine what you would do with the room shown in the picture. Think about:

- how you could use different parts of it (e.g. sleeping, working, watching TV)
- what furniture you might put in it
- where you could put different items (e.g. pictures, a TV, a computer).

b Draw a rough plan of the room to show what you would do. Think how you could use:

- expressions for imagining from 4b on p.87
- vague phrases from 5a and 5d on p.87.

c Show Student B your plan and tell him/her how you imagine the room. Then listen to Student B and ask questions about his/her room.

d Now go back to p.87

9A Student A

a Describe your inventions to Student B, but don't tell him/her what it is. Ask him/her to guess what the invention is. Use these expressions to help you.

This thing's made of …
You can hold it in your hand.
You can put it …
You can put something in it.
You can perhaps find one in …
It might be useful after/when …

Anti-snoring pillow

This pillow uses a sensor to detect snoring and then responds by vibrating. Tests show that this is efficient in reducing snoring. In addition, the pillow has an internal recording device which will allow you to record your snoring and monitor the effectiveness of the pillow.

Ear dryer

You can use this to dry the inside of your ear after you've had a shower, bath or swim. You place the device in your ear and it blows hot air. The makers suggest you use it after you have dried your ears with a towel.

b Now go back to p.106

4A Student B

a Read about Ihsan Khan. Use these questions and keywords to help you focus on the main points.

1 What was Kahn's life like before his win? (job, money)
2 What was his dream? (diamonds, number)
3 How much did he win?
4 What did he do then? (taxi, car, houses, Pakistan, mayor)
5 Then what happened? (earthquake, medicine, school)
6 Why isn't he satisfied? (money, greedy)
7 What happened later? (parliament, votes)

Ihsan Khan

Before he won the lottery, Ihsan Khan used to work as a taxi driver and security guard in the USA – first in Chicago and then in Washington. He would usually send most of what he earned back to his family in Pakistan. 'It was the worst job in the world,' Khan says now. And then, one night, he had a dream in which he saw diamonds and also a number: 246 1725. He played those numbers on the lottery for 10 years. Then one day he struck lucky. Ihsan Khan won the jackpot and found he had $55 million. He immediately gave up his job as a taxi driver and bought an expensive car and two luxury houses.

But then he did something surprising. Instead of living in the USA and spending the money on luxuries, he went back to his hometown of Battagram and ran in the election to become mayor. He saw it as a way to pay back some of what he'd gained. Khan believes that it's wrong to save money for yourself and that we have a responsibility to help others who are not so well off as ourselves. Although he was competing against a candidate whose family had been in local politics for 35 years, Khan was elected mayor. Then, just after he was elected, the region was hit by a huge earthquake which killed 3,000 people in Battagram. Mayor Khan took the opportunity to use his lottery money to help people directly. He spent $300,000 on medicine and on repairs to homes, and he also gave money to build a new school.

But Khan isn't fully satisfied with what he's done and feels that simply giving people money is never enough. He used to think he could use his money to fix everything, but he no longer believes that. He has discovered that people are often greedy and they never seem satisfied with what they are given.

In 2008, he resigned as mayor and ran for election to the Pakistan parliament, but this time he wasn't a winner. The winning candidate received over 22,000 votes. Ihsan Khan only received 5,000. It seems his luck had run out.

b ▶ Now go back to p.45

4C Student A

a Prepare to give an opinion on one of the topics below. Plan what you will say about it.

- a recent sports event
- your classroom
- a famous person

b Tell Student B your opinion about the topic you have chosen.

c Listen to Student B's opinion about their topic. Express careful disagreement. Use language in 4c on p.51.

d ▶ Now go back to p.51

9C Student B

a Have two conversations.

Conversation 1
Your partner has got an entertainment surprise for you. Try to find out what it is. You like going to classical music concerts and opera, but you're not very keen on theatre. Try to be polite and grateful.

Conversation 2
Tell your partner you have a surprise for them to do with a sports game. Make them try and guess. Eventually tell them it's free tickets for them to go to a basketball game. If your partner looks a little disappointed, check that they like basketball – you're sure they told you they did.

b ▶ Now go back to p.111

6A Student A

a Read about the two tourist destinations. Make notes about them. Think about which you prefer and why.

b Tell Student B about the destination you prefer. Try to agree on which of your two destinations to visit. Use your notes from **a** to persuade your partner to visit your place.

Dominica
A small but beautiful Caribbean island with superb beaches. There's also tropical rainforest with exotic bird life. Dominica's biggest attraction is a boiling lake. After a three-hour trek through stunningly beautiful forest you come to a lake that is hot and steaming. No one knows about it – go there now.

Bornholm
Bornholm is Denmark's secret island in the Baltic Sea. You can get there easily by ferry or plane. Bornholm has a unique coastline with dramatic rock formations in the north, picturesque historic towns and dense forests. The island boasts the largest medieval fortification in Northern Europe as well as Denmark's highest lighthouse.

▶ Now go back to p.70

4C Student B

a Look at the photos of Moscow, Russia. Imagine you visited this place. Prepare to present your photos to other students. Decide:

- what the photos show
- what you will say about them
- which expressions in 2a on p.50 you can use.

Notes: The photos show Moscow State University, built in 1953.

A

B

C

b ▶ Now go back to p.50

5A

a Are you an optimist or a pessimist? Read the descriptions below to find out.

Mostly a) answers:

You're an optimist. You expect things to turn out well for you, and when you encounter problems you believe you can overcome them. When things go well, you usually see it as the result of your own ability or hard work. When things go badly, you see it as just bad luck and expect it to be better next time.

Mostly b) answers:

You're a bit of a pessimist. You don't always expect things to turn out well for you, and when you encounter problems you believe you are generally unlucky. When things go well, you usually see it as the result of chance or what other people have done. When things go badly, you see it as a result of your own weaknesses.

b ▶ Now go back to p.56

3C Student A

a You need to buy a new jacket. You'd like Student B to come with you after class, because you need someone's advice on the best jacket to buy. You're not sure if Student B is keen on shopping. Perhaps suggest doing something nice as well, for example having a coffee together. Make careful suggestions and try to agree on what you can do after class.

b ▶ Now go back to p.39

9B

a Read the final part of the story about Rodriguez.

Rodriguez's songs, which were about protest and overcoming hardship, caught the imagination of young people in apartheid-era South Africa and everyone was listening to him. But no one in South Africa really knew who Rodriguez was. People thought he was dead; there were even rumours that he had committed suicide while performing on stage.

Then, one day in 1995, a South African reporter, Stephen 'Sugar' Segerman, became curious about the rumours of Rodriguez's death and decided to trace Rodriguez and find out how he had really died. 'First of all, I tried to find out where the money for his albums had gone. The money never reached Rodriguez and no one knows to this day where that money went or why he was never told about it. I was astounded that no one knew anything about him. When I made enquiries people kept on being very vague.'

This made him even more determined to find Rodriguez. Using words from his songs (the only clues 'Sugar' had), he traced Rodriguez to Detroit, where he managed to get in touch with Rodriguez's producer from the 1970s. He discovered to his amazement that Rodriguez wasn't dead at all – he was alive and living in Detroit, completely unaware that half-way round the world he was a huge success.

Stephen Segerman went to meet Rodriguez and told him about his fame in South Africa. He invited Rodriguez to give a concert there and Rodriguez agreed. In 1998, after years of living from hand to mouth, Rodriguez went on his first South African tour, playing six concerts in front of thousands of fans and being treated like a superstar.

b ▶ Now go back to p.108

6B Pair B

a Prepare for a discussion. You believe that it's important to stop languages dying out. Every time we lose a language we lose part of our culture.

Use these arguments or prepare your own:

- There's no reason why people shouldn't speak several languages: their own language and one or two 'bigger' languages.
- Languages die out because people feel ashamed of them. It's important to educate people to respect and value minor languages.
- The world needs variety – the world would be very boring if people all spoke one language.
- Many tribal languages contain knowledge about plants, medicines and the environment which could be very useful. We need to preserve this knowledge.

b ▶ Now go back to p.73

9C Student B

a Have two conversations.

Conversation 1

Student A is going to draw a picture in four steps. After each step use expressions from 2c (p.110) to show that you're unsure what the picture is. Get Student A to explain or add more detail to the picture until you can guess what it is.

Conversation 2

Look at the guide to drawing a penguin. Follow the steps to draw your own penguin. Student A will try and guess what you are drawing. Be prepared to explain or add more detail.

What on earth is that?

I haven't got a clue what that is.

b ▶ Now go back to p.110

4C Student B

a Prepare to give an opinion on one of the topics below. Plan what you will say about it.

- a film or book
- a café or restaurant
- the town/city you're in now

b Listen to Student A's opinion about their topic. Express careful disagreement. Use language in 4c on p.51.

c Tell Student A your opinion about the topic you have chosen.

d ▶ Now go back to p.51

5B

a Read the text and check your answers to the quiz in 1b on p.59.

Antarctica is the fifth largest continent in the world and is completely surrounded by the Southern Ocean. It is approximately the size of the USA and Mexico. About 98% of Antarctica is covered by ice that averages 1.6 km in thickness. It is the coldest, driest and windiest continent in the world. Temperatures reach minimums of between –80 °C and –90 °C in the winter. The landscape is considered a kind of desert, because there is very little rainfall. There are mountains, glaciers and rivers, but no trees or bushes. There is a variety of animal life on the continent, but the two most well known are penguins and seals. The continent is positioned around the southern-most point of the planet, the South Pole. The first person to reach the South Pole was the Norwegian Roald Amundsen.

b ▶ Now go back to p.59

8B Pair B

a Read the story and answer the questions.

1 Why was the art teacher given the job?
2 What was wrong with his CV?
3 Why did the principal sack him?

The art teacher

A school was looking for a new art teacher. They had received several applications, including one from a well-known local artist who also had many years' teaching experience. He made a good impression in the interview, so they offered him the job.

On his CV, he had listed an MA in art history. After the school had employed him, they discovered that he had started an MA course but never finished it. His CV was clearly wrong.

The principal called him into her office and asked him about it. He explained that he hadn't finished the MA because he'd had to spend a year in the army. He had intended to write 'Course work completed for MA' – it was just a simple mistake.

The principal of the school was faced with a difficult decision. She didn't believe the art teacher, but he had already started working and he was doing his job well. However, after thinking it over, she decided to sack him.

b What do you think the principal should have done? What would you have done?

c ▶ Now go back to p.96

6B Pair A

a Prepare for a discussion. You believe that everything in the world changes and languages naturally die out. There's no point in trying to stop that happening, and it doesn't really matter.

Use these arguments or prepare your own:

- In the modern world, everyone needs to speak a major world language.
- A lot of tribal languages are not adapted to modern life. They belong to a way of life which is dying.
- If young people speak a major language, they can travel and get jobs.
- Languages die because young people don't want to speak them. It's wrong to try to force them.

b Now go back to p.73

7B

a This is a picture from a reality TV programme. Talk about the questions. What do you think?

- Is the woman really suffering or is she acting?
- Would you like to be in her situation? Why / Why not?

b Now go back to p.83

9A Student B

a Describe your inventions to Student A, but don't tell him/her what it is. Ask him/her to guess what the invention is. Use these expressions to help you.

This thing's made of …
You can hold it in your hand.
You can put it …
You can put something in it.
You can perhaps find one in …
It might be useful after/when …

Mobile oxygen booster

This mobile oxygen booster boosts available oxygen from 20% or lower up to 30%. You can use this in the office, while exercising, or anywhere you feel the need for a bit of extra air.

Influenza saver ultraviolet steriliser

This is an ultraviolet steriliser which can stop you getting the flu. You can use it to sterilise everyday things from computer keyboards to kitchen items and even beds. It uses ultraviolet radiation to kill bacteria. It's ideal for any home.

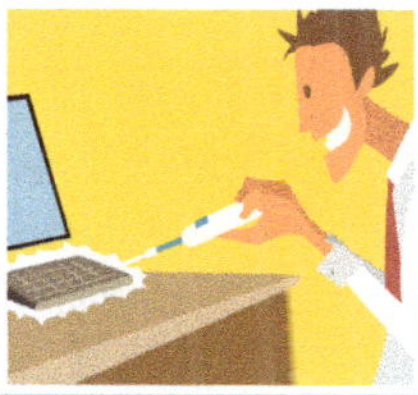

b Now go back to p.106

7C Student B

a Imagine what you would do with the room shown in the picture. Think about:

- how you could use different parts of it (e.g. sleeping, working, watching TV)
- what furniture you might put in it
- where you could put different items (e.g. pictures, a TV, a computer).

b Draw a rough plan of the room to show what you would do. Think how you could use:

- expressions for imagining from 4a on p.87
- vague phrases from 5a and 5d on p.87.

c Listen to Student A and ask questions about his/her room. Then show Student A your plan and tell him/her how you imagine your room.

d Now go back to p.87

8B

Of the 50 letters dropped, only 20 found their way to Mr Fingham. The next day staff from the newspaper were sent to check the places where they had left the envelopes and they had all disappeared. This suggests that many people opened the envelopes and looked inside, and if the envelopes had contained real tickets they would probably have used them. It seems that some Londoners weren't so honest after all!

On the positive side, four Londoners were so keen to show how honest and considerate they were that they didn't post the letter they found – they ran after our letter-dropper to return it.

One of London's good people was 18-year-old Julia Dalrymple, from Notting Hill, who found a letter in a Starbucks café. Not only nice, but also rather smart, Julia wrote her number and a message on the envelope before posting it: "Dear forgetful Mr Starbucks, as I am an honest person I will go on to post this letter that I found … If you have any more where these came from and you're feeling generous, let me know."

Now go back to p.95

Grammar Focus

1A Review of tenses

1.2

Present simple
We use the present simple:
- for habits, repeated actions, facts and things which are generally true
  *I usually **do** my homework in the evening.*
  *She **writes** crime stories.*
- with state verbs for short-term states, verbs of preference and verbs of the senses.
  *I **want** to go home.*

Present perfect simple
We use the present perfect simple:
- for experiences in our life without saying when they happened
  ***I've seen** this film three times.*
- to focus on present states which started in the past and have continued up to the present
  ***I've lived** here since I was a child.*
- to focus on past completed actions which are recent (often with *just*) or which have a connection with the present.
  ***I've posted** your letter.*

Present continuous
We use the present continuous:
- for actions in progress now (at the moment of speaking) or around now
  *Sorry, I can't talk now – I'**m doing** my homework.*
  *She'**s writing** a book about her life.*
- for temporary situations.
  *I'**m studying** English in Cambridge this semester but normally I work in Milan.*

Past simple
We use the **past simple:**
- to talk about completed past actions and states. We often specify the time in the past with the past simple:
  *I **lost** my phone last week, but then I **found** it in my car.*

Past perfect simple
We use the past perfect simple:
- for actions and events that happened before a particular moment in time
- for reasons (after *because*).
  *I decided to walk home because I **had forgotten** my bus pass.*

Past continuous
We use the past continuous:
- to describe actions that were in progress at a particular moment in the past
- for actions or events in progress at the time of a shorter, past simple action.
  *He phoned while I **was doing** my homework.*

1B Question forms

1.13 **Positive and negative questions**
Most questions have an auxiliary verb (e.g. *be, do, have* or modal verbs) before the subject. The auxiliary verb can be positive or negative:
*How **do** you spell that?* *Why **isn't** my computer working?*

Prepositions usually come at the end of questions.
*Where are you **from**? NOT ~~**From** where are you?~~*

In very formal questions they can go at the beginning.

> **Tip** We can make short questions from *who / what / where* + preposition:
> **A:** *I'm going to a party tonight.* **B:** ***Who with**?*
> **A:** *Can I borrow your phone?* **B:** ***What for**? (Why?)*

We use negative questions to express surprise:
***Haven't** they **finished** yet?* (I'm surprised)

When we ask about the subject of a sentence the word order doesn't change and we don't use an auxiliary verb.
***Somebody** wrote this book.* → ***Who** wrote this book?*
NOT ~~Who did write this book?~~

1.14 **Indirect questions**
We use indirect questions to sound polite. Start indirect questions with *Can you tell me… / Do you know…* We don't use an auxiliary verb and the word order doesn't change: Use *if* in indirect yes / no questions.
*Why **did she become** famous?* → ***Do you know why** she became famous?*
***Do you like** foreign films?* → ***Can you tell me if** you like foreign films?*

We can also use indirect questions in sentences starting with: *I'm not sure… I know / don't know… I wonder… I can't remember…* etc.
Is this answer correct? → ***I'm not sure** if this answer is correct.*
Where have they been? → *I **wonder** where they've been.*

> **Tip** We use ***which*** + **noun** when there is a limited number of options and ***what*** + **noun** when there are many possibilities:
> *We can have our meeting at 10.00, 12.15 or 14.30. **Which time** would you prefer?*
> *I'm free all day. **What time** do you want to meet?*

1A Review of tenses

a Correct the mistakes in the sentences. Think about spelling, tense and form.

1 I'm studing hard at the moment because I try to pass my final exams. _I'm studying, I'm trying_
2 Internet shopping becomes more and more popular these days. ______
3 We looking for new members of our group. Do you want to join? ______
4 This food is tasting a bit strange. I think I prefer food from my own country. ______
5 We think of buying a new car but they're costing a lot of money. ______
6 I write to apply for the job of sales assistant. I send my C.V. with this letter. ______

b Match the sentence halves.

1 ☐ When I arrived … a … I was watching television.
2 ☐ While my brother was cooking … b … twice in my life.
3 ☐ I was waiting for the plumber … c … Sally had already left.
4 ☐ I have been to Istanbul … d … when he phoned me to cancel.
5 ☐ Robert stayed in my flat … e … in 2004 to work abroad for a year.
6 ☐ I moved to Singapore … f … both this summer and last summer too.

c ▶ Now go back to p.9

1B Question forms

a Choose the best word or phrase to complete each question.

1 Where *we are* / *are we* going to eat?
2 What *you thought* / *did you think* of the film? Did you enjoy it?
3 We've got cheese sandwiches and egg sandwiches. *What* / *Which* flavour do you prefer?
4 Why *you didn't* / *didn't you* call me?
5 I hear you're a musician. *What* / *Which* kind of music do you play?
6 I got this watch for my birthday. *Who from?* / *What from?*
7 What *happened* / *was happened* to the window?

b Write questions about the underlined words and phrases.

1 _Who discovered pulsars?_ Jocelyn Bell-Burnell discovered pulsars.
2 ______ She's interested in classical music.
3 ______ Over 2000 people watched the match.
4 ______ They haven't started yet because they're waiting for you.
5 ______ My left foot hurts.
6 ______ She heard the news from Ralph.

c Rewrite the sentences and questions using the prompts.

1 What do you want?
I don't know … _what you want._
2 Why didn't they come back?
I wonder … ______
3 Where are they going?
Where do you think … ______
4 Have you ever met him?
Can you tell me … ______
5 Who wrote this story?
Do you know … ______
6 Does this pen work?
I wonder … ______
7 What's your sister's name?
Can you tell me … ______
8 When will it be ready?
When do you think … ______

d ▶ Now go back to p.13

2A Narrative tenses

We use narrative tenses to tell stories about what happened in the past. The most important narrative tenses are: past simple, past continuous, past perfect simple and past perfect continuous.

1.30

We use the past simple for completed past actions and states which happened at a specific time in the past:
*We **spotted** them on the mountain so we **rescued** them and **took** them to hospital.*

We use the past continuous for actions (not states) that were in progress at the time of the main events in the story:
*When we spotted them, they **were standing** next to some stones. They **were waving** their arms but we couldn't hear what they **were shouting**.*

We use the past perfect simple / continuous for events and activities that happened before the main events in the story and to give explanations or reasons. It often occurs after *because*.
*We spotted them because they **had built** the word* help *out of stones.*
*We finally spotted them after we **had been searching** for over a week.*

After we**'d been searching** for them for over a week, we finally **spotted** them on the mountain. They **were** standing next to the word 'Help', which **they'd built** out of stones.

Past perfect simple or continuous?

We use the past perfect simple:

- To focus on the results of an earlier completed action:
  *We **spotted** them (result) because they**'d built** a big sign* (earlier action).
- To talk about 'time up to then' with a <u>state</u> verb (e.g. know, have, be):
  *When we found them, they**'d been** on the mountain for a week.*

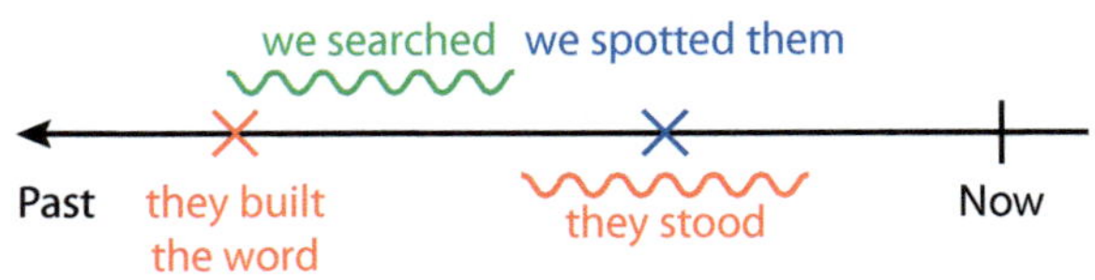

We use the past perfect continuous:

- before a result in the past to show the effect of an earlier activity:
  *They **were tired*** (result) *because they**'d been building** a big sign* (earlier activity).
- To emphasize the duration of time with an <u>action</u> verb (e.g. wait, search, drive):
  *We found them after we**'d been searching** for a week.*

2B Future time clauses and conditionals

We use future time clauses to talk about future possibilities, future plans or to give advice. We can normally use *will, be going to*, or the imperative in the main clause.

We normally use a present tense in the subordinate clause with words like *if, when, as soon as, unless, as long as, provided, in case*, etc. We can also use the same time clauses to talk about facts and things which are generally true. In these sentences we often use a present tense verb in the main clause.

1.31

***When** we **go** hiking next weekend, we'll try a new path.*
***If** you **see** a bear, don't run.*
*It won't attack you **provided** you**'re standing** still.*
***Unless** you know the way well, **bring** a map.*
*Always bring a snack **in case** you **get** hungry.*
***As soon as** it **gets** too cold, we'll go home.*

> **Tip**
> When *if* means *whether*, we normally need *will* or *going to* to refer to the future:
> *I don't know **if / whether I'll** see any wild animals when I'm on holiday.*
> *NOT: ... ~~if I see~~ ...*

1.32 ***as soon as***

As soon as shows that something will happen immediately after another thing:
***As soon as** I get home, I'll email you.*

> **Tip**
> We can use present perfect or present simple after words like *as soon as* or *when* to talk about completed processes in the future. There is little difference in meaning:
> *We'll leave **when / as soon as I've finished** my work.* (Or: ... ***I finish** ...*)

1.33 ***if, unless, as long as, provided** and **in case***

Unless means *if not*. The verb after *unless* is usually positive:
*You won't see any animals **unless** you **stay** quiet.*
(You won't see any animals if you don't stay quiet)

As long as and *provided* are similar to *only if*:
*We'll be safe **provided / as long as** we stay here.*
(But only if we stay here).
*You can go out tonight **as long as** you're back by 10.* (But only if you're back by 10).

We use *in case* to talk about preparations for possible future situations:
*Take your keys **in case** we're out when you get home.*

2A Narrative tenses

a Complete the sentences with the past simple or past continuous form of the verbs in brackets.

1 While he __was walking__ (walk) in the forest, he __tripped__ (trip) and __cut__ (cut) his knee.
2 I ________ (not / notice) what the thief ________ (wear) because I ________ (hide) under the desk the whole time.
3 When I ________ (get) home, everyone ________ (watch) TV. Nobody ________ (even / say) 'hello'.
4 **A:** Where ________ (you / be) when you ________ (hear) the news?
B: I ________ (be) on the bus – I ________ (travel) to work.
5 Fortunately, I ________ (not / hurt) myself when I ______ (fall) because I ________ (wear) a helmet.
6 **A:** What page number ________ (the teacher / just / say)?
B: Sorry, I ________ (not / hear) anything. I ________ (not / listen).

b Choose the best verb form.

1 She was out of breath because *she'd run / she'd been running*.
2 It was sad to sell my old car – *I'd had / I'd been having* it since I was a student.
3 The party was great. *They'd planned / They'd been planning* it for months.
4 We were really pleased because *we'd finished / we'd been finishing* our project.
5 Everything was wet because it *had rained / had been raining*.
6 How long *had they known / had they been knowing* each other when they decided to get married?
7 They weren't very happy because *they'd waited / they'd been waiting* for six hours.
8 I didn't watch the film because *I'd already seen / I'd already been seeing* it four times.

c Choose the best verb forms.

It [1]*happened / had happened* on the last day of our holiday. We [2]*were getting / got* up and [3]*saw / were seeing* that, at last, the sun [4]*was shining / had shone*. We [5]*were leaving / left* the hotel and [6]*were starting / started* walking along the narrow cliff path. Then, after [7]*we'd been walking / we walked* for about two hours, the path [8]*was suddenly becoming / suddenly became* much narrower – it was no more than 10cm wide. There [9]*had been being / had been* a storm the previous night, and the sea [10]*had washed / was washing* part of the path away.

The cliff wasn't very high, so [11]*we'd decided / we decided* to keep going, along the narrow path. I [12]*went / was going* first, and [13]*had made / made* it safely to the other side. But then I [14]*was hearing / heard* a shout and a splash. Mike [15]*had fallen / fell* into the sea below. There were sharp rocks all around him, but luckily [16]*he'd landed / he'd been landing* safely in the water, and [17]*wasn't hurting / hadn't hurt* himself. So I [18]*climbed / was climbing* down the cliff to help him to safety.

Later, back at the hotel, he [19]*had been explaining / explained* what had gone wrong: [20]*he'd been trying / he tried* to take a photograph at the time of his fall.

d Now go back to p.22

2B Future time clauses and conditionals

a Tick (✓) the correct sentences. Correct the mistakes.

1 I'll send you a postcard when we'll be on holiday. ☐ __incorrect when we're on holiday__
2 We'll come out as soon as we've eaten dinner. ☑ ________
3 My parents don't mind if I go out as long as I'll tell them where I'm going. ☐ ________
4 You won't pass the exam unless you don't study harder. ☐ ________
5 If it's still raining when you'll finish work, I'll pick you up. ☐ ________
6 I'm going to leave my laptop at home in case it'll get damaged. ☐ ________
7 I lend you my car provided you won't drive too fast. ☐ ________

b Join the sentences using the words in brackets.

1 Maybe I'll see Joseph. I'll tell him to call you. (if) — I'll __tell Joseph to call you if I see him.__
2 She'll finish university. She wants to be a teacher. (when) — She ________.
3 They'll be late if they don't hurry up. (unless) — They'll ________.
4 I'll check your work. Then I'll send it back to you immediately. (as soon as) — I'll ________.
5 You can take photographs but you mustn't use a flash. (provided) — You ________.
6 You should take some money because you might need to take a taxi. (in case) — You ________.
7 He won't bite you but you must be careful. (as long as) — As ________.
8 You'll only understand if you listen very carefully. (unless) — You ________

c Now go back to p.24

3A Multi-word verbs

1.45 Multi-word verbs consist of a verb and one or two particles:
*We **came up with** some good ideas, and decided to **try** them **out**.*

Sometimes the meaning of the multi-word verb is clear from the meaning of the verb and the particle (e.g. *sit down*), but often you have to learn the meaning of each multi-word verb.

Transitive and Intransitive multi-word verbs

- Transitive multi-word verbs need an object. The object can come before the particle (e.g. *throw **sth** away*) or after the particle (e.g. *look after **sb***), depending on the type of multi-word verb.
- Intransitive multi-word verbs don't have an object, e.g. *go away* NOT ~~*go somebody away*~~

Type 1 has no direct object (intransitive): verb + particle	wake up; go away; fall over; stay up; break up; sit down; take off; calm down
Type 2 has an object (transitive): verb + noun / pronoun + particle OR verb + particle + noun / pronoun	wake up; fall over; take off; calm down; try sth out; figure sth out; make sth up; throw sth away; pick sth up; let sb down
Type 3 has an object (transitive): verb + particle + noun / pronoun	look into sth; focus on sth; believe in sth; live for sth; be into sth; look after sb
Type 4 has two particles and always has an object: verb + particle 1 + particle 2 + noun / pronoun	come up with sth; look down on sb; look up to sb; run out of sth; fall out with sb; go on about sth; get away with sth

Tip Many multi-word verbs are both transitive and intransitive (e.g. *wake up; fall over; take off; calm down*):
*When you **wake up*** (intransitive), *try not to **wake the dog up*** (transitive) *too!*
*After the plane **took off*** (intransitive) / ***took my shoes off*** (transitive). Use a dictionary to find out if a multi-word verb is transitive or intransitive.

Type 2 multi-word verbs

When the object is a long noun phrase, it normally comes after the particle:
*Please **throw away** those old shoes that are nearly falling apart!*
When the object is a pronoun (e.g. it, me, sb), it almost always comes before the particle:
*Those shoes are really old. Please **throw** them **away!*** NOT: ~~*Please **throw away them!***~~
When the object is a short noun phrase (e.g. up to three words), it can come before or after the particle:
*Please **throw** those old shoes **away** / Please **throw away** those old shoes.*

3B Present perfect simple and continuous

1.50 We use the **present perfect simple**:

- to talk about experiences without saying when they happened
  *He**'s tried** to run a marathon four times in his life.*
- for experiences during any present period of time
  *What **have** you **learnt** so far **this year**?*
- with superlatives
  *She**'s the nicest person** I**'ve** ever **met**.*
- for recent completed actions which have a result in the present.
  *Oh no! I**'ve broken** my key.*
- with *already, just* and *yet*
  *I**'ve already done** the shopping, I**'ve just put** the food in the oven, but I **haven't laid** the table **yet**.*
- to talk about *how long* with state verbs (with *for / since*)
  *I**'ve known** them **for** years but I **haven't seen** them **since** January.*
- with *how many, how much* and *how often* to talk about experiences
  ***How many** essays **have** you **written**?*

We use the **present perfect continuous:**

- when a recently completed action has a result now
  *She's tired because she**'s been training** hard.*
- to describe repeated activities which started recently
  *I**'ve been going** to the gym a lot recently.*
- to talk about unfinished activities using *how long* and *for / since*
  *We**'ve been walking since** the sun came up.*

3A Multi-word verbs

a Tick the correct sentences. Sometimes more than one sentence is correct.

1 a I don't **believe in** these new language learning techniques.
  b I don't **believe** these new language learning techniques **in**.
  c I don't **believe in** them.
  d I don't **believe** them **in**.

2 a Do you want **to** try the new guitar I got for my birthday **out**?
  b Do you want to **try out** the new guitar I got for my birthday?
  c Do you want to **try out** it?
  d Do you want to **try** it **out**?

3 a We've **fallen out** with our neighbours.
  b We've **fallen with** our neighbours **out**.
  c We've **fallen** them **out with**.
  d We've **fallen out with** them.

4 a Did you **make up** that story?
  b Did you **make** that story **up**?
  c Did you **make up** it?
  d Did you **make** it **up**?

b Rewrite these sentences replacing the verbs in bold with multi-word verbs. Use a verb from A and one or two particles from B.

A: come be go take look let figure run

B: up into out off about of with into out down on

1 How did you **invent** a name for your shop? *How did you come up with a name for your shop?*
2 Have you **investigated** the cause of the accident? ______
3 I've **liked** jazz since I was at university. ______
4 We've almost **used all** our food. ______
5 I hate to **disappoint** you. ______
6 I can't **understand** it. ______
7 I know I was wrong. Stop **repeating** it! ______
8 Do you think this product will **be successful**? ______

c ▶ Now go back to p.34

3B Present perfect simple and continuous

a What are the most likely combinations? Match the sentence halves.

1 a ☐ I'm really proud of myself because …		1 … I've been building a wall in my garden.
2 b ☐ I'm exhausted because …		2 … I've built a wall in my garden.
3 a ☐ They've been on holiday …		1 … three times this year.
4 b ☐ They've been going on holiday …		2 … to the same place for 20 years.
5 a ☐ I've written …		1 … six emails already.
6 b ☐ I've been writing …		2 … emails all morning.
7 a ☐ She's been playing …		1 … tennis twice this week.
8 b ☐ She's played …		2 … a lot of tennis recently.

b Tick (✓) the correct sentences. Correct the mistakes.

1 How long have you worked here? ☑ ______
2 Please don't come in – we haven't been finishing yet. ☐ *incorrect   haven't finished*
3 Have you ever been sailing? ☐ ______
4 We've been giving three presentations this week. ☐ ______
5 This room has been empty since our son left home. ☐ ______
6 I've been watching a lot of films lately … maybe too many. ☐ ______
7 I haven't been hearing that old song since I was a child. ☐ ______
8 Those people have been calling me five times today. ☐ ______

c Complete the sentences with the correct form of the verbs in brackets. Use the present perfect simple or the present perfect continuous.

1 I *'ve just spent* (just / spend) over £100 on football classes for you, and now you're saying you don't like football!
2 Can you hurry up? We ______ (wait) for ages!
3 How long ______ (you / study) to become a doctor?
4 She ______ (not / say) a word all day – I think she's angry with me.
5 ______ (you / clean) the car yet, or is it still dirty?
6 **A:** Your eyes are red. ______? (you / cry) **B:** No, I ______ (chop) onions!

d ▶ Now go back to p.37

4A used to and would

2.2 ***used to*** **and** ***would***

We often use *used to* to describe past situations. In general, these situations continued for a long time and are not true now. They can be states (e.g. *like, live, have*) or habits (= repeated actions):

When I was a child, I ***didn't use to*** *like vegetables, but now I love them.*

When we were students, we ***used to*** *go dancing every week.*

We can also use *would* to describe past habits. Don't use *would* for past states:

When we were students, ***we'd go*** *dancing every week.*

We often use a mixture of *used to, would* and the past simple when talking about our past:

When I was young, we never ***used to*** *go on holiday. Instead,* ***we'd spend*** *the whole summer playing in the fields near our house. We* ***loved*** *it.*

> **Tip** Don't use *used to* or *would* for things that happened only once, or when we say how many times something happened in the past:
> *I read that book* ***once / a few times*** *when I was a teenager.*
> NOT ~~*I* ***used to*** *read ...*~~

2.3 ***no longer*** **and** ***any more***

We use *no longer* before a positive verb or after *be*:

We ***no longer*** *go to the old forest. It's* ***no longer*** *there.*

We use *any more* at the end of a sentence with a negative verb:

We ***don't*** *go to the old forest* ***any more****. It's* ***not*** *there* ***any more****.*

2.4 ***be / get used to***

Don't confuse *used to* with *be / get used to*. They have very different meanings. After *be / get used to*, we use a gerund or a noun phrase:

I ***used to*** *study for many years.* (This was my habit in the past.)

I'm getting used to *working in an office.* (It's becoming normal for me now.)

I'm used to *the job now.* (It's normal for me. It's not difficult.)

> **Tip** We can also use *usually* + the present simple to talk about habits in the present tense:
> *I* ***usually get up*** *at 6.30 am.*

4B Obligation and permission

2.11

	The speaker is making a rule	The speaker is describing somebody else's rule	
		Present	Past
Strong positive obligation	*You* ***must*** *wear a helmet. I won't let you ride without it.*	*We* ***have to*** */* ***need to*** *wear a helmet. It's the law.*	*We* ***had to*** */* ***needed to*** *wear a helmet to go on the motorbike.*
Strong negative obligation	*You* ***must not*** */* ***mustn't*** *remove your helmet. It's far too dangerous.*	***We're not allowed to*** */* ***can't*** *remove our helmets. The instructor will get very cross with us.*	*We* ***weren't allowed to*** *remove our helmets.*
Positive obligation	*I think you* ***should*** *give /* ***ought to*** *give the money back.*	***I'm supposed to*** *give the money back, but I don't want to.*	*I* ***was supposed to*** *give the money back, but I forgot.*
No obligation	*You* ***don't have to*** */* ***don't need to*** */* ***needn't*** *buy a ticket.*		*You* ***didn't have to*** */* ***didn't need to*** *buy a ticket.*
Permission	*Yes, it's OK, you* ***can*** *go home.*	*I* ***can*** */* ***I'm allowed to*** *go home now.*	*I* ***could*** */* ***was allowed to*** *go home before 5pm.*
No permission	*No, I'm sorry. You* ***cannot*** */* ***can't*** *go home yet.*	*I* ***can't*** */* ***I'm not allowed to*** *go home yet.*	*I* ***couldn't*** */* ***I wasn't allowed to*** *go home early.*

- *must* and *mustn't* are very strong. In most situations, it's more natural to use *have to, need to, needn't, can't, be not allowed to*, etc. Questions with *must* are very rare.
- *should* is much more common than *ought to.* Questions and negatives with *ought to* are very rare.
- *Need to* is like *have to* whereas *need* (usually found in the negative) is a modal.

2.12 ***make*** **and** ***let; be forced to*** **and** ***be allowed to***

make and *let* are special because they are followed by an object + infinitive without *to*:

They ***made*** *me* ***pay*** *extra.* NOT ~~*They* ***made*** *me* ***to pay*** *extra.*~~

They ***let*** *me* ***come*** *in for free.* NOT ~~*They* ***let*** *me* ***to come*** *in for free.*~~

We often use the verbs *force* and *allow* in passive constructions. Both are followed by *to* + -infinitive:

I ***was forced to*** *pay extra.* (Less common*: I was made to pay extra)*

I ***was allowed to*** *come in for free.* NOT ~~*I was* ***let come in*** *for free.*~~

4A *used to* and *would*

a Tick (✓) the possible forms in each sentence.

1 She ________ good at maths when she was little.
  a used to be ☑ b would be ☐
2 Laura was my best friend – we ________ for hours every day.
  a used to talk ☐ b would talk ☐
3 I ________ five swimming competitions when I was at school.
  a won ☐ b would win ☐
4 Our teacher, Mr Williams, was very strict. He ________ allow us to speak at all during lessons.
  a didn't use to ☐ b wouldn't ☐
5 I'll never forget the time I ________ my leg. I couldn't walk for weeks!
  a used to break ☐ b broke ☐
6 We ________ a dog but he died about five years ago.
  a used to have ☐ b would have ☐

b Choose the correct form.

1 I *used to / would be* really good at football when I was young, but now I'm terrible at it.
2 I *didn't use to / didn't used to* like jazz, but now it's my favourite type of music.
3 I*'m used to / used to* living on my own. It was strange at first, but now it's fine.
4 I don't think I'll ever *get used to / get use to* writing on a tablet computer – it's much easier on a laptop.
5 Where did you *use to go / used to go* on holiday when you were a child?
6 How long did it take you to *get used to / used to* working from home?

c ▶ Now go back to p.45

4B Obligation and permission

a Rewrite the sentences using the words in brackets.

1 You can wear whatever you want. [need to]	___You don't need to wear___ a uniform.
2 I think you should write to them. [ought]	I think ________________.
3 They made me give them my phone. [forced]	They ________________.
4 They won't let you park there. [allowed]	You won't ________________.
5 You don't have to stay here. [can]	________________ if you like.
6 They advised us to bring strong shoes. [supposed]	We ________________.
7 I wasn't allowed to use a dictionary. [let]	They ________________.
8 It was raining so we were forced to stop. [made]	The rain ________________.

b Look at the rules for a computer training course. Andy explains the rules to his friend Dan. Complete the conversation with one word or a contraction (e.g. mustn't) in each space.

- All users must change their passwords after first logging in.
- You are not allowed to access the computer system without a new password.
- You can choose your own password.
- Your new password must be at least 20 characters long.
- Your password should be easy to remember but it shouldn't be easy to guess.
- You must not tell anyone else your password.

Dan: So how was the course?
Andy: It was OK, but the security was really tight. We ___had / needed___ to change our password straight away.
Dan: Why?
Andy: They said we [2]________ access the system without a new one. We were [3]________ to choose our own passwords, but it [4]________ to contain at least 20 characters?
Dan: Wow … that's long!
Andy: Yes, but it was [5]________ to be something that's easy to remember.
Dan: OK, so the name of your football team then?
Andy: No, it was [6]________ to be something that's not easy to guess.
Dan: So what was it?
Andy: I [7]________ tell you! We're not [8]________ to tell anyone else!

c ▶ Now go back to p.49

5A Future probability

We use a wide range of modals verbs, adverbs, adjectives, etc. to describe what we think is the probability of future events:

Degree of probability	Modal verbs	Other expressions	Adjectives
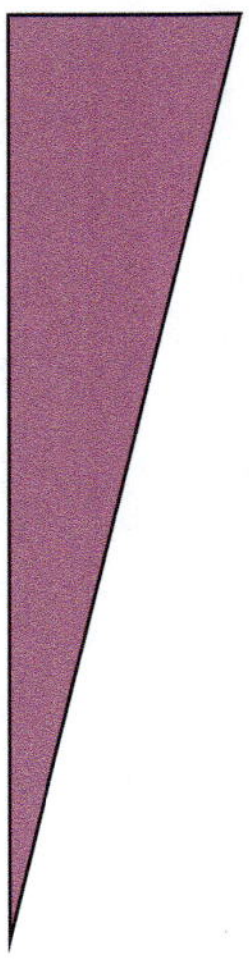 100% high	*We **will** go.* *We **will certainly** go.* *We **will probably** go*	***I'm sure** we'll go.*	*It's **certain** that we'll go.*
	*We **could well** go.* *We **may well** go.* *We **might well** go.*		*It's (very) **likely** that we'll go.*
50% medium	*We **could** go.* *We **may** go.* *We **might** go.*	***There's a (good) chance that** we'll go.*	*It's **possible** that we'll go.*
	*We **probably won't** go.*	***I don't suppose** we'll go.* ***I doubt if** we'll go.* ***I shouldn't think** we'll go.*	*It's (very) **unlikely** that we'll go.*
0% low	*We **won't** go.* *We **certainly won't** go.*	***There's no chance that** we'll go.* ***I can't imagine that** we'll go.*	

2.25 Positive and negative forms

We can make negative statements of probability with *might not* or *may not*. Don't use *couldn't* in this way – it refers to the past ability, not future probability:

We **could** *go out on Friday.* (= it's possible that we'll go out next Friday).
We **couldn't** *go out on Friday.* (= we weren't able to go out last Friday).

Adverbs like *certainly* and *probably* increase or decrease the level of certainty and come after *will*, but they come before *won't*:
*It'll **probably** be a nice day today but it **probably won't** be nice tomorrow.*

2.26 Adjective + *to* + infinitive

With the adjectives *sure / likely / unlikely / certain / bound* we can use the pattern: *be* + adjective + *to* + infinitive:

*They**'re sure to be** late.* (= I'm sure that they'll be late.)
*He**'s certain / likely / unlikely to see** you.*
*There**'s bound to be** someone who knows the answer.*
(= I'm sure someone knows the answer)

5B Future perfect and future continuous

2.28 Future perfect

Positive	Negative	Question	Short answer
We'll have left.	She won't have left.	Will they have left?	Yes, they will / No, they won't.

We use future perfect to describe what we expect to happen before a specific time in the future:
*I don't know exactly when somebody will buy my car. I hope **I'll have sold** it by the end of the month.*

Tip We often use future perfect with *by*.
*We'll have finished **by Friday / by the time** they get here.*

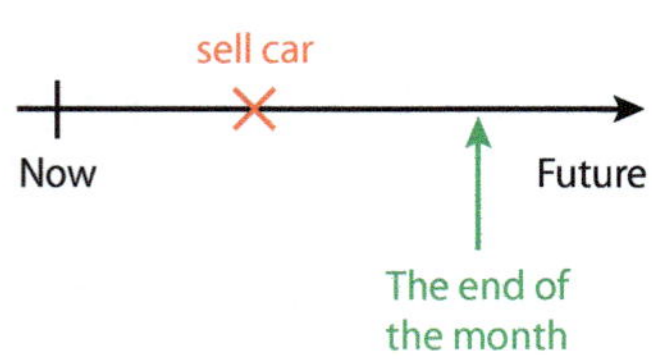

I don't know exactly when somebody will buy my car.
I hope **I'll have sold** it by the end of the month.

2.29 Future continuous

Positive	Negative	Question	Short answer
He'll be driving.	We won't be driving.	Will you be driving?	Yes, I will / No, I won't.

We use future continuous for activities that will be in progress around a particular time in the future:
*Don't phone me at 5pm. **I'll** still **be driving** home from work at that time.*

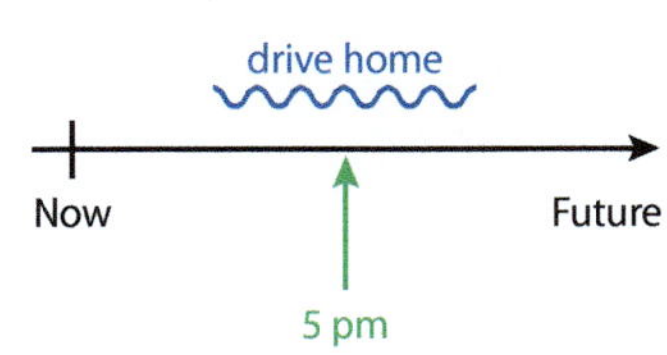

We can also use future continuous for things that are already planned:
*It'll be tough in my new job – **I'll be getting** up at 4am every day.*

5A Future probability

a Complete the sentences with one word from the box. Use each word once.

can't chance if likely might no
probably shouldn't suppose sure

1 I'll _probably_ get up at about 8 tomorrow.
2 I don't __________ I'll ever see them again.
3 It's very __________ that you'll get a better job soon.
4 I __________ imagine that they'll move to another country.
5 There's __________ chance that we'll win, but we can try.
6 That __________ well be the best idea.
7 I'm __________ you'll have a brilliant time.
8 I __________ think too many people will be interested.
9 There's a good __________ that I'll be back before 10.
10 I doubt __________ they'll be able to fix my printer.

b Rewrite the sentences using the words in brackets. Keep the meaning the same as the original.

1 It's certain that he'll pay you. (to)
He's _certain to pay you._
2 It's very unlikely that we'll leave. (probably)
We__________.
3 He'll certainly win a medal. (bound)
He's __________.
4 These new phones are unlikely to sell well. (unlikely)
It's __________.
5 It's possible that she won't notice. (might)
She __________.
6 I'm sure there'll be another chance. (to be)
There's __________.

c Now go back to p.58

5B Future perfect and future continuous

a Tick (✓) the sentences which are correct. Correct the mistakes.

1 I'd prefer to visit you in August because I'll be finishing my exams then. ☐ _incorrect I'll have finished_
2 I don't want to be late – they'll have eaten all the food before we get there! ☑ _correct_
3 I can't take you to the airport at 10 because I'll have attended a very important meeting at that time. ☐ __________
4 The presentation is scheduled for the 15th, so I'm sure I'll be writing it then. ☐ __________
5 Thursday is the best day to call me at home because I'll have worked from home then. ☐ __________
6 I can pass the message on to Arthur – I'll be seeing him tomorrow at college. ☐
7 A: How will I recognize you at the airport? B: I'll have carried a sign with your name on it. ☐ __________
8 I can't access the internet right now. Can you try again in 10 minutes – hopefully it'll be working again then. ☐ __________

b Look at Christina's calendar for tomorrow. Complete her conversation with Zofia with the future continuous or future perfect form of the verb in brackets.

Zofia: So, what time can I come and visit you tomorrow? What about 8.30?
Christina: No, sorry, 1 _I'll still be taking_ (I / still / take) the kids to school at that time.
Zofia: OK, so maybe when you're back home. 2 __________ (you / get) back by 9.30?
Christina: Yes, probably. But 3 __________ (I / still / deal) with my emails then. I've got some urgent emails that I need to reply to. But you could come at about 11. I'm sure 4 __________ (I / finish) before. Does that suit you?
Zofia: Er … not really. Could we make it a bit later? What about 14.00?
Christina: Yes, that's fine, but it'll only give us an hour. 5 __________ (I / leave) about 15.00 to pick the kids up from school.
Zofia: OK, yes, an hour should be perfect. Oh, one thing. Can you lend me that DVD you were telling me about?
Christina: Well, Hannah's got it at the moment. She wants to watch it tonight. But 6 __________ (I / see) her tomorrow, so I can ask her to bring it. 7 __________ (she / watch) it by then.

Monday

8.00 – 9.00
Take children to school

9.00 – 10.45(?)
Deal with emails

12.30 – 14.00
Meet Hannah

15.00 – 16.00
Pick up children from school

c Now go back to p.61

6A Gerunds and infinitives

2.41 verb + *-ing*

When verb + *-ing* functions like a noun it is called a gerund. We use gerunds:

- when a verb is (part of) the subject of a sentence: ***Swimming*** is good for you. / ***Meeting*** *you last week was a real pleasure.*
- after prepositions (e.g. *about, by, without, of,* etc.): *I worry too much* **about making** *mistakes.* *They escaped* **by digging** *a tunnel under the wall.*

2.42 *to* + infinitive

We use *to* + infinitive:

- after adjectives (e.g. *happy, pleased, easy, difficult, dangerous, safe, possible*): *It's* ***easy to find*** *your way into the city centre, but it's very* ***difficult to get*** *out again.*
- to express purpose (= what a person wants to achieve): *We're going to the beach* ***to lie*** *in the sun.* (= because we want to lie in the sun) ***To watch*** *the clip again, press 'replay'.* (= if you want to watch again)

> **Tip** Be careful with verb forms after *to*. The word *to* is sometimes a preposition and sometimes part of *to* + infinitive.
> *I'm looking forward* ***to seeing*** *you.*
> *I hope* ***to see*** *you.* (NOT ~~*I hope **to seeing***~~)

2.43 verb + verb

There are many verbs which are followed by gerunds (e.g. *I* ***enjoy painting***) and many which are followed by *to* + infinitive (e.g. *I* ***want to watch***). There are also a few which allow both patterns with a change of meaning:

- *try* + *to* + infinitive: *I* ***tried to talk*** *to him, but he didn't answer his phone.* (= I attempted to do it)
- *try* + gerund: *I* ***tried talking*** *to him, but he's still angry.* (= I did it but it didn't work)
- *remember / forget* + *to* + infinitive: *Please* ***remember*** */ don't* ***forget to buy*** *some milk.* (= a job for the future)
- *remember / forget* + gerund: I ***remember*** */ I'll never* ***forget hearing*** *that tune the first time.* (= an experience in the past)
- *go on* + *to* + infinitive: *After explaining the theory I'll* ***go on to describe*** *some examples.* (= stop one thing and start the next)
- *go on* + gerund: *The professor* ***went on talking*** *for over an hour.* (= didn't stop)

> **Tip** *stop* can be followed by a gerund, or an infinitive of purpose:
> *I* ***stopped drinking*** *coffee.* (= I don't drink it now)
> *I* ***stopped to drink*** *coffee.* (= I stopped because I wanted to drink coffee in a café)

2.44 Sense verbs

Verbs connected with senses can be followed by an object and verb + *-ing*. (e.g. *look at / see / watch / notice / observe / hear / listen to / feel / smell / taste*):

I ***watched*** *the people* ***walking*** *around.*
I could ***smell*** *something* ***burning***.

6B The passive

2.52 We can use the passive:

- when we don't know who did something / what caused something, or when this is not important. *These words* ***were written*** *thousands of years ago.*
- when the agent (the doer) is very obvious. *Which languages* ***are spoken*** *in your family?*
- when the main thing we are talking about is the object of the verb. *I read a really interesting article today. It* ***was written*** *by someone who spent a year living in a jungle.* (*It* = the article)

The passive is formed with the verb *be* in the appropriate tense + past participle.

	Active	**Passive**
Present simple	*They* ***use*** *it.*	*It* ***is used***.
Past simple	*They* ***used*** *it.*	*It* ***was used***.
Present continuous	*They* ***are using*** *it.*	*It* ***is being used***.
Past continuous	*They* ***were using*** *it.*	*It* ***was being used***.
Present perfect	*They* ***have used*** *it.*	*It* ***has been used***.
Past perfect	*They* ***had used*** *it.*	*It* ***had been used***.
Future	*They* ***will use*** *it.* *They* ***are going to use*** *it.*	*It* ***will be used***. *It* ***is going to be used***.
Infinitive (e.g. after modal verbs)	*They* ***can use*** *it.* *They* ***might use*** *it.*	*It* ***can be used***. *It* ***might be used***.

2.53 Prepositions after *made*

We can use a range of prepositions after passives with *made*:

- Made + *by* + method: *These cakes* ***are made by hand*** */* ***by mixing*** *cornflakes with chocolate.*
- Made + *with* + tool: *I think these marks* ***were made with a knife***.
- Made + *of* + material: *The wings* ***are made of very strong plastic***.
- Made + *from / out of* + original object: *Our table* ***is made from*** */* ***out of an old door***.

Our table **is made from** */* **out of** *an old door.*

6A Gerunds and infinitives

a Underline the correct verb form.

1 I was looking forward to *hear* / *hearing* your ideas.
2 We need to book an appointment to *see* / *seeing* them again.
3 I'm still getting used *to be* / *being* a manager
4 Riding an elephant is similar *to ride* / *riding* a horse.
5 He doesn't find it easy *to talk* / *talking* to anyone.

b Match the sentence halves.

1 ☐ Oh no! I forgot …
2 ☐ I'll never forget …
3 ☐ Why don't you try …
4 ☐ We're going to try …
5 ☐ Can you please stop …
6 ☐ You'll have to stop …
7 ☐ Did you remember …
8 ☐ I don't remember …
9 ☐ Start with the easy questions and then go on …
10 ☐ We started in the morning and went on …

a … to win the match. It'll be hard but we've still got a chance.
b … to turn off the lights before you went out?
c … playing until it was dark.
d … to pay the phone bill. I'm really sorry.
e … to buy some petrol. You're going to run out soon.
f … restarting the computer? That usually works for me.
g … to try the ones that are left.
h … making that noise? I can't concentrate.
i … meeting the President – it was the most memorable day of my life.
j … buying these shoes. Are you sure they're mine?

c Complete the sentences with the correct form of the verb in brackets.

1 I'll be happy _to help_ (help) you find somewhere to stay.
2 He spent two years without ________ (speak) to another person.
3 ________ (live) in another country is the easiest way of ________ (learn) a foreign language.
4 Can I borrow your laptop ________ (check) my emails?
5 Suddenly, I noticed a young man ________ (run) towards me.
6 I'm afraid of ________ (be) alone in the dark.
7 ________ (avoid) the risk of misunderstandings, I'll explain everything twice.
8 Would it be possible ________ (leave) five minutes early?
9 ________ (spend) a year as a volunteer teacher was one of the best experiences of my life.
10 As he waited for his results, he could feel his heart ________ (beat) in his chest.

d ▶ Now go back to p.69

6B The passive

a Complete the sentences with the correct passive form of the verb in brackets.

1 The local people are angry because these old trees _are going to be cut_ (cut) down next week.
2 The first email between two organisations _____ (send) in 1971.
3 Currently, English _____ (use) as an official language in almost 60 countries.
4 I promise that you _____ (inform) as soon as your bags arrive.
5 The thief _____ (not / catch) yet, but I'm sure they'll catch him soon.
6 By the time we arrived, all the best seats _____ (already / take), so we had to sit right at the back.

b Rewrite the sentences in the passive.

1 I wrote that report. — That report _was written by me_.
2 My sister told us about this restaurant. — We ________________.
3 We can only dream of the technology of 2100. — The technology of 2100 ________________.
4 Someone had already built this bridge 1000 years ago. — The bridge ________________.
5 You can't always depend on Martina. — Martina ________________.
6 I'm sure they'll look after you well. — I'm sure you ________________.

c Complete the sentence with the correct preposition.

1 Jam is made _out of_ fruit.
2 This toy car was made _____ an old shoe box.
3 I can't believe this music is made _____ computer.
4 If you want a perfect paper aeroplane, it must be made _____ scissors and glue.
5 Windows in a plane are made _____ special glass, so they don't break easily.
6 All our clothes are made _____ local wool and _____ local people.

d ▶ Now go back to p.73

7A too / enough; so / such

3.2 ***too* and *enough***

We use *too* and *not enough* to explain problems, when something is more than the right amount or less than the right amount:
*Oh no, there are **too** many people and there is**n't enough** food! What's everybody going to eat?*

We often use *enough* to tell somebody not to worry:
*Don't worry. We've got **enough** food. I bought lots of food this morning.*

We use adjective + *enough* and *enough* + noun

	More than the right amount	The right amount	Less than the right amount
With adjectives	*It's **too** warm to play tennis.*	*It's warm **enough** to go to the beach.*	*It is**n't** warm **enough** to have a picnic.*
With countable nouns	*There are **too many** people. I can't see anything.*	*There are **enough** people for a game of volley ball.*	*There are**n't enough** people for a game of football.*
With uncountable nouns	*I spend **too much** time in internet chat rooms.*	*I have **enough** time to bake a cake.*	*There is**n't enough** time to go shopping.*

3.3

Tip After *too* and *enough*, we often use *to* + *infinitive*:
*It's **too** late **to walk** home but I don't have **enough** money **to pay** for a taxi.*

3.4 **so / such**

We use *so* and *such* to draw attention to the extreme quality of something. We can use *so* before an adjective and *such* before adjective + noun.

- *so* + adjective: *Why are you **so happy?*** (= why are you as happy as you are?)
- *such* + *a / an* + adjective + singular noun: *It's **such a beautiful day!*** (= it's a very beautiful day)
- *such* + adjective + plural noun: *They're **such friendly people!***

Tip We can use *such a* + noun to express a positive or negative opinion:
*It's **such a pity / shame** you missed the beginning!* (= I'm so sorry / sad.)
*You're **such a genius**!* (= You're so clever!)
*The meal was **such a waste** of money!*
*It's always **such a pleasure** to talk to you.*

3.5

After *so / such*, we often use a *that* clause:
*It was **such** a nice place **that** we decided to stay another week.* (= we decided to stay because it was extremely nice)
*I ate **so** much food **that** I felt ill.*

7B Causative *have / get*

We use the structure *have / get* + object + past participle to talk about things that we arrange or pay for but don't actually do ourselves. *Have* is slightly more formal than *get*.

3.9

	have / get	Object	Past participle
They're	*having*	*their kitchen*	*painted.*
When are you going to	*get*	*your hair*	*cut?*
I've	*had*	*my car*	*fixed.*
She wants to	*have*	*her book*	*published.*

We can mention the agent (the person who did the action) after *by*:
*She had her dress made **by a top designer**.*

3.10

Tip We use a reflexive pronoun (e.g. *myself, herself, ourselves*) to emphasize that we **didn't** arrange or pay for somebody else to do something:
*I wanted to get my trousers shortened, but it was too expensive, so I did it **myself**.*

We can use the structure *have* + something + past participle to talk about experiences that are caused by other people. These experiences are usually negative:
*He **had his phone stolen**.* (= He experienced the situation where somebody stole his phone)

We can use the structure *get* + something + past participle to focus on the end results of an activity rather than the activity itself:
*I don't care how you do it – just **get this work done**!* (= finish it or pay for somebody to finish it)

7A too / enough; so / such

a Complete the sentences with one phrase from the box in each space. Use each phrase twice.

enough | too | too many | too much

1 She speaks quite quickly but she makes _too many_ mistakes.
2 Oh no … we haven't got ________ milk. Can you go to the shop and buy some?
3 They're nice children, but they make ________ noise.
4 We wanted to go out, but it was ________ cold.
5 They spend ________ time watching TV. It's not healthy!
6 Your project isn't brilliant but it's good ________. You don't need to do it again.
7 You should take a bus – it's ________ far to walk.
8 ________ people attended the meeting – everyone was talking at the same time and they couldn't make any decisions.

b Match the sentence halves.

1 ☐ They're so …
2 ☐ It was such a …
3 ☐ You've read that book so many …
4 ☐ She wrote her complaint in such a …
5 ☐ There was so much …
6 ☐ They're such …

a … times that you must know every word by now.
b … way that we thought she was being kind.
c … nice people that I'm sure you'll like them!
d … boring film that we left halfway through.
e … lazy that they never do any homework.
f … food that we couldn't eat it all.

c Rewrite the second sentence so that it means the same as the first. Use the words in brackets and *so*, *such*, *too* or *enough*.

1 They went by plane because they're rich. (that)
They're _so rich that_ they went by plane.
2 I'm so sorry that we didn't see you. (pity)
It's ________ that we didn't see you.
3 He's too young to be a doctor. (old)
He isn't ________ be a doctor.
4 I didn't go out because I was so tired. (too)
I was ________ go out.
5 That player's so good that he plays for his national team. (such)
He's ________ he plays for his national team.
6 It was such a serious situation that they had to call the police. (so)
The situation ________ they had to call the police.

d ▶ Now go back to p.81

7B Causative *have/get*

a Match the sentences with reasons A–C for using causative *have/get*.

1 ☐ Have you had your hair done? It looks lovely.
2 ☐ My boss isn't very good at getting his team motivated.
3 ☐ I've had my heart broken too many times – I don't want to fall in love again.
4 ☐ I need to get my eyes checked. I can't see very well.
5 ☐ My neighbours had their car stolen last week.
6 ☐ I just want to get this work done quickly so I can relax again.
7 ☐ I had my portrait painted by a wonderful artist.
8 ☐ Last time I went to the dentist I had to have two teeth taken out.

A The subject arranges or pays for somebody to do something

B The subject has a bad experience caused by someone else

C The speaker focuses on the end result rather than the activity itself

b Rewrite the phrases in bold with causative *have/get*. Don't include the words in brackets.

1 I'm going to **(pay sb) to clean my flat.**
2 I'll **(arrange for sb) to install the new programs**.
3 Can you try to **finish the project** as quickly as possible?
4 **(sb) stole my email password** last week.
5 Robert, would you like to **start the meeting**?
6 We **really need to tidy the flat** – it's such a mess.

c ▶ Now go back to p.84

8A First and second conditionals

3.20 We can use both first conditionals and second conditionals to talk about future possibilities.

The first conditional:
The first conditional describes possible or likely future events and the expected results of those events:
if + present simple, *will* + infinitive
If I save *a little every month,* ***I'll be able to afford*** *a new car soon.*

The second conditional:
We use the second conditional to talk about imagined events or states and their consequences. They can be about the unreal present or unlikely future events:
if + past simple, *would* +infinitive
If I ***had*** *£1 for every time I've heard that, I'****d*** *be a millionaire.*
If *I* ***saved*** *£50 every month,* ***I'd have*** *enough for a new computer by the end of the year.*

> **Tip** We use the phrase *if I were you* to give advice:
> ***If I were you,*** *I* ***wouldn't*** *borrow so much money.*

> **Tip** We can use *going to* instead of *will* in first conditional sentences.
> *If I see her tomorrow, I'm* ***going to tell*** *her my news.*

We often use other past / present tenses in the *if* clause:
*If you****'ve finished*** *your test and you****'re waiting*** *to leave, you* ***should come*** *to my desk.*

We can also use imperatives in the main clause:
If you've finished your test and you're waiting to leave please ***come*** *to my desk.*

We often use other modals than *will* / *would* in the main *clause* (e.g. *might, could, can*, etc.):
If I ***weren't feeling*** *so tired, I* ***might*** *go for a run.*

8B Third conditional; *should have* + past participle

3.23 ***should have*** **+ past participle**
We can use the structure *should have* + past participle to criticise other people's past actions:
You ***shouldn't have told*** *them about the party – I wanted it to be a surprise.*

Third conditional
We use the third conditional to talk about imagined past events or states and their consequences:
If *I****'d arrived*** *five minutes earlier,* ***I'd have seen*** *the robbery.* (But I arrived after the robbery, so I didn't see it.)

if clause	Main clause
If + past perfect	*would* + *have* + past participle
If you hadn't told *me the answer,*	***I 'd have checked*** *on the internet.*
If there had been *more time,*	***we wouldn't have had*** *to hurry.*

> **Tip** Be careful with *'d*. It's short for *had* in the *if* clause but *would* in the main clause. *If I****'d*** *known earlier,* ***I'd*** *have told you.*

We can use past perfect continuous in the *if* clause. We can also use *might* or *could* in the main clause:
It was a nasty accident. If I ***hadn't been wearing*** *a helmet, I* ***might*** *have been very badly hurt.* (But I was wearing a helmet, so I wasn't badly hurt.)

3.24 **Mixed conditionals**
We combine clauses from the second and the third conditional to talk about past conditions with a result in the present, or present conditions with a result in the past.

if clause	Main clause
If those burglars ***hadn't damaged*** *that painting last year, …* [Third conditional – unreal past]	*… it* ***would be*** *worth a fortune now.* [Second conditional – unreal present]
If I ***didn't have*** *such a good relationship with my family, …* [Second conditional – unreal present]	*… I* ***would have left*** *the city years ago.* [Third conditional – unreal past]

8A First and second conditionals

a Complete the sentences with a first or a second conditional.

1 [likely]: Be careful with my phone! If you __lose__ (lose) it, I __'ll be__ (be) very angry.
2 [unlikely] If somebody __spoke__ (speak) to me like that, I __'d be__ (be) really angry.
3 [likely] It ______ (be) much cheaper if you ______ (come) by bus.
4 [likely] If you ______ (not spend) more money on advertising, your sales ______ (go) down.
5 [unlikely] I think you ______ (have) a great time if you ______ (study) abroad.
6 [likely] If Tony ______ (not finish) work soon, he ______ (not be) here on time.
7 [unreal] If you ______ (know) how to drive, I ______ (not have) to drive you everywhere.
8 [advice] If I ______ (be) you, I ______ (not say) anything about this to Ricky.
9 [likely] I'm sure they ______ (not be) angry if you ______ (tell) them the truth.
10 [unreal] She ______ (not have) a chance of getting that job if she ______ (not speak) English so well.
11 [likely] If it ______ (not rain) tomorrow morning, I ______ (walk) to work.
12 [advice] I ______ (not touch) that wire if I ______ (be) you.

b Look at the pictures. Write sentences using the prompts. Use the first or the second conditional.

1 OK, so I promise __I'll give you 50p if you wash my car__
[give you 50p / wash / my car]

2 Sorry. ______
[love / go dancing tonight / not / have / so much work.]

3 ______
[if / I / you / buy / new shoes]

4 Watch out! ______
[if / fall / might/ hurt yourself]

5 Wow – just imagine! ______
[if / we / find / that gold / rich]

6 Of course it's not working! ______
[it / not / work / if / turn it on]

c ▶ Now go back to p.93

8B Third conditional; *should have* + past participle

a Write sentences about each situation. Use the third conditional with the past perfect simple or continuous in the *if* clause.

1 I didn't take the exam because I didn't know about it.
I __would have taken the exam if I'd known about it.__
2 They went to the same university so they met and fell in love.
If ______
3 It was raining so we took the metro.
If ______
4 We didn't buy the picture because it was so expensive.
We ______
5 You didn't hear the phone because you were listening to music.
I ______
6 My parents gave me some money so I was able to buy a car.
If ______

b Write sentences about these situations using *should have* + past participle. Use the words in brackets.

1 Oh no, they're going to be late again. [leave home earlier]
__They should have left home earlier.__
2 The customer was really rude. [he / not speak to me like that]
______
3 You've made the alarm go off! [not press that button]
______
4 I had no idea it was your birthday. [you / tell me]
______
5 That car drove across the red light. [it / stop]
______
6 She failed her driving test. [she / take / more driving lessons]
______

c Match the sentence halves.

1 ☐ If we'd had more time, …
2 ☐ I'm sure Walter would have lent you some money …
3 ☐ If you hadn't driven me home, …
4 ☐ They'd be a lot richer …
5 ☐ I wouldn't have bought so much food …
6 ☐ If Gloria wasn't so nice, …

a … if they'd sold their flat when prices were still high.
b … I'd still be at the station now.
c … if you'd told me only four people were coming.
d … we wouldn't have invited her to stay with us.
e … we'd have done a bit more sightseeing.
f … if you'd asked him.

d ▶ Now go back to p.96

9A Relative clauses

3.38 Defining relative clauses
Defining relative clauses give essential information about a noun.

They've invented a car. **The car** stops people crashing.
They've invented a car ***that*** *stops people crashing!*

- *who* describes a person, and *which* describes a thing. In defining relative clauses, you can use *that* instead of both *who* and *which*:
  This is the work ***which*** */* ***that*** *has to be finished today.*
  The man ***who*** */* ***that*** *I needed to talk to wasn't available.*

When *who / which / that* replace **the object** of the clause, we can omit the relative pronoun:
You're applying for **the job** (= object)
*What's the job (****which*** */* ***that****) you're applying for?*

- *where* describes a place:
  There's a new shop in town ***where*** *you can buy furniture.*
- *whose* describes possession:
  The woman ***whose flat*** *was burgled is called Mrs Plater.*
- *when* describes times (e.g. *day / year / time*):
  The days ***when*** *I have to collect the children are stressful.*

We sometimes use *who* and *which* with prepositions. The prepositions usually come at the end of the sentence:
There is a place nearby ***which*** *we can stop at.*

3.39 Non-defining relative clauses
Non-defining relative clauses give extra information about a noun. The clause is not necessary for the sentence to make sense. A non-defining clause has a comma before it and either another comma, or a full stop after it:
*My new doctor****, who I had my first appointment with on Thursday,*** *recommended the medicine to me.*

In non-defining clauses, *which* can relate to a single noun, or to the whole main clause:
I'm going to Thailand next week, which *is very exciting.*

There are two main differences between defining and non-defining clauses.

- we cannot use *that* in a non-defining clause:
  Revolutionary technology, ***which*** *is rare, usually costs a huge amount to develop.* NOT ~~*Revolutionary technology, that is rare…*~~
- we can never omit the relative pronoun in a non-defining clause:
  Jane, ***who*** *I have always trusted, was the only person I told about the situation.* NOT ~~*Jane, I have always trusted…*~~

Tip Be careful when you describe places with *which* and *where.*
- *which* replaces a noun or pronoun:
  *I grew up in the house (****which / that****) you're buying!*
  (you're buying **the house**)
- *where* replaces *there* or preposition of place + noun:
  I still live in the house ***where*** *I grew up.*
  (I grew up **in the house** / **there**)

9B Reported speech; reporting verbs

3.40
When we report what people said or thought in the past, we usually change the tenses, pronouns, possessives and references to time and place:
Anna: 'I won't go out ***tomorrow****.'*
Anna ***told*** *me she* ***would*** *not go out* ***the following day.***

present tenses → past tenses
past tenses → past perfect tenses
will, can and *may* → *would, could* and *might.*
Past perfect, *would, could* and *might* don't normally change.

When the reporting verb is in a present tense, we don't change the tenses:
*'I****'ve*** *never* ***seen*** *them in concert.'* → *She* ***says*** *she****'s never seen*** *them in concert.*

When we report questions, the word order is the same as in sentences. Use *whether* or *if* to report *yes / no* questions. *Whether* is more formal than *if*:
'Where do you live?' → *They asked me where* ***I lived.***
NOT ~~*They asked me where* ***did I live.***~~
'Are you famous?' → *They weren't sure* ***if / whether*** *I was famous.*

Reporting verbs
After some reporting verbs there are different verb patterns:

Verb + (*that*) + clause	agree, believe, complain, discover, find out, insist, promise, realise, say, state, …	*He* ***stated that*** *he would stay with us.*
Verb + sb + (*that*) clause	inform, tell, warn, assume, …	*We* ***informed them that*** *it was ready.*
Verb + *to* + infinitive	agree, promise, refuse, …	*They* ***refused to speak*** *with us.*
Verb + sb + *to* + infinitive	ask, order, tell, remind, …	*She* ***ordered me to leave.***
Verb + gerund	admit, apologise for, deny, regret, suggest, …	*He* ***admitted taking*** *the money.*
Verb + (sb) + reported question	ask, discover, know, realise, wonder, …	*I* ***wondered where they were.***

Tip With negatives use *not to* + infinitive or *not* + gerund.
We agreed ***not to go.***
He apologised ***for not stopping*** *at the red light.*

9A Relative clauses

a Complete the sentences with the correct relative pronoun. If no word is needed , put (–).

1 This is my best friend, Kim, ________ I've known since we were tiny.
2 There are three things ________ I need to tell you about today's event.
3 Everybody congratulated the team, ________ hard work had won the contract.
4 The receptionist recommended the restaurant ________ we ate.
5 We never worried about money until the year ________ we bought our first house.
6 Who are the people ________ arrived late?
7 My job, ________ I love, is also really demanding.
8 They discovered a treatment ________ had no side-effects.
9 I wish I could move to a seat ________ I could see out of the window.
10 The singer, ________ voice I have loved all my life, seemed to be singing directly to me.

b Correct one mistake in each sentence.

1 This is the book what I was telling you about.
2 There's a new machine at the gym I think you would really like it.
3 We're travelling to Dubai, where I've always wanted to visit.
4 I was worrying about my luggage, that I'd forgotten to weigh before we left.
5 Chris, who his father owns the company, always works really hard.
6 I've finally had to replace my old car, I've had since I passed my test.

c Rewrite the two sentences into one making all necessary changes to punctuation and word order. Remember to cut unnecessary words.

1 The band didn't come on stage until nine o'clock. They were supposed to start at eight-thirty.
2 The rail company refunds passengers. The passengers' trains are delayed.
3 I looked in all the places. I thought I might have left my phone there.
4 The idea worked wonderfully well. We came up with the idea together.
5 Morocco is my favourite place for a holiday. We spent our honeymoon there.
6 The neighbours get back from holiday tomorrow. I'm looking after the neighbours' cat.

d Now go back to p.106

9B Reported speech; reporting verbs

a Look at the direct speech in the left-hand column. Complete the reported speech or thoughts in the right-hand column.

1 'I don't understand what you want.' — He told me … *that he didn't understand what I wanted.*
2 'Harry can't ski.' — I didn't realise …
3 'You may feel a little sleepy after you take the tablets.' — The doctor warned her that …
4 'The exam will be really easy.' — I assumed …
5 'No, I wasn't walking past the bank when I heard the alarm.' — The witness denied …
6 'We've been trying to call you since we heard the news.' — They informed us that …
7 'Margaret won't be happy when she finds out.' — I warned you …
8 'I couldn't open the door because I'd forgotten my key.' — He discovered that …

b Look at the questions from a job interview in the left-hand column. Complete the reported questions.

'What do you know about this company?' 'Do you have any experience of this sort of work?' 'How fast can you type?' 'Why did you leave your last job?' 'Are you good at dealing with customers?' 'Have you ever managed a team?' 'Why have you applied for this job?'	They started by asking me [1] *what I knew* about the company. Then they wanted to know [2] ________ any experience of that sort of work. They even asked me [3] ________ type! Then I had to explain [4] ________ my last job! The worst question was when they asked [5] ________ good at dealing with customers. They also wanted to know [6] ________ a team – I didn't know what to say! By the end, I wasn't sure [7] ________ for the job!

c Complete the reported speech, thoughts and questions with **one or two** words in each gap. Contractions (e.g. *didn't*) count as one word.

1 'I promise that I'll be really careful.' — I promised *to be* really careful.
2 'You must explain what you're doing here.' — The guard ordered ________ explain what we were doing there.
3 'Yes, OK. I told somebody about the accident.' — Amanda admitted ________ somebody about the accident.
4 'How did they find out?' — I wondered how ________ found out.
5 'I'll pay for the meal – no discussion!' — Robert insisted ________ for the meal.
6 'I'll send you a postcard.' — Sam told ________ send me a postcard.
7 'We're really sorry that we lost your order.' — They apologized ________ our order.
8 'OK, I can give you the money.' — Patricia agreed ________ us the money.

d Now go back to p.108

10A Past Modals of deduction

We can use modal verbs to show that we are making a deduction, not stating a fact. We use the modal verbs *must*, *may*, *might*, *could* and *can't* + *have* + past participle to make deductions about the past.

3.52

Deduction	Meaning
They are late.	I know for certain that they are late.
*They are never late. They **must have got** lost.*	I believe they've got lost.
*They **may** / **might** / **could have** gone the wrong way.* *They **might not have** found the right street.*	I believe it's possible that they've got lost.
*They **can't have got** lost. They have a satnav.*	I believe they haven't got lost.
They haven't got lost. I can see them coming up the street now.	I know for a fact that they haven't got lost.

The opposite of *must* for deductions is *can't*.

We can also use *may not have or might not have / mightn't have*:
*Try calling them at home. They **might not have** gone out.* (= It's possible that they haven't gone out).

10B Wishes and regrets

3.58 When we make a wish, we imagine an unreal situation in the past, present or future.

Wishes about the future	We use *would* to make wishes about the future. Don't use *would* to make a wish about yourself – use *could* instead.	*I **wish** it would stop raining.* *I **wish** I **could** get a better job but I haven't got enough experience.* (= if I had more experience, I would be able to get a better job.)
Wishes about the present	We can use the past simple to make wishes about the present. We can also make wishes about the present with *could* + infinitive.	*I **wish** I **had** more time.* (= I would like to have more time.) *I **wish** I **could** speak French – it's such a beautiful language.* (= I wish I was able to speak French, but I'm not.)
Wishes about the past	We use the past perfect to make wishes about the past.	*I **wish** I **hadn't been** so lazy at school.* (I was lazy when I was at school, and now I regret it.)

Tip To talk about something that we see as realistic, possible or likely in the future use *hope*, not *wish*:
*I **hope** you get better soon.* NOT ~~*I **wish** you would get better soon*~~.

I wish ... / if only ...
If only ... means the same as *I wish* ..., and we use it in the same way.

Tip When making wishes about I / he / she / it, we can use *were* instead of *was*. *Were* is preferred in formal English, but in normal spoken English, both versions are common:
*If only it **were** that simple.* (Or: ... *it **was** that simple.)*

3.59 ***should have*** **+ past participle**
We use *should have* + past participle to express regret about our own past actions:
*It's my fault. I **should have locked** the door.*
(But I didn't lock it so the burglars got in.)

10A Past Modals of deduction

a Tick (✓) the correct sentences. Correct the mistakes.

1 I said hello but he didn't reply. He mustn't have heard me. ☐ *incorrect* *can't have heard*
2 Sorry, I may not have made myself clear. ☑ ______
3 I can't find my purse … someone might stolen it. ☐ ______
4 I don't know who wrote the report – it could had been anybody. ☐ ______
5 They can't have just disappeared! It's impossible! ☐ ______
6 It might haven't been such a good idea to walk home alone. ☐ ______
7 They look sad. They must lose the match. ☐ ______
8 Wow! That's a nice car! It had to cost a fortune. ☐ ______

b Complete the sentences with one of the phrases in the box and the correct form of the verb in brackets. Use some of the phrases twice.

must have   may have   can't have   might not have

1 **A** We walked all the way home in the snow.
B Wow – that *must have been* (be) cold!
2 **A** I think I saw Angela on the bus today.
B No, it ______ (be) Angela – she's on holiday in the mountains this week.
3 **A** I saw a beautiful sweater in the shop but I didn't buy it. It's probably too late now.
B Maybe, but let's go back and check – they ______ (sell) it yet.
4 **A** That's strange. My bicycle tyre's flat. How did that happen?
B I'm not sure. You ______ (ride) over some broken glass or something.
5 **A** Where have all the sandwiches gone? The plate's empty!
B Tom ______ (eat) them. He was the only person who came into this room all day.
6 **A** I think I've broken my arm – it really hurts.
B I don't know … you ______ (break) it. I'm not an expert, but it doesn't look broken.

c ▶ Now go back to p.117

10B Wishes and regrets

a Match the sentence halves.

1 ☐ Hmm … I don't like the look of those dark clouds.
2 ☐ I really regret leaving my old job.
3 ☐ I was sure the bank would lend us the money if we filled in a few forms.
4 ☐ It's really annoying that you told me the match result.
5 ☐ I don't know why they're so late.
6 ☐ I really miss you.
7 ☐ You never do any cleaning around the house.
8 ☐ It looks like a lovely place for a holiday.

a If only it were that simple.
b I hope nothing has happened to them.
c I wish you'd kept quiet about it.
d I wish you'd help out a bit more.
e I hope it doesn't rain.
f If only it weren't so expensive!
g I wish I hadn't resigned from it.
h If only I could see you again.

b Write wishes or hopes for each of these situations. Use *If only*, *I wish* or *I hope*

1 Why didn't you remind us? *If only you'd reminded us.*
2 I don't know what to do. ______
3 If I do this course, I might be able to speak Korean next year. ______
4 They didn't warn us in advance, unfortunately. ______
5 Maybe Rebecca will help me. ______
6 I'm angry that they cancelled the flight. ______

c Write sentences about these situations using *should have* + past participle. Use the words in brackets.

1 Oh no, we're going to be late. [leave home earlier]
We should have left home earlier.
2 I regret buying that new bag. It was too expensive. [not buy it]
______
3 I feel terrible after running so far. [stop earlier]
______
4 I really wanted to see that new film and now it's too late. [go to the cinema yesterday]
______

d ▶ Now go back to p.120

Vocabulary Focus

1A Character adjectives

a Read the descriptions of people's characters. Which is personal and which is more formal?

Fred currently works as a researcher here at Bio-Tech. He's been a very **loyal** member of our staff, and has worked here for over ten years now. He's **passionate** about alternative energies and this can be seen in the energy and enthusiasm he puts into his work. He's also **self-confident**, so he is never afraid to work independently or to work on difficult tasks. Finally, he's always **optimistic**, even when he comes across problems in his work.

We've got this new colleague at work, Sheila. She's only been here for two weeks and already I don't like her very much. She's one of those **ambitious** people who's got lots of plans, but she's so **arrogant** about it all. She thinks she's better than everyone else. But if you try and suggest a different idea, she gets really upset. So she's a strange mix of being very sure of herself, but incredibly **sensitive** at the same time. She told me that she wants to be our team leader. If she thinks that's going to happen overnight, she's really **naive**!

b Match the bold character adjectives in **a** with the definitions.

1 when you don't have much experience of the world and believe things too easily
2 when you easily get upset by what people say about you
3 when you believe or behave as if you know more or are more important than other people
4 when you feel sure about yourself and your abilities
5 when you like something and have strong feelings about it
6 when you have a strong wish to be successful, powerful or rich
7 when you always support something or someone, even when other people don't
8 when you always think good things will happen

c 1.7 Complete the sentences with the adjectives from the texts in **a**. Listen and check.

1 He's very ________. If I give him any negative feedback, he gets angry and shouts at me.
2 I'm sure he won't be nervous when he gives the speech. He always seems very ________.
3 I feel quite ________ that this project will be successful – everything is going according to plan.
4 They both think they're fantastic and everyone else is stupid. I've never met a couple who are so ________.
5 She's helped and supported me since we were at school. She's a very ________ friend – I know I can always rely on her.
6 Phil is really ________ about being a doctor. He loves the job and looks forward to going to work every day.
7 She works really hard because she's ________ and wants to do well in her career.
8 Martin is a little ________ – he honestly thought his boss would listen to his suggestions but of course in the end he didn't. He really is very young.

d Think of three family members or friends. Make notes on their character. Tell your partner.

My father's very passionate, particularly about his work.

I really like my aunt. She's a very successful lawyer. Some people think she's arrogant, but I don't.

PRONUNCIATION Word stress

a 1.8 Listen to these adjectives and underline the stressed syllable. Which syllable is stressed: the first, second, third or fourth?

optimistic unsympathetic arrogant ambitious

b 1.9 Write these words in the table. Then listen and check your answers. Practise saying the words.

passionate self-confident sensitive determined determination pessimistic environment environmental influential television

1st syllable stressed	2nd syllable stressed
3rd syllable stressed	**4th syllable stressed**

c Test each other. Student A: Choose a word from **b** and say a sentence.
Student B: Did Student A say the adjective correctly?

I'm determined to become a millionaire.

d Now go back to p.10

2A Expressions with *get*

a Read what Emma and Martin say. Who did they have a problem with?

Emma:
Last year I decided to join the social club at work. I always thought the social club was a bit boring and I wanted to improve it. I talked to some other people in the club and we tried to work out a way to **get rid of** the man running the club – the secretary – because we really thought he was the problem. Everyone liked this idea and we all **got a bit carried away** and decided a direct approach would be the best one. At the next meeting, we were about to say something when all of a sudden he said, 'Look, I'll **get straight to the point**. I think the social club's getting a bit boring and we need some fresh ideas.' We couldn't believe his sudden change. Now the club is much more interesting and lots of new people have **got involved**.

Martin:
My son's really **getting on my nerves** at the moment. He won't study at all. I can't **get across** to him the importance of doing well at school. He just won't listen and it's **getting me down**. The problem is he **got through** his exams very easily last year without studying. He thinks he can do the same thing this year, but I'm not so sure.

b Match the *get* expressions in bold in a with definitions 1–8.

1 to say something important immediately and in a direct way
2 to make someone understand something
3 to take part in an activity or organisation
4 to be successful in an examination or competition
5 when something annoys you
6 to become excited about something so that you are no longer careful
7 when something makes you feel sad or depressed
8 to send or throw someone or something away

c 1.26 **Pronunciation** Notice the linking between ***get*** and the word after in this example.

Lots of new people have got‿involved

Listen to these examples. In which sentences is there linking between *get* and the word after? What does that tell you about linking?

1 We tried to work out a way to get rid of the man running the club.
2 We all got a bit carried away.
3 I'll get straight to the point.
4 I can't get across to him the importance of doing well.

d Think of examples of these things.

1 a time that you got rid of something you didn't want
2 something that gets on your nerves
3 a time when you got through an exam, test or interview
4 a situation where you got a bit carried away
5 a club or organisation you got involved in

e Tell each other about your examples in d.

PRONUNCIATION Sounds and spelling: *g*

a 1.27 Listen to the words. In which words does *g* have … ?

1 a hard sound /g/
2 a soft sound /dʒ/

get negative manage

b 1.28 Decide which sound the *g* has in these words – /g/ or /dʒ/. Then listen and practise saying them.

guard gymnastics guide generous
biology together religion agree
dangerous forget bridge gardener

c Look at your answers to b.

1 If *g* is followed by a consonant or *a*, *o* or *u* is it hard or soft?
2 If *g* is followed by *e*, *i* or *y*, is it hard or soft? Are there exceptions to this rule?

d Now turn to p.21

3B Words connected with sport

Jack Taylor will once again **represent** Australia at next year's Olympics. He already holds the **world record** for the 400m after his brilliant performance in 2011. During that race, he **led** from the start.

Referee Eno Koskinen gave Rodriguez a red card and **awarded** a penalty kick to Chelsea. But the **spectators** weren't at all happy with the decision and **cheered** Rodriguez as he left the **pitch**.

a Find words in the sports reports which mean:

1 play for your country or city
2 the people watching a match
3 be ahead during a game or competition
4 give (a prize or a point) for something you have done
5 shout to show you think someone is good
6 the best or fastest that has ever been achieved
7 the person who makes decisions during a sports game
8 the area where a football match is played

b Underline the correct words.

1 Even though she holds the *world record / spectator* in the 1500m, Kirabo Sanaa probably won't *represent / award* her country at next year's Olympic Games.
2 The spectators *cheered / represented* as the players walked onto the *pitch / referee*.
3 Sasha Spyridon *cheered / led* the race from the beginning and was *awarded / cheered* a gold medal.

c Write two short sports reports, using two of the sentence starters. Use the words in bold in the texts and your own ideas.

1 Ten minutes into the match ...
2 18-year-old Martina Bereskova from Belarus ...
3 Kenyan runner Pamela Abasi ...

d Read out your reports. Who has the most interesting sports report?

PRONUNCIATION Word stress

a Add the words in the box to the table.

training ~~competition~~ victor competitor performance championship trainer athletic competitive athletics victorious performer professional

Verb	Noun (event or activity)	Noun (person)	Adjective
compete	*competition*		
		athlete	
	victory		
		champion	
train			
perform			
	profession		professional

b 1.46 Which syllable is stressed in each word in the table? Does the stress stay the same in all the word forms or does it change? Listen and check.

c 1.47 How does the vowel sound in **bold** change in each pair of words? Listen and check.

athl**e**te athl**e**tics
vict**o**ry vict**o**rious
comp**e**te comp**e**titor

d Work in pairs. Cover the table and test each other.

Student A: say a sentence with one of the words.
Student B: make a follow-up sentence with a similar meaning, using a different word.

He entered the championship.

He wanted to be the champion.

e Now go back to p.36

4B Talking about difficulty

a Underline a word or phrase in each sentence that means (*to be*) *difficult*.

1 Working as a waiter in a busy restaurant is one of the most demanding jobs I've ever had.
2 I find it quite awkward when I have to speak to my staff about mistakes they've made.
3 Teaching a class on my own for the first time was a very testing experience.
4 Doing the outdoor survival training course really challenged me.
5 I have to talk to my teacher because I'm not happy with her lessons; it's a very delicate subject and I'm not sure what to say exactly.
6 Unfortunately, it's often not very straightforward for students here to find part-time work.
7 When I lived in Budapest, it was a struggle to learn Hungarian well.
8 I think I understand how computers work, but learning a programming language really stretched me.

b Which two words in **a** do we use to describe situations that are embarrassing or need to be dealt with very carefully?

c Complete the sentences with words from **a**. There may be more than one answer.

1 My final exams at university were really ________ / ________ – I needed a long holiday after I finished!
2 I can't come to my best friend's wedding because I'm going on holiday. It's a really ________ / ________ situation and I'm not sure how to tell her.
3 I'm really busy at work at the moment and I'm finding it a ________ to get my work done by the end of the day.
4 I thought connecting my new printer to my computer would be easy but actually it's not ________ at all.
5 I'm not very confident, so giving a presentation at university last week in front of 50 people really ________ / ________ me.

d Think of an experience you've had for three of the things below:

1 an outdoor experience that stretched you
2 the most demanding thing about learning a language
3 a book you once read that wasn't straightforward
4 an awkward meeting you once had
5 a sport that it was a struggle for you to learn
6 a delicate question that you had to ask someone
7 something you studied that really challenged you
8 a testing experience you had in a new place or country

e Now tell each other about the things you chose in **d**.

PRONUNCIATION Sounds and spelling: *u*

a 2.8 Listen to the words.

include struggle cushion busy

b Match the vowel sounds in the words in **a** with the sounds in words 1–4.

1 cup
2 put
3 true
4 thin

c 2.9 What sound does *u* have in these words? Listen to check and add them to the table.

subject	focus	punish
pullover	amusing	assume
unfortunately	super	pudding
business	supper	helpful

sound 1 /ʌ/	sound 2 /ʊ/	sound 3 /uː/ or /juː/	sound 4 /ɪ/

d Write a sentence with two of the words in **a** or **b**. Read out your sentence to other students and check if you pronounced *u* correctly.

e Now go back to p.49

5A Adjectives describing attitude

a Read about Tamara's family and add adjectives in the gaps.

thoughtful critical disorganised unreliable
well-organised irresponsible sympathetic competitive

My brother Nick is very ¹_____ – his desk is a mess and he can never find anything. But my sister Vera is a very ²_____ person. She plans her day carefully and she always knows exactly where everything is. She's also so ³_____. She wants to be the best – it's all she thinks about. I would say my grandmother is a very ⁴_____ person – you can go to her if you're in trouble and she'll always listen and make you feel better. My cousin, Maude, is very ⁵_____. She's always thinking about how she can help other people. She remembers everyone's birthday and always sends presents. I like my other cousin, Becky, but she can be quite ⁶_____. She never tells anyone where she's going when she goes out, and she sometimes leaves the front door open or doesn't lock her car. She's also terribly ⁷_____. If you arrange to meet her somewhere she'll probably be late or she won't even show up. And what about me? Everyone in the family complains that I'm always commenting on what people are like. Some of them say I'm too ⁸_____ and I only see the bad things in them. I can't imagine why they should think that.

b Complete the table with the opposite of the adjectives in **a**.

thoughtful	
well-organised	disorganised
	unreliable
	irresponsible
sympathetic	
competitive	
critical	

c Make a list of the prefixes and suffixes we can add to adjectives to make them negative.

d 2.20 Look at the sentences. Decide if the word in bold is correct or not. Then listen and check.

1 He often arrives late to meetings and doesn't bring everything he needs.
He's very **disorganised**.
2 She always makes sensible decisions and she never does anything silly.
She's very **irresponsible**.
3 She often expresses negative opinions about things and other people. She's very **critical**.
4 If he says he's going to do something, he always does it.
He's very **reliable**.
5 He doesn't think about how the things he says might affect other people.
He's totally **thoughtful**.
6 When you tell her your problems, she listens and tries to understand how
you feel. She's **unsympathetic**.
7 He always wants to do better than everyone else. He's quite **competitive**.

e Look through the adjectives and their opposites and note down your own personality 'profile'.

f Tell your partner and mention a few examples of things you do.

I think I'm fairly thoughtful and caring. For example, I always phone my grandmother once a week to ask how she is ...

PRONUNCIATION Sounds and spelling: *th*

a 2.21 Listen to *th* in these words. What two different sounds do you hear?

thoughtful clothes
weather seventh
sympathetic

b 2.22 Which sound does *th* have in these words? Listen to check, then add them to the table.

leather north
thumb northern
month Netherlands
together healthy
something enthusiastic
therefore worth

/θ/ (think)	/ð/ (the)

c Now turn to p.58

6A Travel and tourism

a Put the correct word from the box in the gaps. The definition of each word is given in brackets.

feature setting constructions outskirts

1 … and there are waterfalls on the ________ of the city. (just before the city finishes and becomes countryside)
2 However, the most amazing ________ you can see here is the nearby volcano, Paricutin. (an important thing that you notice)
3 … the whole island is like a museum of breathtaking wooden ________ that date from the eighteenth century. (things that you build)
4 In many ways it's the perfect ________ for them. (the position of a building)

b Match pictures a–f to examples 1–6 from a tourist guide.

1 Remember to tell your taxi driver which **terminal** your flight's leaving from.
2 We also recommend a visit to the **studio** where he painted in the last years of his life.
3 We're both a hotel and a conference **venue**.
4 You can dine in the open air on our **terrace**.
5 High tea is served every afternoon between 2.00 pm and 4.00 pm in the **lobby** opposite reception.
6 If you would like to go **hiking**, there are trails of different levels of difficulty.

c 2.46 Listen to Annie's story about going to Malaysia. Put one word in each gap.

Last year we wanted to [1]________ away for a couple of weeks so we decided to go trekking in the forests of Malaysia. We thought it would be cheaper to catch a train to the airport rather than go by taxi. But we were a bit upset to discover that the trains weren't [2]________ on time. We [3]________ up at the check-in desk very late and just managed to catch our flight. The flight took 17 hours because we [4]________ over in Dubai for a couple of hours. By the time we got there we were exhausted and not really in the mood for trekking.

d Think about answers to the following questions. Then ask and answer them with a partner.

1 When you go travelling, do you usually turn up at the station or airport early or on time?
2 Imagine you have to go on a long flight from your country to another one. Where would you like to stop over? How long would you like to stop over for?
3 Have you ever been trekking? If yes, where did you go? If not, would you like to try?

PRONUNCIATION Consonant groups

a 2.47 Listen to the underlined sounds in these words. What do they have in common?

studio outskirts construction

b 2.48 Listen to these words. Underline where two or more consonants occur together in the same syllable.

approval discussion expensive apply
hungry transfer contrast destroy

c Write two sentences. Each sentence should contain at least two words from **b**. Read your sentences to each other.

d Now go back to p.70

7B Film and TV

a Look at the words in bold in sentences 1–8. Find two:

- words that refer to people who work in film and TV
- verb forms that refer to when a film or TV show is shown
- words that talk about the way TV shows are divided up
- verb forms that talk about what can happen during the making of a TV programme or film.

1 The longest-running science fiction TV **series** is the British production *Doctor Who*.

2 As she walked through the front door, her look of complete surprise **was captured** on film.

3 The first *Star Wars* film **was released** in 1977.

4 After filming, the **editor** began the work of choosing the best shots and putting together the film.

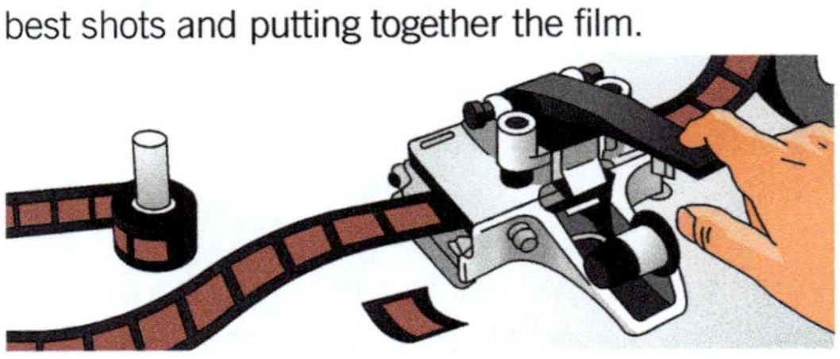

5 He appeared in only one short scene of the film, but that **was cut** after filming finished.

6 Any big international sports event **is broadcast** live all around the world.

7 It's a really good news programme because the **presenter** is completely neutral and you never know what her opinion is.

8 There's a brilliant crime show on TV at the moment. Tonight it's the final **episode** and we'll find out who the murderer is.

b Answer the questions.

1 Does a TV series normally include more than one episode?
2 Viewers normally see a presenter on TV. Do they usually see the editor of a TV programme?
3 When a film is released, where do we usually see it, in a cinema or on TV? Are TV programmes normally released or broadcast?
4 Who normally captures something on film, an editor or a camera operator? Who normally cuts something?

c Are the four verb forms in **a** in an active or passive form? Is this form more typical for these verbs?

d Put one word in each gap. Use a word from **a** or from p. 84.

1 The ________ of the new comedy programme is made up of actors who aren't famous.
2 The scene where he gets home has been ________. It's not necessary and it's a bit boring.
3 Every summer, a lot of big action films are ________ because studios think they'll do good business.
4 Some people think the way a film ________ puts together a film is just as skilful as the work of the director.
5 The film looked beautiful and was full of wonderful ________ of scenery, but the storyline and the ________ were terrible. I couldn't understand what was going on.
6 The UK soap opera *Coronation Street* has been running since 1960. He maintains that he's seen every single ________.
7 Having talked to the director about his ideas for the film, the ________ felt enthusiastic and began thinking how he could get finance.
8 The accident was ________ on video by a member of the public using her phone.

e Discuss the questions.

1 What's a TV series that you've enjoyed recently? What's it about?
2 What kinds of things do you think shouldn't be broadcast live on TV?
3 What do you think is more important in a film – a good script or great shots? Why?
4 Which job do you think would be most interesting: producer, director or editor? Why?

PRONUNCIATION Sounds and spelling: *o*

a How many different pronunciations of the letter *o* are in the words below?

editor broadcast episode director company

b Which of the symbols and examples match the sounds in **a**?

sound 1 /ɔː/	sound 2 /uː/	sound 3 /ə/	sound 4 /ʌ/	sound 5 /aʊ/	sound 6 /əʊ/
four	food	professor	mother	now	road

c 3.8 Match the pronunciation of *o* in these words to the correct sound in **b**.

show bought police support young
correct chose throw nothing corner

d Write two sentences. In each sentence try to use two *o* words that have a different sound. Read your sentences to each other.

e Now go back to p.84

8B Crime

a Read the two news reports. Match the illustrations to the underlined words and phrases.

NEWS

Thieves [1]broke into a jeweller's shop and stole £5,000 worth of jewellery and watches. However, they were seen on CCTV and [2]two suspects were arrested yesterday. They will appear in [3]court on Wednesday.

The [4]trial of Rebecca Rivers, who [5]was accused of theft, is finally over. It continued for over three weeks and around 50 [6]witnesses were called to give evidence. Yesterday the [7]jury gave a verdict of guilty. The [8]judge sentenced Ms. Rivers to five years in prison.

b 3.25 Choose the correct words to complete the dialogue. Then listen and check.

A Did you hear about the [1]*court / trial* of that company director?

B Oh, you mean the one who was [2]*accused / arrested* of bribery. I knew he'd been [3]*arrested / sentenced*. What happened?

A It was incredible. He appeared in [4]*trial / court* yesterday and five [5]*suspects / witnesses* all gave [6]*evidence / verdicts*. They all said he had asked them for bribes.

B Wow. So, what was the [7]*verdict / trial*? Was he found [8]*accused / guilty*?

A No, the [9]*jury / witnesses* said he was not guilty.

B Hmm. What did the [10]*judge / jury* say?

A Nothing. She didn't [11]*arrest / sentence* him. She let him go free.

B Hmm. That's a bit odd, isn't it?

c Think of a famous court case from your country or from a film you've seen. Make notes on what happened. Think about:

- the crime and when it happened
- any suspects who were accused and/or arrested
- the trial and the witnesses who gave evidence
- the jury's verdict
- the judge's sentence

d Discuss the court cases. Which one is the most interesting?

PRONUNCIATION Sounds and spelling: *l*

a 3.26 Listen to the words. Is the letter *l* pronounced in all of them?

stole	talk
will	trial

b 3.27 Underline the word in each group where *l* is not pronounced.

1	called	could	cold
2	milk	incredible	walk
3	should	guilty	told
4	film	gold	calm

c Practise saying all the words in **a** and **b** with and without the /l/ sound.

d Now go back to p.97

9A Health

a Match the texts to the illustrations.

① Last night I **bumped** my head against the kitchen cupboard door so hard that I collapsed on the ground and **lost consciousness**. I didn't cut myself badly, so I won't have a **scar**, but this morning there's quite a large **bruise** on my forehead.

② A few months ago I woke up feeling very ill. My face was very **pale** and my head was **aching**. I also felt really **dizzy**. I went to the doctor and he said it was probably just an **infection** so I stayed at home until I felt better.

ⓐ

ⓑ

b Match the words in bold in the texts to the definitions 1–8.

1 a temporary dark mark on your skin
2 to hurt part of your body by hitting it against something hard
3 when your face has less colour than normal because you are ill
4 when you feel the world is spinning around
5 a more formal way of saying 'pass out'
6 to have a continuous pain in a part of your body
7 a disease in a part of your body that is caused by bacteria or a virus
8 a permanent mark on the skin after you cut yourself

c Complete the sentences using the correct form of a word from **a**.

1 When I sit at my desk behind my computer all day, my back often starts to ________.
2 I almost ________ ________ so he poured cold water on my face to keep me awake.
3 I hardly slept last night so now I feel exhausted and my face is ________.
4 I've got a small car and I often ________ my head when I get in.
5 The ________ on my stomach is from an operation I had when I was a child.
6 He fell over and hit his leg on a chair yesterday. Now he has a big ________ on his knee.
7 My throat is very sore today. I've probably got an ________.
8 I always eat breakfast because if I don't, I usually start to feel ________ with hunger at about 11 o'clock.

d Choose five of the words from **a** and **b** and tell a partner something that happened to you or someone you know, using the words. Ask and answer questions.

I had an infection last month after I had a cold. I was off work for a week.

PRONUNCIATION Sounds and spelling: *ui*

a 3.35 Put the words in pairs of the same vowel sound. Listen and check.

bruise	quiet
wire	guitar
dizzy	shoes

b 3.36 What sound does *ui* have? Put the words in the correct box.

fruit	require
inquire	guilt
suit	nuisance
build	circuit
biscuit	acquire

/ɪ/	/uː/	/waɪ/
guitar	bruise	quiet

c Write three sentences. Each sentence should contain a *ui* word with a different sound. Read your sentences to other students. Check each other's pronunciation.

d Now go back to p.106

10A Adjectives with prefixes

a Read about William and his change of lifestyle. What part of his life does he change?

William was working as a **legal** adviser. He was an **experienced** and **responsible** employee with **regular** working hours. But he was bored. He was not a **patient** man either and wanted to change his life before it was too late. So he handed in his notice, and explained in a **formal** and **polite** manner that he was not **satisfied** with his situation.
He then started working for himself as a gardener and discovered that it was even better than **expected**. He enjoyed working outdoors, he loved seeing all the wildlife around him, and he felt like a very **fortunate** man. He was happy that he had been **honest** with himself and followed his heart.

b Look at the adjectives in bold in the text. Add the opposite of the adjectives in the correct place in the table. Use a dictionary to help you.

un-	in-	im-
ir-	il-	dis-

c Look again at the adjectives in the blog on p.118. Add them to the correct places.

d Complete these rules:

We use *im-* instead of *in-* before adjectives beginning with the letter ________.
We use *il-* instead of *in-* before adjectives beginning with the letter ________.
We use *ir-* instead of *in-* before adjectives beginning with the letter ________.

e Use adjectives from the table to complete the sentences.

1 Karen left top-secret documents in her car with the window open. It was very ________
2 I inherited my grandmother's jewellery when she died. I had no idea she wanted me to have it, so it was completely ________
3 Be careful of Alex. He may try to cheat you! He's a bit ________
4 My sister always reads the last chapter first because she wants to find out what happens in the end. She's so ________
5 I stayed in a hotel with terrible service. My friend recommended it to me, but I was very ________

f Choose two of these questions and discuss them with a partner.

1 Do you ever get impatient? When?
2 What is the most unbelievable piece of news you've heard recently?
3 What's the most unexpected thing that's ever happened to you?

PRONUNCIATION Word stress

a 3.54 How many syllables have these words got? Put them in the correct place in the table. Listen and check.

impatient	illegal
unfortunate	irregular
dishonest	inexperienced
irresponsible	dissatisfied

3 syllables	4 syllables	5 syllables

b 3.54 Listen again and mark the main stress in each word. Which two words also have a secondary stress?

c Where is the stress in all the 3- and 4-syllable words? What's different about the 5-syllable words?

d Choose three words with a different number of syllables. Say the word in a sentence to your partner. Check that your partner's stress is correct.

e Now go back to p.118

Audioscripts

Unit 1

1.4

CHLOE What's that book you're reading?
AMELIA It's about astronomy – black holes, planets, the big bang …
C Hmm, not exactly a light read, but I suppose you like that sort of thing. Me, I like to relax when I read.
A It's just I read this article online the other day.
C Uh-huh?
A It was about this physicist. She discovered these things called pulsars which are like … well, they're an incredible kind of star.
C Uh-huh … She?
A Yeah, yeah, her name's Jocelyn Bell-Burnell. She's a respected physicist. Well, that's the thing, that's what got me interested. There aren't many women working in that area.
C But hang on, she discovered these stars?
A Yeah, she was a postgraduate student at the time, but the guy who was her supervisor got all the credit.
C You're kidding?
A No, he won the Nobel Prize.
C So who did you say this woman was?
A Jocelyn Bell-Burnell.
C But I've never even heard of her.
A Well, no. That's the point. On this website it talks about … well, it's got a whole lot of information on people like her … you know, people who work behind the scenes and don't get the credit or don't become famous. It was really interesting.
C Yeah, I bet there are a lot of people like that.
A I mean, she really is an inspiring woman. Even when she was at high school, they weren't going to let her join the science class …
C When was this?
A Back in the fifties.
C Really? Even in the fifties?
A Yeah. And then at the end of the year, she came top of her class! And when she was doing her PhD and made her amazing discovery, she had a young child and was having to manage a whole lot of things in her private life, too. I mean, she was really determined, but in a quiet way. And then, when the newspapers wanted to interview her, they didn't want to know about her research, they just asked a lot of stupid questions about her height, her clothes, that sort of thing.
C That's terrible, isn't it? So is that a biography of her that you're reading?
A Well, no, it's just a book about astrophysics.
C Astrophysics? Just? So you're going to become … what? A rocket scientist or something?
A Well, no … I don't know. The thing is … after I read the article, I found an interview with Jocelyn Bell-Burnell online. And she was talking about how even today there still aren't many women who go into science and become scientists.
C So now you want to go back to university and do a physics degree?
A Maybe. But, you know, why not? I've always been good at science and I used to really enjoy physics.
C But are you really prepared to study and put in all that effort?
A Yeah, I think I am.
C Well, you've always been motivated, that's for sure. And stubborn …
A But I'm still thinking about it … doing some reading, that kind of thing.
C Well, actually … good on you. Why not make a change – take a risk? I admire that.
A Yeah. Actually that's what she says in the interview: 'Be prepared to take a risk – you'll probably surprise yourself.' And she said something else very simple about women wanting to be scientists: 'Go for it!' And I thought, yeah, why shouldn't I?

1.10

INTERVIEWER So Alison, you went to find out about the 30-day challenge. What is it and how does it work?
ALISON Yes, I went to a one-day seminar about it. The basic idea is that, according to psychologists, 30 days is about the time it takes to really develop a new habit because that's how long it takes for our brains to shift to a new direction. So often if we try something new, we give up after about a week or two because our brain hasn't adapted. So the idea of the 30-day challenge is, you choose something you want to do, like drink less coffee, for example, and you keep going for exactly 30 days.
I So, if you manage to do it for 30 days and you feel good about it, you'll probably keep to it, is that the idea?
A That's right, yes. But the other thing about it is that 30 days isn't a very long time. 30 days goes past quite quickly anyway. So if you decide to do something completely new – let's say you decide to get up at dawn every day and see the sun rise – maybe you wouldn't want to keep it up for your whole life, but it might be fun to do it for just 30 days. So it's also a chance to try something different, and if you're successful it's great, but if it doesn't work out it doesn't matter too much.
I I see, so it's not just about giving up bad habits. The idea is really that you try out something new.
A Yes, very much so. There were people at the seminar, for example, who'd written a short poem every day for 30 days, and someone else had tried to eat something new every day for 30 days. So it's a chance to do something you've always wanted to do or maybe something new that you'd never thought of doing.
I It sounds a lot of fun, if you've got time for it.
A Yes, well you can either do something that doesn't really get in the way of your life, like writing a poem – you can do that in your lunch break, it's easy. Or you can take time out and have a go at something you've always wanted to do, like paint a picture or climb mountains or something. Obviously to do something like that you need to make an effort and, of course, you have to give yourself a time limit of 30 days.
I So, it sounds like you think it's a good idea.
A I think it's a great idea, yes. I came away convinced!
I So, are you planning to try the 30-day challenge yourself?
A Yes, in fact I already am. I decided to put my car keys in a drawer and I'm going to cycle everywhere for 30 days, even if it rains.
I And how's it going so far?
A Really well. I'm finding it much easier than I expected.
I And when did you start?
A Erm … this morning.
I Well, good luck with that, Alison. Now, Alison's only just started, but next up on the Life and Style podcast we're going to talk to a few more people who've been doing the 30-day challenge. They're all about half-way through, and they've done it successfully so far …

1.12

INTERVIEWER What made you decide to become vegetarian, Farah?
FARAH Well, for quite a long time now I've been trying to eat less meat, partly for health reasons. I think vegetables are better for you.
I But didn't you ever think of being vegetarian before?
F Yes, but I always thought I'd miss meat too much. But the idea of being a vegetarian for 30 days was really good, because I could give it a try and then see how I feel.
I And how do you feel? Are you finding it difficult?
F No, I feel really good. Actually, I don't miss meat at all, so I think I'll easily manage the 30 days and I might try carrying on longer. I certainly think I'm a bit healthier than I used to be.
I Mona, why did you decide to draw something every day?
MONA Well, I've never been very good at drawing, but I've always thought I'd like to start drawing things around me. It's one of those things that you think about doing, but you never get round to.
I What have you drawn pictures of so far?
M All kinds of things. At the start I drew objects around me at home. Then I went out in my lunch break and started drawing things outdoors, like yesterday I drew a duck in the park – that was really difficult!
I So do you feel it has been worthwhile?
M Oh yes, definitely. I'm still not very good at drawing, but it's been lots of fun and it's very relaxing.
I Steve, what language did you decide to learn?
STEVE Well, I thought I'd choose a language that isn't too different from English, so I decided to try Italian.
I Isn't it difficult to keep going with it?
S Yes, it is. I've had to be very strict with myself. I'm using a book with a CD, so I usually try to cover one lesson a night.
I And who do you practise with? Or are you just working alone?
S Well, there's an Italian restaurant just round the corner and I'm friends with the owner, so I go there and I chat to him. That's one reason I chose Italian.
I And do you think you'll carry on after the 30 days?
S Maybe, or I might try a different language every month. I'm thinking of trying Japanese next.

1.15 **PART 1**

BECKY That was a really interesting lecture. There's so much to learn, though. I'm going to try and get all my homework done tonight.
TESSA Oh, I'm going out tonight. Can't be bothered with homework. I'll do mine later. You always study too much! Do you want a coffee?
B Sorry, I can't. I've got to go to work. It's my first day!
T Oh, of course, at your cousin's café. Well, good luck! Oh, by the way, when is that assignment due?
B Friday. Really must go now, I'll be late. See you tomorrow.
T Bye!

1.16 **PART 2**

BECKY Hi, Tom. I'm just on my way to the café.
TOM Oh OK …
B I'm late.
T Look, this evening … do you want to come over? I wanted to talk over a few things … about the wedding …
B I'd love to but I've got to study tonight.
T OK. Never mind. Well, good luck with your first day at work.
B Thanks. I'm sure it'll be fine.
T Don't spill coffee over anyone!
B I'll try not to. Oh, must run. Here comes my bus. No time to talk now. See you tomorrow. Bye.

1.19 **PART 3**

SAM OK, so what was I showing you? The food. The sandwiches are all here. The most important thing is, don't touch the food. Remember to always use these tongs to pick food up. And what else? Oh, the espresso machine. Uh, the coffee goes in here, the cup there, and you press this button. Is that clear?
BECKY OK, I'll remember that.
S Another thing to remember is the tables – they're all numbered. So it starts with one over there and goes round to fifteen. OK, have you got that?
B Yes, sure. I think I can count to 15!
S Hah – I still get them mixed up myself. Oh, say hello to Phil. He's our most regular customer. This is my cousin Becky. She's just started here.

PHIL Hi, nice to meet you.
B Hi.
S Phil's writing a novel.
B A novel! Amazing.
P Well, it's just a science fiction story. Haven't got very far yet.
S He comes to the café to write. We call him JK. You know – like JK Rowling. She wrote the first Harry Potter book in a café.
B Oh, right!
EMMA Oh, there you are. Lovely to see you, Becky. We're really pleased you're working here.
B Me too. I'm going to enjoy it, I'm sure.
E Is my husband looking after you and explaining everything?
B Oh yes, I'm getting the hang of it – slowly.
P She's doing really well.
E And I see you've met Phil. He's going to make the café famous one day, you'll see.

1.20 PART 4

TOM Large cappuccino please, with extra milk.
BECKY With extra m – oh Tom! Sorry. Wasn't expecting you.
T I was just passing by. How's it going?
B There's a lot to learn, but I think I'll be OK. Is it OK if I take my break now?
SAM Yeah.
B I'll make a coffee for both of us.
T Sure that's OK?
B Yeah, it's fine. You came at a quiet time. So, what was it you wanted to talk to me about tonight?
T Er, the wedding?
B The wedding?
T Yes, our wedding!
B Of course. We need to start thinking about it.

1.23

GITTA Most people at work think my boss, Michaela, is an inspiring woman who's had an amazing career – we work for a public relations company. She always looks very busy and people find that impressive, but I find her a bit arrogant, to tell you the truth. The other day, we were having a performance review meeting – she was reviewing me – and in the middle of the meeting her mobile phone rang. She answered the call and just ignored me! When she finished the call, she then spent a long time writing an email on her phone whilst I was just sitting there – waiting. When she'd finished, she didn't apologise or anything and just said, 'OK, what were we talking about?' Maybe I'm being too sensitive, but she didn't seem to care about our meeting – or me – and was far more interested in her phone call and email. I really think people should switch off their phones during meetings. I was really upset, to be honest.
DEREK For years, I resisted getting a mobile phone. Don't get me wrong – I'm not a techno-phobe. I've been using a computer for years; in fact, I have two: a desktop and a laptop. It's just that mobile phones annoyed me. I didn't want to be available all the time and I thought the language people used in text messages was a bit silly. However, my niece, Emma, was determined that I should get a mobile phone. I run a small firm of accountants and she felt someone in my position needed to be 'more connected', as she put it. Emma has a smartphone and she explained to me how they were just like mini computers that you carry around in your pocket. And, of course, she was right. She let me borrow hers for a weekend. I didn't actually phone anyone, but she had a lot of clever apps on her phone and I found out that I could go online and check email really easily. Of course, I went out and bought a smartphone the following week. Emma was delighted – she had finally managed to convince me. I haven't told her that I still don't ring anyone or send text messages, but now she thinks I'm more connected. For me, it's a great new toy – lots of fun.

Unit 2

1.25

ABBY So, when are you off to South Africa?
ROB End of next week. I can't wait to get away.
A I absolutely loved it when I went there last year. So, what have you got planned?
R You know – the usual things – Cape Town first. I'll definitely go to Robben Island.
A Great.
R And one thing I want to try while I'm there is surfing. Apparently, there are some really great schools you can go to.
A Yeah, there are loads.
R I've always wanted to learn how to surf and I'll finally get to do it – you know, with proper waves! Cool!
A That's a great thing to do – I went to one of those schools.
R And was it good? Did you learn a lot?
A Yeah – yeah I did. But … but you've got to be a bit careful in the water there. Actually, I got into a bit of trouble once.
R What, in the water?
A Yeah, when I was first learning to surf I went out one time by myself. I was trying to catch this wave, but I came off my board, and stupidly, I'd forgotten to attach a leg rope from my ankle to the board.
R So you lost the board?
A Yeah, I tried to get hold of it, but it got swept away by the wave.
R So what did you do – just swim to the shore?
A Well sort of. I started swimming and I soon realised that I wasn't getting anywhere. Then very gradually I got the feeling I was being pulled out to sea.
R You were caught in a current?
A Yeah, and when I realised this, I began to panic a bit. So I waved to get someone's attention. Luckily a life-guard had already seen that I was in trouble. And he came to rescue me in his lifeboat.
R Bet you were pleased to see him!
A Yeah! But the idea of being carried right out to sea is really frightening. I don't think you could survive very long. I'm quite a strong swimmer, but even so …
R Yeah I think you'd start to really feel the cold in the water.
A Well, I was wearing a wet suit. But they say if you get caught in a current you shouldn't try and swim against it. The thing is, the water there is ocean, not sea. The waves are really powerful.
R Hmm, maybe I'll have another think about it.
A About surfing you mean?
R Yeah.
A No, honestly you'll love it. It really is the most amazing feeling. I just had a bad experience. I got myself a new surfboard, and as soon as I'd had some lessons and knew what I was doing, it was fantastic. It's just you and the board, and you have this incredible sense of freedom. And when you catch the wave at the right time …
R Yeah, you're right, it sounds amazing.
A Yeah, it's fantastic. Oh, but, just watch out for sharks.
R Yeah, I'll … watch out for what?!

1.34

INTERVIEWER Miles, tell us about the story. What happened?
MILES Well, one day in the winter of 1997, in eastern Siberia, one of the wildest and most natural habitats on Earth, a hunter came across a Siberian tiger. He shot the tiger and wounded it and then took part of the dead animal that the tiger was about to eat. Of course, the tiger wasn't happy. It attacked and killed Markov but it didn't do this immediately. It waited 48 hours before attacking. In other words, it remembered what had happened and carefully planned the attack. So while Markov was away hunting, the tiger found its way to his hut in the forest and broke in through the door. The tiger then took Markov's mattress outside and laid on it, waiting for him to return. When Markov finally appeared, the tiger dragged him into the forest and ate him, leaving only his boots. They found the boots later and figured out what had happened.
I So these are very dangerous animals, obviously.
M Yes, very dangerous if you make them angry, certainly. They're also not just any tiger, they're the largest species of cat walking on earth. The Siberian Tiger is a very impressive animal. They can be up to four metres long and they weigh more than 250 kilos. They can jump about ten metres if they need to. So imagine a creature that's as active as a cat and has the weight of an industrial refrigerator – that's what a Siberian tiger's like! …

1.35

INTERVIEWER … So what happened then?
MILES Well of course, a group of men hunted the tiger down and killed it.
I I suppose they had to, really.
M But did they?
I What do you mean?
M Well, when you read the story, you're not sure whose side you're on, the tiger's or the humans'. As Vaillant says, the tiger's response is quite 'logical' and the tiger is 'just trying to be a tiger', and it's a human who interferes with that.
I So in a sense, it's the humans who are dangerous, rather than the tiger?
M In a way, yes. What's interesting is that humans and tigers hunt the same animals and share the same environment, and they've done this in Siberia for years but they don't normally disturb each other. But if you make the mistake of attacking a tiger, you're in trouble. People who live in the area say this has never happened before. There is no record ever of a tiger hunting a human being.
I So is that the message of the story – leave tigers alone?
M Well, yes, don't make a tiger angry, certainly, or it will take revenge. But also it makes you ask the question, 'Which is the dangerous animal, tigers or humans?' We think of tigers as dangerous, but of course we're not at risk because of tigers, they're at risk because of us. There are 40 million humans but only 500 tigers, so they really are an endangered species, and that's mainly because of us hunting them and living in their habitat and taking away their natural food.
I Miles, thank you. You heard Miles Holman talking about the book *The Tiger* by John Vaillant …

1.37 PART 1

BECKY Could you give me a hand with this please, Tessa?
TESSA Sure.
B I just, I just can't get the right height.
T OK.
B Great, thank you.
T No problem.
T Good shot?
B Not really. I think I need to be closer. It's quite difficult.
T Yeah, it's hard, isn't it? … Do you need all this equipment?
B I find it helps.
T Do you?
B Usually. Ah, this is fun.
T Yeah, much better than sitting in a lecture at college. All that theory!
B Well, that can be interesting …
T I'd really like to take a photo of something a bit more exciting – maybe a squirrel.
B A squirrel? That'll be good … if we can find one …

1.39 PART 2

TESSA Nice daffodils.
BECKY Gorgeous, aren't they?
B Can I have a look? Wow, what a great shot!
T It's all right.
B You know just how to get a really good shot. The light is amazing.
T Thanks. Guess it's not bad. Can I have a look at yours?
B It's pretty boring.
T Don't you want me to?

B No – I mean it's not a problem. I just feel it's a pretty ordinary shot. You know, just … nothing special. Compared to yours.
Have you ever worked as a photographer?
T Me? No. It was just something I kind of got into. Kind of a hobby. How about you?
B No, never. I used to have this job working in HR, but I've just given that up.
T Too stressful?
B Sort of.
T Or too boring?
B Well … both! My café job's enough to pay the bills – just. You?
T I'm just studying at the moment; I haven't got a job …
B Oh right …
T Shhh!
B What?
T Squirrel. Over there.
B Oh right. Great.
T We'll need to get a bit closer. But quietly.
B You go first.
T No, no. You go.
B No, really – you should go.
T It's fine. This is your shot.
B Sure?
T Yeah.
B OK. Oh no! It's run away. Ah, this is a really bad shot. The light's all wrong. I need a reflector.
T Can I have a look?
B I don't like it.
T This is great.
B Really?
T Yeah, it's your best shot.
B But I didn't have a chance to set it up.
T Maybe sometimes you don't need to.
B Hm. OK. Maybe not. You know, one thing I don't like about this assignment.
T What's that?
B It's so cold!
T Yeah, it's freezing, isn't it?
B My flat's not far away. Do you fancy a nice warm cup of coffee?
T OK. Yeah. Why not?
B Great. Let's go.

1.41

LUIZA I spent a year in Vancouver in Canada. I loved the National Parks there – they're very special environments full of rare and protected plants and animals. This one particular day I'd been exploring in the Pacific Rim National Park when I got in trouble in the forest. I'd been to see this waterfall. It was a very easy walk from the main track – less than an hour. On the way back I saw what I thought was a short cut that would get me back to the main track more quickly – a big mistake. After a couple of hours I realised that I was going round in circles and I wasn't getting anywhere. I'd got completely lost. I was beginning to get worried – that's for sure. All I had to eat was an energy bar and I had nothing to drink. Well, I waited until later in the afternoon because then I knew the sun would go down in the west and I knew roughly I should be going in an easterly direction. And I had a bit of luck – I came across a stream with fresh water. I followed the stream for a bit and I came to an open area – a kind of a clearing. I knew that eventually people would start looking for me – I'd told the forest ranger when I would be back and I was more than four hours late. And I knew it's better to sit in one place where you can be seen. So I was sitting quietly and thinking about how I could spend the night in the forest and I suddenly had this strange feeling I was not alone.

1.42

LUIZA I looked around the clearing and on the edge of it I saw a bear looking at me. I knew that you shouldn't run away or show fear. I stood up and said in a clear voice "I have a right to be here" and moved slowly backwards without looking at the bear in the eyes. I could sense the bear watching me. I tried to keep calm but inside I was really panicking. I was terrified. Suddenly, it started moving – thankfully it was away from me. It just disappeared back into the forest. I didn't know if I should stay where I was or keep moving. But then I could hear a helicopter in the distance coming towards me. I thought it might be looking for me. I jumped up and tried to see it, but it flew away before I could get its attention. It was so frustrating. But about fifteen minutes later it flew back and I was ready. I took off my jacket and turned it inside out – the lining was red and easy to see. This time they saw me and waved back. About a half an hour later rescuers arrived and guided me out. What I couldn't get over is the fact that I was only 10 minutes away from the main track.

Unit 3

1.43

NARRATOR My teacher will get angry if I make mistakes.
TEACHER I don't really think that's the case. Teachers really do prefer students who try hard, you know, make an effort. It doesn't matter if they make mistakes. In fact, it's better if they do because if we know what their mistakes are, we can help fix them.
N Children learn faster than adults.
T I guess you could say that children aren't as busy as adults – they probably have a bit less going on in their lives. And that helps. They're less distracted and, you could say, a bit more open to learning. But adults – well, they often have really good motivation. They're often quite focused and they're really keen to learn. So this motivation can make them faster learners than children.
N I must practise every day in order to make progress.
T Well, in my experience you can practise too much! It's actually better to take two or three days off each week. The thing is our brains need a bit of a rest. It's like muscles when you're doing physical exercise – you need to rest them. So we need to rest our brains when we're learning and practising something new.
N If something seems very easy, I must be doing it wrong.
T Yeah, a lot of people believe this, but I think the opposite is true. In reality, if it's easy, it probably means you're doing it right. But if something's difficult or it's a physical activity that's causing you pain, then you're probably doing something wrong. Learning doesn't always need to be hard!
N Long practice sessions are best.
T It's much, much better to have shorter practice sessions. You've got to remember that most people get tired after about fifteen minutes and they need a short break. The thing is, though, during the fifteen minutes of practice, you really want people to concentrate on what they're doing – really focus. They'll get more benefit that way.

1.44

SEAMUS Ever since I was first able to read I've loved comic books. I just think it's a brilliant way of telling a story. I've read literally thousands of them. But, at the same time, I discovered I was quite good at drawing. When I was about eight years old I started copying some of the pictures in comics and even my parents were surprised by how good my copies were. It wasn't long before I started making up my own stories. All of my friends were also really into comics, but none of them tried coming up with their own stories. But they quite liked reading mine, so I'd share the comics I wrote with them. This was helpful because it gave me a good idea of what worked and what didn't. I studied design at university and then got a job as a graphic designer. But all the time I was writing and drawing my own comics – comics for adults and children. I've just signed a contract with a major comics publisher in the USA and I can now give up my job as a graphic designer. I think my career in comics is beginning to take off … well, I hope to do really well. Ten thousand hours? You bet. I've probably spent more time than that, but I loved every minute of it.
FIONA I'm a chemist and I've been lucky enough to get a research position at a university. I love chemistry because it's all about the things that make up the world we live in. I find it fascinating. It's funny, whenever I say that I'm a chemist, one of the first things people mention is the table of elements – you know, all the symbols for all the different metals and gases. They can never figure out all those symbols. Well, I have this system where the letter or letters remind me of the name of a person, and that reminds me of a face and something about the way he or she looks reminds me of the element. One colleague pointed out that this wasn't a very scientific way of remembering these elements. In fact, some scientists look down on this kind of thing, but it works for me. I find all these ways of making your memory stronger really interesting and I think making associations to help you remember is really useful. I have to remember so much information in my research work, so I want to look into these techniques in more depth.
HENRY I'm a musician – I play saxophone in a band. We're just about to go on a tour so we're practising full-time to get ready. We've got so much to do before the tour – so much that it's getting us all down a bit. Apart from needing to practise playing together, we've got to write some new songs and learn some others. I read about this idea of learning different things at different times of the day, so we decided to try it out and see if it'd help. So now we focus on writing new material in the morning, and we also use that time to learn the words and music of some classic songs we want to play – actually studying the notes and remembering the words of songs. After lunch we play together – you know, do the physical learning. And I have to say it's working pretty well. We're putting in a lot of work and we feel we're using the time well. The songs are getting easier to remember and I think our playing in the afternoon is tighter – we're producing a better sound. The only problem is that some days we get a bit carried away in the afternoon and keep playing into the evening, which means we stay up late and aren't so good in the morning!

1.48

PETER This week on The Book Show we're talking about David Epstein's *The Sports Gene*, in which he claims that many sports professionals are so good simply because they're lucky enough to have the right genes. According to him, top athletes and other sportsmen are simply different from the rest of us. With us is athlete Barbara MacCallum, who is a professional runner and trainer. Barbara, you've read the book. Do you think Epstein is right – is it all about having the right genes?
BARBARA Well, I think he's right that genes are important. And, of course, we all know that many Kenyans are tall and thin and so on, and also as the book says they live at a high altitude – 1,000 metres – so they have more red blood cells. So these things are important. But I think there's much more to it than that.
P You've lived in Kenya yourself.
B Yes, I've lived in Kenya myself and I've trained with Kenyan runners, I've also worked with Kenyan children. And there really are lots of very good runners in Kenya. But it's not just about having long legs. They also have a culture of running, everyone runs, even small children, so they have this background, they all see themselves as runners, as good runners. And if you're poor in Kenya, becoming an athlete is a way to change your life, so everyone wants to be a runner.
P And they run in bare feet. Does that help?
B Yes, it does. It gives you a much better running technique, so that's important, too. So yes, I think it is partly genetic, but it's also to do with lots of other factors, like having lots of practice, lots of encouragement to run, believing in yourself, and also learning to run in the right way.
P So could I run as fast as a Kenyan?
B Well, yes, you could, but you'd have to start early in life and you'd have to get very fit.
P Well, I haven't run anywhere for years, so maybe it's a bit too late to start.
B Absolutely not, it's never too late. Start training now and you'll be amazed at what you can achieve.

1.49

PETER Thank you, Barbara. Well, also with us now is Marta Fedorova. Marta, you've been playing tennis since you were a child and you've been a professional player for ten years.
MARTA Yes.
P You've also read the book. Do you think he's right? Are some sports people naturally better? Or is it a question of technique and practice, as Barbara says?
M Well, yes, I've been thinking a lot about this recently. I used to think that it was mainly practice and technique that were important. You know, if you practise a lot, if you get fit, if you improve your technique, then you'll win. But after reading this book I'm not so sure. For example, I've played maybe 50 serious matches this year. And I've won about half of them. If I think about the people who beat me, they all have certain things in common physically. Short bodies but longer arms, for example.
P Like you.
M Well, yes, I suppose so! And very good eyesight, obviously. And mostly aged 18 to 25. And these are things that you can't really change. So yes, there is something in it.
P So sport isn't as fair as we like to think?
M That's right, and that's really what he's saying in this book. When we watch the Olympics, for example, we think it's a fair competition between equals, but it isn't. We're watching a competition between very different types of people who have different natural advantages. So there will be people who need to train very hard to get where they are and others who don't need to train so much, and there will be some people who can naturally finish 40 seconds ahead of all the others, and so on. So fairness in sport doesn't really exist.

1.51 PART 1

BECKY So when are you going to tell your parents about your promotion?
TOM This weekend, I think. We're seeing them on Saturday, remember?
B Oh yes. Anyway, as I was saying – about Tessa …
T Tessa, yes, your classmate …
B She's just got this amazing natural ability.
T So have you.
B But I've been taking photos for years …
T Very good ones too …
B … and I've gradually got better, but Tessa …
T Maybe she's been practising for years, too. In secret! … So what's for dinner then?
B Well, I got some cheese, some chicken and some salad.
T Cheese? You mean the one on offer?
B Yeah. Two for one – bargain.
T Yes, it was a bargain. That's why I got some.
B Well, I guess I know what we are having for dinner.
T Cheese on toast?
B Cheese on toast.

1.52 PART 2

TOM Anyway, as I was saying … about the wedding. I was thinking we should start making some decisions if we want to get married in June.
BECKY Yes, you're right.
T So what do we need to think about?
B Well, the usual things … guests, a venue for the reception, the cake.
T So maybe the first thing to decide is …
B … who should we invite?
T I mean, do we want a large wedding with lots of guests or just a small one?
B How about … how about we invite no one?
T What?
B We can just have a secret wedding. You know, go to Las Vegas in America – or something like that.
T Seriously?
B It's an idea …
T Seriously Becky – don't you think it's a good idea to set a limit? Say, no more than 80 guests?
B Yes, I suppose it is.
T OK.
B And … Tessa!
T Sure – we can invite her.
B … well, yes … but I was thinking … we'll need a photographer.
T Well, yes.
B But don't you agree that Tessa would be perfect as the photographer?
T Um … Becky .. that's kind of an unnecessary detail right now.
B Yes. Of course.
T To go back to the guests …
B OK, so how many relatives, how many friends?

1.55 PART 3

TOM So, if we just invite close family and friends …
BECKY We'll have to invite Aunt Clare.
T Your mad Aunt Clare?
B We have to invite her.
T Of course, we could sit her next to my Uncle Fred.
B But he never says anything.
T Exactly – the perfect pair.
B Who else? What about the people you work with?
T Hmm – I don't know about that.
B We could always invite them to the evening reception.
T Don't you agree that it'd be easier not to invite them?
B But I would like to invite Tessa.
T As I said – that's fine. Anyway, I think we need to limit it to close friends and family members. Even the scary ones.
B I sort of get both excited and nervous when I think about it.
T It'll be fine. So the next question is where?
B Well, there's that lovely old hotel … you know, near where my cousin lives.
T Oh … 'Regent's Lodge'.
B Actually … thinking about where … after we're married. Where are we going to live?
T Hm. Good question.
B What you might call a necessary detail?

1.57

REPORTER This is Marco Forlan reporting from the multi-million-pound Market Street Sports Complex. It's huge – it's got so many different courts for different sports – tracks for athletics and cycling. It's even got its own indoor snow slope. It's been up and running for a year now, so I've come down to see just how much use it's getting. So, Lizzie, you haven't been doing this long, have you?
LIZZIE No, just over six months.
R And before that?
L Well, nothing. I was one of those people who was pretty hopeless at sport at school. In basketball I could never catch the ball very well and I couldn't throw it far enough. And I've never been a fast runner.
R So you were always last to be picked for a team?
L Yeah, that was me! Everyone else was so much more talented and they looked down on me. But I wanted to do some kind of exercise, and, to be honest, I almost don't consider this a sport – it's just something I used to do to get to school. I train four days a week now and I do a mix of track and open road. It's my favourite part of the day.
R And in the future?
L Next month I'm going to compete in a race. It's just a small local one, but it gives me a goal to aim for. I've been training quite hard for the past six months now. I train here on the track, but also on the open road.
R Good luck with your race.
R Hey, Barry – that was quite an impressive jump.
BARRY Thanks.
R So how long have you been doing this?
B Just over a year. I took it up after I recovered from a foot injury. You see, I used to run marathons, but now I find it really uncomfortable to run long distances.
R And did you get started here at the centre?
B Yeah, that's right. In the beginning I was just having fun – you know … And then I realised I was quite good at it. What I enjoy is … it's mostly about skill and the way you use your whole body – it's not just about strength.
R And have you ever tried it out in the open?
B Yeah, last winter I went to France and had my first go on real snow. I met a lot of amazing people there including a few professionals. They told me that I've got a naturally good style.
R Any plans for the future?
B I'm going to compete in some championships this winter and I've just bought myself this new board. I just wish we had real mountains in England.
R That's a great-looking board. Have fun! That was a pretty energetic game, Patricia.
PATRICIA Yeah, it was fun.
R So you're new to the game?
P Yeah, I started about nine months ago.
R How did you get into it?
P I took it up because I wanted a sport for myself. You see, I've spent the past six or seven years taking my two children to different sports events. They're older now and can get to sports practice on their own. So I had to figure out what I'd like to do.
R How did you decide?
P Well, I was always quite good at basketball, but I wanted to try something new. And I wanted a sport that would get me fit, and this certainly does. Once I'd looked into a range of options – the choice was easy.
R This is a fairly new sport in the UK …
P Yeah.
R So how is it different from basketball?
P Well, you can actually take three steps with the ball – so long as you do it in three seconds.
R That's not long. And how often do you practise?
P Once a week and then we have a friendly game. I enjoy the social side of things as much as the competing. Next year my team's thinking about entering some championships.
R Well, I hope you continue to enjoy it.

1.58

1
A Oh no. There's glass all over the floor.
B Well, you dropped it so I think you should clear it up.
A I can't, I've got to go. Couldn't you do it? Please?
2
A What does 'potential' mean?
B Um, I don't know. I'll have to look it up. I'll tell you in a minute.
3
A Did you manage to learn Spanish?
B Yeah, it was easy. I picked it up in about six months. But I never really learned the grammar.
4
A I think we should talk about having longer lunch breaks. Thirty minutes is much too short.
B Yes, I agree. Why don't you bring it up at the meeting?

Unit 4

2.5

PRESENTER Monica, we often hear stories about lottery winners who were unhappy or who spent their money unwisely.
MONICA Yes, that's true, you often read about lottery winners whose lives turned bad. For example, the Griffiths family recently – that was a big story. They won £1.8 million on the lottery and they spent it all on houses and cars and I don't know what else. And they ended up losing all their money, and soon after that their marriage broke up – it was a very sad story. And you do certainly hear stories like that.
P So does suddenly having a lot of money really influence people's behaviour? Or are these just isolated or unusual cases which make a good story?
M They're just isolated cases; in fact winning doesn't usually have a negative influence on people. Of course, people like to believe that winning money leads to disaster because that makes them feel better about not winning. But the idea that winning a lot of money causes misery is actually a myth, it's simply not true.
P There have been studies done on this, haven't there?

M Yes, that's right. According to most studies, suddenly having a lot of money is just as likely to have a positive effect on you as a negative effect. And most people don't in fact spend all their money.

P Can you give us some examples?

M Yes. For example, a recent study in Britain looked at how much of their money people spent if they won the lottery. And it found that people spent a lot in the first five years, but very few people spent all the money in their lifetime, only about 2–3%. So most people do spend a lot, but they save a lot as well. And then there was an interesting study in California, and they measured how happy people are as a result of winning the lottery. And they found that people get very happy when they win, which isn't surprising, but as they adjust to the idea of being rich and go back to normal again after a few months – they end up feeling just the same as before. So over the long term, getting richer doesn't actually affect how happy you are, you just stay the same ... but with more money, of course.

P So, if you're happy anyway, you'll stay happy even if you get rich, is that the message?

M Yes, that's right. Money won't make you happy, but it won't stop you being happy either. And studies have also shown that it depends on how you spend the money. So people who buy lots of things, like clothes or houses or cars, are often not very happy. As soon as you've got a car you want a better car and so on, so that doesn't make you happy for long. But spending money on experiences usually results in longer-term happiness.

P Experiences?

M Yes, for example, going on the holiday of a lifetime or doing something you've always wanted to do. That'll make you happy while you're doing it, and it'll make you happy later because you also have good memories of it. So it's a better way to be happy.

P OK, so there we have it. When you win that £5 million, forget the cars and the new house, and go for a long holiday instead.

2.7

ALPHONSO For me, the thing that's changed my life most is having a baby. Things are just completely different now. We used to go out a lot, we used to travel as well, we'd go somewhere different every year, and we didn't use to care much about money, we both had good jobs and we had a small flat in town so we didn't need to care about money very much. But now of course the baby's the most important thing, so I'd say I've become a bit more cautious than I used to be. I used to be quite an adventurous person, I used to take all kinds of risks without thinking much about it. Whereas now I think more about having a family, having a home, having a steady job, things like that. Sounds terribly boring, doesn't it, but it doesn't feel boring!

DRAGANA A very big change in my life was going abroad to study. I grew up in Croatia in a fairly small town and I went to university there. But then I had the chance to go to Berlin for a year to study. And of course I had a good time there and I made new friends, but I think it also changed the way I look at life. Before I went I was quite shy and not very self-confident and I had quite a protected life, I suppose, and then in Berlin I had to look after myself and also adapt to a new culture, of course. And as a result of being there, I think I no longer see everything from a Croatian point of view but more internationally, so I'm much more open to different ideas than I used to be – I hope so, anyway.

2.10

MIRANDA I think the hardest part of drama school was actually getting into it. The audition process took for ever. First of all we had to perform two scenes from plays – one modern, one Shakespeare. Then we got called back to do the scenes again. I was supposed to prepare a song as well, but they forgot to let me know. So I just sang the first song that came into my head – can't even remember what it was. After that, there was a workshop for a day where they made us work on new scenes from plays and do movement and voice classes. After all of that I felt really lucky to get selected. There's no doubt the training was very thorough, I mean, we did everything – the usual voice and movement classes, but also specialised things like learning how to pretend to fight on stage. I really enjoyed those classes. The tutors were all very different – some were really strict and tough. For example, we had a movement teacher and in her class we weren't allowed to talk or use our voices in any way. That was really difficult. But our voice teacher was really relaxed – she was cool. During my second year I went through a bit of a difficult time because I wasn't sure if acting was what I really wanted to do. I mean, drama school is a huge sacrifice. The training sort of swallowed my life – like, I lived it every single moment of the day. I kind of felt like I wasn't having what you'd call 'a normal life' for a 20 year-old. The school was really flexible about this and they let me take a couple of weeks off to make up my mind. I decided to keep going and I'm glad that I did. I graduated last year and I've got an agent and I've just got a small part in a production at the Royal Shakespeare Company. So I guess you could say I'm on my way ...

FRED I got into a football academy when I was eleven years old. I was playing at my local club and a scout from a professional club saw me and invited me to play in a trial match. I was really excited about this. My parents had their doubts – they were worried about me not having a normal childhood – but they could see this was a pretty unique opportunity, so they let me do it. Dad was really pleased about one thing – we were allowed to see all the club games for free. But I don't think any of us really understood just how difficult a commitment it would be. Mum and Dad were more or less forced to act as my chauffeurs and they had to drive me to practice three times a week and then to a match every Sunday. I had to do this and keep up with my school homework at the same time. And that meant I often wasn't allowed to go out and play with my friends when I wanted to. Still, in the academy we had the best coaches and there's no doubt that my playing got so much better. We also used to watch videos of matches all the time and analyse the strategy of the different players. I enjoyed this a whole lot more than I thought I would. In fact, one of the coaches once told me that this is one of the reasons why I stood out from some of the other boys in the academy. It's a really competitive environment and at the end of every year, there were some boys who were forced to give it all up because they didn't get invited back for the following year. I had one mate, Jack. We started at the same time, but when we turned 16, and it became possible for some of us to earn a salary, Jack wasn't selected. And it was like the previous five years were all for nothing. And he was like my best mate and I really missed him. I did get selected though, and now I've got a full professional contract, so things are pretty good. Did I have a normal childhood? No, probably not. I kind of regret that, but then I've been given an opportunity, haven't I? I guess you can't have it both ways.

2.13 PART 1

BECKY Now let's have a look at some of the most successful ones. Tessa took this one.

TESSA We really like the way the light is hitting the tree.

B And here's a similar shot, but from a different angle with a plane crossing the sky. We got some close-ups of flowers. We managed to get some good shots of daffodils.

T The light was really good for this one.

B And we were lucky and managed to get a couple of wildlife shots. Here's a shot of a swan that Tessa took. And finally ... my shot of a squirrel.

B Thank you for listening.

TUTOR OK, thank you, Becky ... and Tessa. Some very good work. There were some interesting close-up shots there, very sharp details and clear colours. Yes, a very good first assignment. Well done both of you. OK. Now for your next assignment - Bridges. Pick a bridge that you like. Photograph it and then write an essay to go with it. OK? We'll see how you get on. You've got one month.

2.14 PART 2

BECKY That went quite well.

TESSA Yeah.

B It was fun. So, bridges for the next assignment.

T Yes, bridges. So boring.

B Oh, I don't know, it's not that boring. All that fantastic architecture. That could be quite interesting.

T Yeah, maybe you're right, I'm not sure. But there's all that theory for the essay. I didn't take any notes in yesterday's lecture.

B Don't worry, I took loads of notes. You can borrow mine.

T Can I?

B Sure. Come round to the café later and I'll give them to you.

B Must go now. Bye!

2.16

1

A I thought the goalkeeper was useless. He was the weakest player in the team.

B Really, did you think so? I thought he played quite well.

2

A €60 for fish and a salad! That's far too much.

B I'm not sure about that. It doesn't seem that expensive.

3

A Did you see that bank managers earn an average of £100,000 a year? It's crazy!

B I know what you mean, but on the other hand it's a very responsible job.

4

A She's having a fancy dress party on her birthday. How boring!

B Oh I don't know. I think it could be quite good fun.

5

A It was a very boring film. I thought it was far too long.

B Maybe you're right, but I enjoyed some bits of it.

2.17

1

A I thought that was a really interesting lecture.

B Oh, I don't know. It wasn't that interesting.

2

A I find photography a very difficult subject.

B Oh, I don't know. It's not that difficult.

3

A Look at that bridge. It's so unusual.

B Oh, I don't know. It's not that unusual.

4

A I thought the questions in the exam were incredibly easy.

B Oh, I don't know. It wasn't that easy.

2.18 PART 3

BECKY Here you are. My lecture notes.

TESSA Ah great, thanks.

B And these...

T Thank you.

B And here are some other notes I made earlier.

T Ah, OK, thank you. Plenty to read here.

B It's not too much, is it?

T Um, well ... no, thank you. You've saved my life.

B Don't worry, that's OK. I'm more into the theory than you are.

T You can say that again. I hate it.

B By the way, Tom and I were sorting out details of the wedding last night.

T Oh yeah?

B And well we thought – if you're interested – we'd love you to take the photos.

T Me? Are you serious?

B Yeah, why not?

T Well, I'm not ... I don't think I'm good enough.

B Oh don't be silly. Of course you are. Oh, will you? Please?
T Well, yes, if you want me to. I mean … I'd love to.
B Great. Better get back to work.
PHIL Oh no. No!
B What is it, Phil?
P I've just deleted the whole chapter. I only meant to delete the paragraph.
B Oh no.
T Who's that?
B That's Phil. He's always here. He's writing a book. Well, trying to, anyway. When he isn't accidentally deleting his work!
T A writer … that's interesting.
B See you later.
T Hi.
P Hi.
T Becky tells me you're writing a book.
P Sort of.
T That's great. I like books.
P Mm.
T I'd like to see what you've written, anyway. I'm sure it's really good.
P Thanks. I haven't written much yet.
T Ah well, I'd better let you get on, bye. …
P Bye …

2.19

EVA I got a chance to go to Toronto in Canada for a year to work for my company – I didn't have to go there, but I chose to go because I thought it would be interesting. And it was a great experience. And, of course, at the start it was all new and exciting, and there was so much to see, so many places to go out. I'm from quite a small town in Colombia, so it was a huge difference. The most difficult thing, I think, was getting to know people. I think in a big city everyone's busy with their own life, you know, everyone's in a hurry. It was really hard to meet people and make friends. Also, because it's really cold in winter, nothing goes on outside in the street, everyone does things indoors in their own homes and that's quite a big difference. Sometimes you walk down a street and you think, where is everyone? And it was so cold, that really affects your mood, it makes you just want to stay indoors and as a result I felt quite lonely sometimes. So yes, it was a good experience, I'm very glad I went there, but I was quite glad to come back home again and see all my friends.
NICK I got a job teaching English in a town called Katowice in Poland. When I first went there I was very lucky, because I stayed with a family who didn't speak English, so I was really forced to speak Polish. It was very difficult at first, I couldn't understand a word. But because I learned Polish, I very quickly got to know lots of people. I think a key to understanding a country is to learn the language – without that you only ever meet the people who speak English and you can't ever get to know the culture. Another thing is that people often go to places that are beautiful to look at, and that's fine if you're a tourist. But to live in a place, I think what it looks like is the least important thing. People are much more important. For example, I come from a very beautiful old town in England – it looks great in photographs, but there's not much going on there. Where I was in Katowice, it's just a big industrial town, nothing special about it, but the people were very friendly and welcoming, so I very quickly felt at home there and I had a really good time. I was supposed to stay there for three months but I ended up staying for a year!
JEAN I work for a large engineering company and I went to work in Oman, in the Gulf, for a year. And I had a very good time there. I had a good salary so I ate out a lot and, at weekends, I went diving and swimming and went on trips into the mountains or the desert. It's a very beautiful country. So, as I say, I had a good time there, but I don't feel I ever really got to know the culture. I never got under the surface of it, so as a result I remained an outsider. People were very friendly, very hospitable, and I spent some time with the local employees who worked with us – we often went out together. But I suppose because the culture is very different and you're working hard every day, it's easier to spend your time with other foreigners, so my friends were mostly Europeans. I know it's not a good excuse, but it's what most foreign visitors do – they end up in a group of expatriates and have their own lifestyle, and that results in them being like a separate community. Maybe I should have tried harder to learn Arabic, I did try to learn a bit, but I never learned to speak it well enough to have a real conversation with people.

Unit 5

2.23

Lots of people get scared when they fly and they're sure the plane's going to crash, but in fact it's one of the safest ways to travel. The odds of a plane crashing are only about one in a million and obviously they're much less if you use an airline with a good safety record. It's very unlikely that your plane will crash but even if it does you'll probably be fine, because 95% of people in plane crashes survive. If you sit at the back of the plane or over the wing, near the exit, your chances get even better. So, if you're worried about getting on that plane, don't be, because you'll almost certainly survive the journey. You're more likely to have an accident in the car going to the airport – your chances of having a road accident are 1 in 8,000. So the safest way to travel is to take a train to the airport and then fly.

More good news is that you have quite a good chance of living to be 100, especially if you don't worry too much. According to a recent report, in richer countries of the world, women who are 25 now have a 1 in 4 chance of reaching their 100th birthday – men of 25 only have a 1 in 6 chance, not quite so good. But the chances are getting better all the time, so a girl born now has a 1 in 3 chance of living to 100 and a boy has a 1 in 4 chance. Of course, this depends on what country you're in. In some countries like Japan the chances are even higher and modern medicine may well make the chances higher still during your lifetime.

So, that's the good news. You probably won't die in a plane crash and you, or at least your children, could live to be 100. But the bad news is, you almost certainly won't win the lottery. The chances of winning a big prize in the lottery are only about 1 in 18 million – so that's extremely unlikely.

2.27

JOE So, when are you off?
MARTHA Monday of next week.
J Exciting.
M Sure is – this time next week I'll be settling into my accommodation.
J So, I mean, what is it you'll be doing? From what I understand … well, you're going down there to keep your eye on some penguins. Is that it?
M Well, I suppose that's one way of looking at it!
J Yeah, but, you know, what will you be doing on a daily basis?
M Well, I'm not entirely sure, but I think I'll be doing similar things every day. It's more or less a question of observing the penguins – counting them, taking photos, checking tags on some of them – that kind of thing.
J OK – so, just kind of standing around in the cold?
M Yes, well, that's the downside of the job. That and the attacks.
J What? From polar bears?
M Erm … at the South Pole? No, from penguins.
J You mean those sweet little birds attack you?
M Oh yes, they're full of attitude – if you get too close.
J And will they be waiting for you when you get there?
M Well, of course – they know I'm coming.
J Very funny. So, there they are – Mr and Mrs Penguin about to play happy families and …?
M Yeah, so, by the time I arrive the penguins will already have got into pairs and then, by the middle of November, each pair of penguins will have laid two eggs.
J You just watch them sit on their eggs? That must be … 'really interesting'.
M I'm sure they'll do something to keep me entertained.
J And then?
M Well, by the end of December, most of the chicks will have arrived and then after about three weeks we put metal tags on them.
J Unless you get attacked by those nasty, aggressive parents.
M We have our methods of defence.
J Sounds scary. OK this is all very interesting, but, I mean, why? Why's it useful to know what these penguins do? It sounds like they kind of do the same old thing year after year.
M Nothing wrong with predictable – we scientists like that – but sometimes there can be changes, like maybe there are fewer chicks or maybe the parents aren't able to feed the chicks and not as many survive. This can tell us a lot about what's happening in the Antarctic ecosystem.
J Like what exactly?
M Ah, I'm a scientist – I never jump to easy conclusions.
J That's no fun.
M But, in a general sense, if there are changes in the number of penguins or changes in their behaviour, this can tell us that there has been a change in the climate of some sort. It's part of the evidence – the bigger picture, if you like. The work I'll be doing is just a small part in a big project that's been going on for some time. But because Antarctica is such an unspoilt environment the changes that take place there can tell us a lot about what's happening on the rest of the planet.
J And you get to hang out with those cute little penguins.
M Yeah, well … it's just one big penguin party.
J Sounds pretty cool to me.

2.30 PART 1

BECKY Phil? We're closing.
PHIL Nearly done. I'm just finishing this chapter. That's it – done. See you tomorrow, then. What's wrong, Sam?
SAM The usual. Not enough money coming in. I need to do something to get more customers.
P Hmm. You could stay open longer? In the evenings? You could serve meals. I'd eat here.
B You practically live here anyway. But it's an idea, why not?
S It'd be a long day
B You could do just Friday and Saturday to start with.
S Hmm, I'd need to hire a cook. Set up the kitchen properly. On the other hand, the extra money would be good … I don't know.
B Anyway, time to go. Are you ready, Phil?
P Yeah, coming. Bye Sam.
S See you.
P Umm … that friend of yours … curly hair …
B Tessa?
P Tessa. Is she at college with you?
B Yeah.
P OK.
B Bye Phil.

2.31 PART 2

EMMA Bad day?
SAM The café. We're not making enough money.
E Come on, you're doing fine. Mid-week, it's bound to be slow.
S I'm just worried. We've put all our money in this. I don't want to lose it.
E No, of course you don't. I can see that.
S Phil had an idea today.
E Yeah?
S Stay open Friday and Saturday evenings and serve food.
E Interesting.
S Of course, the trouble is we'd have to invest even more money – money that we haven't got.
E Yes, but the good thing about it is, it might be a way to get more business.

S Well, we'd need to put in a proper kitchen, and that'll probably cost a fortune. And we'll have to hire someone to cook. People do often ask if we're open in the evening, so there is a demand … I don't know, it's a big risk …
E I think it's a lovely idea. I know the perfect person to do the cooking.
S Who?
E Me.
S You? Seriously?
E Why not? Promise I won't charge much!

2.36 PART 3

EMMA And maybe we could do a few other things.
SAM Such as?
E Well, how about entertainment? We could have live music, get locals to play at the weekend.
S Hmm, that might be worth a try … if they didn't cost too much. In fact, we can probably get some students to do it for free.
E No!
S If we give them some food or something.
E Sam! You should pay them. That's not fair!
S Hmm, maybe you're right.
E Or display paintings or photos.
S That's not a bad idea. Becky could help with that … or Tessa.
E I know what you're thinking.
S What?
E Look, if you want to use Tessa's photos you should pay her for them. What I mean is, that she can display them and we can sell them.
S Hmm …
E Or readings. Have poetry readings.
S Hmm, that's a possibility … I know who you're thinking of ….
BOTH Phil!
S And he'd definitely do it for free.
E *[sighs]*
S What?

2.38

1
Large areas of farmland were under water and cattle had to be moved to higher ground. Several villages were completely cut off and fire services rescued 53 people from their homes. More rain is expected, so river levels may rise further over the next few days and there is a chance that larger towns will be affected …

2
Temperatures around Boston dropped to –25°. Drivers on the main Boston to New York highway had to abandon their vehicles and several small towns were entirely cut off. Residents were warned not to go out unless absolutely necessary. Temperatures are likely to remain below –20° at least until the weekend, with further heavy snow expected. …

3
March is normally one of the wettest months in the region, but this year's rainfall was the lowest ever recorded, with only three days of rain in some parts of the country. Emergency supplies of water were brought into areas most badly affected. According to a government statement, if the dry weather continues the rice harvest could be severely threatened.

4
Winds of over 150 kilometres an hour are expected to strike the coast on Tuesday evening, and residents in coastal areas have been advised to leave. Centres have been set up in towns further inland to provide food and shelter for families who were forced to abandon their homes.

Unit 6

2.39

DI Because I was travelling on my own, I decided to book myself on a coach tour. I thought it'd be fun and, you know, it would be easy to meet people and hang out with them in the evenings. Well, that was true – I made friends quite easily. But the tour itself … well, I'd never do it like that again – not ever. The problem is the people organising these tours try to include too much in the timetable. It's madness. Some days you have to be up, packed and ready to go by about 7.30am. And all the time they'd say, 'Remember to do this, remember to be back at such-and-such a time.' I mean, I was on holiday – this felt like being in the army! And they never allowed enough time to visit places. Like, I remember visiting this really beautiful palace just outside Vienna – the Schönbrunn Palace, it's called. In the gardens they have this really cool maze – you know, where they plant a whole lot of trees and hedges and it feels like you're getting lost. Anyway, we were all having a great time in the maze, but no, we had to get on the bus and go to the next thing. Before arriving in Rome, I became friendly with a woman, Sue – she was travelling alone too. We decided to leave the tour – didn't care about the money – and we found our own hotel to stay in. It was just a small place near a market. Every morning when I woke up I could hear the sellers setting up their market stalls. So Sue and I spent a week in Rome and then went on to Florence and Venice. Visiting these cities was a real highlight. And one of the reasons why it was great to do things in our own time. It was like getting out of school.
BERNIE I worked in London over the winter months and then I got together with three other mates and we bought this van from a South African couple and we took off together to travel around Europe. We had a great time and there were just a couple of times when we sort of disagreed about what we'd do. The only thing is finding your way round these European cities and getting from one place to another, it's … well, it's a bit of a nightmare really. I mean, we had guidebooks and maps and things, but often what you read about didn't really match reality. And there are just so many cars and so many people. Driving in Paris was really hard work. It was the first really big city we went to. On the second day there, we were driving down a road and I noticed all these people waving their arms at us. We were driving on the wrong side of the road! It was difficult to get used to that. We were only there for three days and we didn't really know where to begin. We went to the Louvre to see the Mona Lisa and all that. But the painting's in this room and there were all these people there with their phones taking a photo – without looking at the painting. And, actually, I couldn't really see it at all. Sometimes I'd see other tourists on some kind of tour and it all looked nice and organised for them, so I guess you get to see a bit more that way and you don't waste a whole lot of time trying to work things out. Next time I go away I might try going on a tour of some kind.

2.46

ANNIE Last year we wanted to get away for a couple of weeks so we decided to go trekking in the forests of Malaysia. We thought it would be cheaper to catch a train to the airport rather than go by taxi. But we were a bit upset to discover that the trains weren't running on time. We turned up at the check-in desk very late and just managed to catch our flight. The flight took 17 hours because we stopped over in Dubai for a couple of hours. By the time we got there we were exhausted and not really in the mood for trekking.

2.49

INTERVIEWER With us this week is Professor William Barnett, who is a specialist in dying languages. Professor Barnett, first of all, how many languages are there in the world? It must be more than the number of countries in the world?
PROFESSOR Oh yes, much more. There are about 200 independent countries in the world but we think there are around 7,000 different languages.
I 7,000?
P Yes, more or less. We don't know exactly, because there may well be languages in areas like the Amazon that we haven't even discovered yet. In fact we only have detailed knowledge of about 15% of the world's languages.
I And some of these are very widely spoken.
P Yes, that's right. Spanish, for example, is spoken by over 400 million people as a first language, English has about 500 million native speakers, Arabic has about 300 million. And the language with the most native speakers is Mandarin Chinese. It's spoken by over 900 million people, that's 14% of the world's population. So these languages are very big, and they're doing fine. In general, the languages that are widely spoken are increasing while the languages that are spoken by smaller groups of people are declining.
I And is this something to worry about?
P It certainly is, yes. The number of languages in the world is decreasing very, very quickly, roughly one language every two weeks – that means that about 30 languages are lost every year. The situation is deteriorating because of globalisation – people have more contact with each other, and they start to speak English or Spanish or Chinese instead of their own language, and their own language dies out. We think that over the next 100 years about half of the world's spoken languages will die out. That means 3,500 languages will disappear completely in just a hundred years.
I Yes, that's serious. Is there anything we can do about it?
P Well, one thing we can do is record the languages and find out more about them. Most 'small' languages are spoken in certain regions of the world – we call these 'language hotspots'. These are areas which have a lot of different languages but each language is spoken by very few people. In one small part of Northern Australia, for example, there are around 135 different tribal languages, but they're all in danger of disappearing. So we're focusing on areas like these, and we're writing the languages down and recording the voices of the last remaining speakers. So it may not be possible to revive the language, but at least we can try and preserve it for future generations.

2.54

INTERVIEWER Professor Barnett, your job is to try to preserve endangered languages. Does it really matter if small languages die out and bigger languages take over? Why is it so important?
PROFESSOR Well yes, it does matter, it matters very much. First of all, of course it matters to the people who speak that language. Your language is part of your identity. Imagine if English died out and no one spoke it any more, how would you feel?
I OK, that's on a personal level. But what about for the wider world? Is it really important?
P Well, yes. If we lose a language, we're losing a part of human culture, there's all that knowledge that the language contains. It's like losing a painting or a building. Every language has its own way of seeing the world.
I How do you mean? Could you give an example of that?
P Well, one example, it's very well known, is a language called Inupiaq, it's spoken in northern Canada. Now they have over 100 different ways to describe sea ice. It's unique to that language, you couldn't translate that into English. And you can find examples like this in every language – every language has a different way of looking at the world.
I OK, I can see that, but isn't it a good idea if everyone learns a global language, say English or Spanish or Chinese, or whatever? Then they can talk to other people. That's what language is for, surely?
P Yes, of course it's a good idea, but that's not the point. People often think you have to give up your own 'small' language to learn a 'big' language, and in the past that often happened, but in fact you don't have to do that. You can keep your language and learn the big language – in other words, teach children to be bilingual.
I So, do you think it's really possible to stop languages from dying out?
P Yes, I think it is if we want to enough, and it's already being done by people all around the world. One important thing we can do is change attitudes,

especially in children, make them feel proud of their own language, because unless children want to speak their own language, the language dies. And another thing is we can use technology, and this is quite new. We can record people speaking the language, and we can create apps so kids can practise the language, for example. I think that's really important because it gives a feeling that the language is something modern and fun, and something for young people to learn.

2.55 PART 1

EMMA So, if we leave late afternoon on Friday …
SAM I need to check with Becky though.
E Do you think it'll be a problem?
S Well, it's asking quite a lot.
E She knows what to do, doesn't she?
S Yeah, but it means she'll have to look after the café for a day and a half by herself. Open up, set things up, deal with the cash, clean up – everything.
E True.
S That doesn't seem very fair – she has only just started. Becky?
BECKY Yeah?
E Do you mind if we ask you a favour?
B Of course not. What is it?
S Feel free to say no, but we – that is, Emma and I – we were hoping to get away … on Friday afternoon … for the weekend.
B Oh, lovely! Where?
S Paris, actually.
B Fantastic.
S So we were wondering …
B Do you want me to look after the café?
E Would you?
B Of course. I can close up on Friday and sort everything out on Saturday. Just tell me what you need me to do.
S Are you sure?
B Of course. I'm happy to help.
S Thanks. That's really nice of you.
E Yes, thanks, Becky. It's just … Sam hasn't had a weekend off for more than nine months.
B My pleasure – it's about time you two had a break together. And I know how everything works now – it's no trouble at all.
E We really appreciate it.
B And if I don't know what to do I can always ask Phil. Can't I, Phil?
PHIL What's that?
B You know all about the café.
P Do I?
S Don't worry, JK. Go back to your book.
E Yes, make us all famous.
S I really am very grateful.
B It's not a problem.

2.56

SAM Becky?
BECKY Yeah?
E Do you mind if we ask you a favour?
B Of course not. What is it?
S Feel free to say no, but we – that is, Emma and I – we were hoping to get away … on Friday afternoon … for the weekend.
B Fantastic.
S So we were wondering …
B Do you want me to look after the café?
E Would you?
B Of course. I can close up on Friday and sort everything out Saturday. Just tell me what you need me to do.
S Are you sure?
B Of course. I'm happy to help.

2.58 PART 2

BECKY Hi there.
TESSA Hi. Just returning your notes.
PHIL Great!
T Great?
P Yes.
T Great what?
P I've just had a great idea. For the story.
B Great!
T So … um … What is it you're writing?
P A science fiction novel.
T Oh. I'm quite into science fiction.
P Oh. Really?
T You must tell me about it – I mean, your story … your ideas. One day.
P Oh right. Yeah. Sure. One day. Love to.
B So … my notes.
T Oh sorry. Thanks for the loan.
B No problem.
T Hey, I was thinking. You know this project – photographing bridges. We should probably make a start soon. I know somewhere great we could go.
B Good idea. When were you thinking?
T How about this weekend?
B Sorry, I can't. I've just told Sam I'd look after the café.
T No problem – how about the weekend after then?
B It's a date.
T Do you want a hand on Saturday?
B Here?
T Yeah. I could help clear tables and … things like that.
B Great, thanks. That's really kind of you.
T I'm more than happy to help out.
B And if things are a bit slow …
T What?
B Phil can tell you all about his book.

2.61

ALEX So where did you go?
KIRSTEN We went camping in the Grand Canyon. It was amazing, a real experience. But before we drove through the Mojave Desert – that's a big salt desert, just salt for miles and miles.
A Wow amazing.
K And we saw cowboys, didn't we, John? Where was that?
JOHN I don't know, some town near there. It was like a cowboy show, they had a shootout.
A You mean like a gun fight? For show?
K Yeah, that's right. Then we stopped for something to eat, and we were really lucky cos it was getting late and we had nowhere to stay, but the owner of the restaurant was really nice, wasn't he?
J He let us camp behind the restaurant.
K Yeah, the people were really friendly, weren't they?
J Yeah. It wasn't very comfortable, though.
A Why not?
K We couldn't blow up the airbed. It had a hole in it.
J So we slept on the ground. Really uncomfortable.
K Anyway, the next day we actually saw the Grand Canyon.
A Oh, that must be incredible.
K It is. It's breathtaking. I've never seen anything like it
A Did you walk through it, or what?
K No, we just drove round it. Round the south rim, that's where the best views are. And we camped there too.
J We were lucky to find a place. It was peak season.
K Yeah. So, anyway, then we watched the sunset over the Grand Canyon. Pretty amazing. And the next day we got up at 4.45 and saw the sunrise.
A 4.45!
J Oh, it was worth it. It looks completely different at dawn. Um, what else did we do?
K We saw a condor.
J Oh yes, they're really rare apparently. Only 30 birds left. Really impressive birds.
A Mm, sounds great.
K And then we went on to Las Vegas.
A Wow, Las Vegas? Hope you didn't lose all your money!

Unit 7

3.6

A So what exactly is a smart city?
B Well, it can be all kinds of different things, but there are two basic ideas. One is that the city uses technology to improve the quality of life of the local residents, so that they can live more slowly and with less stress. And the second one is that the city itself reacts to problems, rather like a living person would.
A Can you give me some examples?
B Yes, London is a good example. They have a system where they monitor cars driving into the centre and automatically charge the driver for the time the car spends there. So it cuts down traffic congestion and pollution, but it also means the driver doesn't have to stop and buy a ticket or look for money – so it saves time, too. And to use the public transport system you just need a single card and you can go everywhere with it. So you don't need to spend time queuing for tickets. Or in Dublin, in Ireland, they have a system which monitors traffic congestion, so drivers can avoid streets with traffic jams, and it also tells drivers where they can find a free parking space. Apparently 30% of traffic congestion in most cities is caused by people looking for parking spaces, so that's a huge saving in time and money.
A So the main point of smart cities is to improve the environment?
B Yes, but it can take many different forms, it's not just about traffic congestion. For example, there's a new city in the UAE called Masdar. It's in the middle of the desert and the whole city is powered by solar panels, and public transport is electric. So it's a 100% sustainable city – it uses zero energy and there's no air pollution. Or there's another new city in Korea called Songdo, which is planned around a central park. So from all the residential areas there's a fifteen-minute walk across the park to get to work and people can also use the park in their lunch break. I read a report recently that said that green spaces in cities really improve people's mental health, so the park sounds like a great idea.
A So it's not just about the environment. It's about urban development in general?
B Yes, exactly.
A So do you think this is how cities will be in the future?
B Oh I'm quite sure of it. The technology is there already. We're all connected now on the internet, so the next step is to connect the people with the city – and it's already happening very quickly.

3.7

DANIELA I think it's a good idea to make cities better places to live because a lot of cities have developed on a kind of American model. In other words, the city centre is taken over by big companies so there are hardly any shops or people living there. Instead, most people live in big high-rise blocks around the edge of the city and they go to big shopping centres in their cars. So it's really good to change that balance and make the city centre a place for people to live. I live in Munich, in Germany, and in a number of ways I think it is a 'smart city', because it's been developed to suit the people who live there. The centre's a pedestrian zone, closed off to traffic, people cycle everywhere, and there are plenty of good cafés and parks and places to sit outside. So you can wander through the city and take your time, and it's nice and quiet. Also, there's a very good public transport system, so people don't need their cars as much.
RICHARD I don't think you have to design a city to make it a nice place to live. I live in Bangkok, the capital of Thailand, and it certainly isn't a planned city – it's just grown naturally. In some ways it's quite a chaotic city, there are cars everywhere, lots of traffic jams, a lot of noise, and there are very few green spaces where you can sit, so if you want a bit of peace and quiet, forget it! But I love living here. It's so full of life and there are people everywhere. In the street where I live, there are lots of ordinary apartments plus a few hotels, there's a very good vegetable market, there are quite a few restaurants, and there are people selling things in the street. So there's everything you need, plus lots of traffic, of course. So it certainly isn't a 'smart city', but it's very exciting to live here!

3.11

ANTONIA As with most things in life, I started small. Not long after I bought this apartment, I suddenly decided that the cabinet in the kitchen was ugly. It was modern and beige and I couldn't stand it. A few days later, I found this absolutely gorgeous, old, wooden cabinet from the 1920s in a second-hand shop. I pulled out the original cabinet and replaced it with the one I found. And then everything looked wrong. I also discovered that the original fireplace and chimney were covered up and underneath there were these lovely, old red bricks. The cover had to come off. Then the paint work looked just awful … and so it went on. Now, I've got a lovely home-style kitchen. I'm really satisfied with that. But I wasn't at all satisfied with the layout of the dining room and the sitting room. They were two very small rooms. And I thought – just imagine – knock down the dividing wall and I could have this lovely open living space. So, one weekend, I got busy and the wall came down! I've still got some work to do there. Then there's the bedroom … I haven't had time yet … and the bathroom needs major attention. OK – I admit it – I'm addicted to renovation. I can't help myself. I love doing these things myself. Getting it done by a professional isn't nearly as much fun. But, hey, there are lots of worse things to be addicted to and my apartment's looking better and better with every day!

ROB You see, under our house, there was a kind of cellar and a garage. And there was also a small passage between the two. They're the kind of places where we keep things we no longer use. But I suddenly had this great idea. What if I knocked down a few walls and made the cellar and the garage one big area – a kind of basement that the kids could use as their space. I got a friend of mine who's an engineer to have a look and make sure it was possible – I mean, I didn't want the house to fall down! And he said, sure, no problem. And I've helped a lot of friends and family do this kind of thing in the past – like, I've got a pretty good idea about what to do. So, I had this great weekend where I knocked down the walls – I loved that – you can really see the potential – immediately. Problem is – once you knock something down, you kind of have to build a few things in their place, so it doesn't look like a worksite. But, well, things have been busy at work and at weekends there are lots of things to do with the kids – sports matches and stuff like that. I mean, I fully intend to finish it all off. That's what I keep promising my wife. But she thinks I've got a 'commitment problem'. You know, I'm not committed to finishing off the renovation. Maybe she's right – but these things aren't as easy as they look. I suppose I could have it done by a professional – but that's expensive. I just say that it's a 'work in progress'. It'll get there. Eventually.

3.12 PART 1

TESSA This is a really good angle.
BECKY Let's have a look. Oh that's great. We can use that one in the competition.
T What competition?
B Didn't you get the email?
T I don't think so. I don't remember.
B It's called 'London architecture in photographs'. It's a free competition. The college said they'll enter our bridge photos.
T I'm not sure I can be bothered. I don't really see the point.
B Well, the first prize is £500.
T OK, that's different! Let's take some more.
B Oh! I completely forgot the time – I've got to go. I'm meeting Tom at 12.00.
T Why don't you call him? Tell him you'll be late.
B I can't. We're meeting the estate agent.
T Estate agent?
B Yeah, we're looking at flats. You know, we want to rent a flat. For after we're married.
T Oh right. You'd better go then.
B Yeah. See you later.
T Bye. Good luck.

3.15 PART 2

BECKY Hi sorry I'm late. I was taking photos with Tessa.
TOM That's OK. This is Katie West. She's from the estate agent's.
B Hi, lovely to meet you. I'm Becky.
KATIE Very nice to meet you, Becky. Good. So I'll show you the first flat. We've had a lot of interest in this already. As you can see, it's in a great location, right by the shops, close to the station. Follow me. …
B Great.
K Here it is. It's a lovely flat for two people. Not too big. Just right for the two of you.
T Two rooms and a kitchen?
K Yes, two rooms, a kitchen – and a bathroom.
T OK.
K So here's the living room. Quite a good-sized room. And a nice view of the street … And here's the second room. It's a bit smaller, but it's perfect as a bedroom. Nice and quiet in here – cosy … And here's the kitchen. Quite practical and er … yeah, has everything you need for a kitchen. It's very convenient. I'll leave you to it.
T Well, I can see why the price is low.
B Tiny.
T Yeah, and too noisy. Right on the main road.
B Yeah. And it smells all damp. Horrible.
T Yes, awful.
B Oh dear.
T Well, let's see what the next one's like.
K So, what do you think?
T Yeah, um, it's nice.
B It's lovely! But maybe not quite what we're looking for.
K OK.

3.16 PART 3

KATIE This one's just come on the market. I think you might like this one better. Have a look round, see what you think.
BECKY Thank you. This is a lovely flat. But can we afford it?
TOM Well, with my promotion … I have got a bit more money now.
B It really is lovely.
T Look, this could be a kind of sitting area by the window …
B Yeah, that's a great idea. And we could have some plants and some bookshelves, or a big lamp.
T Mm, that would work well.
B And this would make a great dining area, we could have a table and some interesting lights.
T Yeah, and I can imagine a big TV right here.
B *[laughs]*
K So, what do you think?
T Yeah … it's a brilliant flat, um …
K Well, we have had one other enquiry this morning. But if you're definitely interested …
T We'll think about it. Can I let you know this afternoon?
K Of course, no problem.

3.18

RYAN I think it's a really bad idea. What do we need a shopping mall for? I mean, we've got a local shop and that sells quite a good range of things – anything you need in an emergency. There's a supermarket only about five kilometres away and it's so easy to get there by bus. A mall's going to ruin this neighbourhood. Why can't they create a nice green living space instead?
SUSIE I think it's great. It's going to be really convenient to have plenty of shops nearby. If I have to do anything like, I don't know – go to the supermarket or get my hair cut or something – I have to go into town and it takes such a long time in the traffic. Can't wait for them to build the mall – it's exciting.
CAROL Well, I am looking forward to having a range of shops nearby. There aren't enough in this part of town. But I know this will change the neighbourhood. It'll make it a lot busier and noisier. And there'll be so much traffic. But I guess that's the price you pay for convenience.
DUNCAN The idea of a mall doesn't particularly bother me, but I guess there'll be a large number of the same old shops – very boring. Everything's part of a chain these days. I wouldn't mind so much if they had a few more interesting shops in the mall – you know, something like an independent music shop or something. But I know that won't happen.
MILES Well, it's about time. That local shop we have is useless. They never order enough of anything and they're always running out of milk and bread and basic things like that. But a new supermarket and lots of shops … that's progress. It'll be great.
MARION It's going to completely change the community. I mean, a number of families live in this part of town and we have young children. Apart from the traffic, we'll have so many people passing through our streets … I really don't know how safe it'll be to live here. It's just … well, I'm thinking about my children. I want them to be safe.

Unit 8

3.19

MICHAEL Welcome to this week's edition of *The Money Pool*. Today, we've invited personal finance expert Mia Radkin on the show to answer questions about your money. Hi Mia.
MIA Hello Michael.
MIC And welcome.
MIA Thank you.
MIC The number is 0800 666961. Give us a call now with your personal finance question, but I believe we already have Jacob on the line.
JACOB Hello
MIA Hello Jacob.
MIC So, Jacob, you've got a question about savings goals, is that right?
J Yeah, that's right. My income's OK and I more or less manage to keep up with my bills and everything, but I never seem to get much ahead. I'd like to start saving for a home, but it feels like a bit of a waste of time.
MIA OK, Jacob, I noticed that you said you 'more or less' keep up with your bills. What's your biggest monthly bill?
J Well, probably my credit card.
MIA Hmm … thought so.
J But I always pay at least the minimum amount each month – sometimes a bit more.
MIA Do you mind my asking, Jacob, how much do you owe on your credit card?
J Well, it's about £15,000.
MIA And I imagine you're paying about 18% interest.
J Yeah, about that.
MIA OK, here's what I'd suggest you do Jacob. Find another credit card provider who will let you transfer your balance to them and pay a very low interest rate. If you transfer your balance, you'll probably pay as little as 3%. And then start paying off that debt as fast as you can. The first step to serious saving is to get out of debt.
J Right.
MIA And then I'd like you to do something else. Get a pair of scissors and cut up your new credit card.
J You mean get rid of it?
MIA That's right, so you don't use it.
J But if I did that I wouldn't be able to afford things like holidays and going out for dinner.
MIA Well, no. Looks like you might have to make some lifestyle changes too, Jacob. But the first step is to manage your debt – sensibly. OK?
J Yeah, good point. Thanks.
MIC Thank you for calling us, Jacob. So, now we go to Sophie. Sounds like she's got money to spare. Is that right, Sophie?
SOPHIE Hello?
MIC Yes, hello Sophie, you're on air now.
S Oh, right.
MIA How can I help Sophie?
S Well, I just want a bit of advice, really. I've been putting aside money for the past five years or so. I've got savings of just over £17,500 in a long-term interest account and it's earning about 2.5%. But I worry if this is the best place for it. Should I be investing the money somewhere else?

MIA So, tell me, Sophie. Have you got debts?
S Not really. Well, just my student loan, but money gets taken out of my salary for that. It's automatic; sort of like paying tax.
MIA But you're still paying interest on that loan. If I were you, I'd use the money to pay off your student loan.
S But if I did that, I wouldn't have any spare money, you know, for an emergency.
MIA £17,500 – what kind of emergency are you expecting?!
S Yes, I see.
MIA Look, it sounds to me like you're a pretty sensible person when it comes to money. And I always say before you worry about investment, free yourself from debt.
S Actually, I think my student loan is now about £16,000. If I pay it off, I'll be debt free.
MIA And that's a very good thing to be.

3.21

SPEAKER 1 Well, I think if I'd found it in the street, I would have posted the letter. It seems quite clear to me. Obviously the person should have been more careful, but it wasn't addressed to me, so it would have been quite wrong to open it. It would have been theft; it doesn't matter what was in it. If I'd found it in a café, I would have given it to one of the staff to keep for Mr Fingham.
SPEAKER 2 I probably would have opened it to check that there really were tickets inside, but then I would have posted it to Mr Fingham. I'm sure the Closing Ceremony was wonderful, but if I'd used the tickets I would have felt guilty, so I wouldn't have enjoyed it. If I'd wanted to go, I would have bought my own tickets.
SPEAKER 3 If I'd found this letter, I certainly wouldn't have just posted it. First, I would have looked at it to see what it was, and I think I would have opened it to see if there really were tickets inside, just out of curiosity. Then I would have thought about it. Maybe I would have used the tickets myself, I don't know. I would have been tempted, certainly. Maybe I'm just not a very honest person – but I would have thought, 'Well, it wasn't my mistake; he shouldn't have dropped the letter. So tough luck.'
SPEAKER 4 If I'd seen a letter like this I probably wouldn't have picked it up; I would have just walked on past and left it for someone else. It's better to mind your own business – you never know what you might find if you pick something up in the street. You hear so many stories about letter bombs these days. I think I would have been afraid to touch it.

3.25

A Did you hear about the trial of that company director?
B Oh, you mean the one who was accused of bribery. I knew he'd been arrested. What happened?
A It was incredible. He appeared in court yesterday and five witnesses all gave evidence. They all said he had asked them for bribes.
B Wow. So, what was the verdict? Was he found guilty?
A No, the jury said he was not guilty.
B Hmm. What did the judge say?
A Nothing. She didn't sentence him. She let him go free.
B Hmm. That's a bit odd, isn't it?

3.28 PART 1

TOM The estate agent just called me back.
BECKY And?
TOM We didn't get the flat. We just missed it. Someone came in and signed a contract about an hour ago.
B Oh no. So we just missed it?
T Afraid so.
B That's really disappointing.
T I know. I did try ringing earlier, but kept getting the estate agent's voice mail.
B Don't worry. It's not your fault – we're just unlucky.
T Yeah. I'll go and see what else they've got a bit later on.
B Good idea. I'm sure there'll be plenty of other places. We'll find somewhere.
T Of course we will.
B Bye.

3.29 PART 2

SAM I'm just popping out for an hour.
BECKY Sure.
S What's up?
B Oh, flat hunting – you know …
S Yeah, it's never easy. Don't give up hope – you'll find something.
B Yeah. You look very smart! What's the big occasion?
S The bank.
B Oh … scary!
S Well, if I want to make improvements to the kitchen …
B Yeah, that's going to be expensive.
S Yeah. We need a new cooker, a bigger fridge – that sort of thing.
B Well, the evening meals have been popular though, haven't they?
S Yeah, better than I thought.
B Emma's a great cook.
S Well, I always knew that!
B And it's good to make changes.
S I hope the bank agrees.
B I'm sure they will. Good luck.
S Thanks!

3.31 PART 3

TOM Sam!
SAM Hi Tom!
T Hi Sam. Escaped for a few minutes?
S I've just been to the bank.
T Oh yeah?
S To see about a loan to improve the kitchen.
T Oh right. How did it go?
S I don't really know. You know banks … they never say much at first. And then they say no!
T Yeah, the same thing happened to me.
S At the bank?
T No, at the estate agent's. They weren't very helpful.
S Yeah, right, finding somewhere to live. It's really difficult, isn't it?
T Yeah, it is. Sorry. I've got to get back to work. Are you going this way?
S Yeah. Erm, Becky said it's been hard work.
T Yeah, we missed out on the perfect flat.
S Hmm, I know the feeling.
T Oh?
S It was just like that when I was looking for the café.
T But you found a good place. The café's great. And it's in a good location.
S In the end. Someone else got it first – then they changed their mind.
T Oh right.
S So you never know …
T Well, I've learnt one thing.
S What's that?
T The next time we find the perfect place, I'll say yes straight away.

3.32 PART 4

KATIE Hello, Tom. It's Katie here from Barkers Estate Agents. Thanks for coming in earlier. Something interesting's just come up. Can you call me back on 249 456?
TOM Hi, Katie? Katie – hi. Hi, it's Tom Gibson here. Yes I just got your voice mail …

3.34

PAUL Did you see that reality crime show on TV last night?
ZOE The one about the young woman using the old man's credit card to buy things for herself?
P Yeah. It made me really angry. It was like a lesson on how to commit a crime. You know, get friendly with the old person – get them to trust you and then offer to get a credit card for them. I mean, if you show people this stuff, then other people will just copy what that young woman did.
Z Do you think so? But it showed you'll get arrested in the end.
P That's only because the old man's niece happened to see the credit card statement and notice all those purchases for women's clothing.
Z Actually, what amazed me about that is the way the niece spoke to the young woman first. If it had been me, I'd have gone straight to the police.
P But I still think the whole programme was sort of saying it's OK to do this. Like, the interview with the young woman. She had all this make-up on, a beautiful dress – it was like she was some kind of star or something. I couldn't believe it!
Z That's true and they hardly spoke to the old man. Poor thing, he looked terrified by the whole experience of being filmed.
P Exactly and he really didn't want to be on TV. I thought the presenter was really pushy with him – she kept repeating the same question – 'but didn't you realise, didn't you realise?'
Z But he must have agreed to it all. They usually have to sign something for those TV programmes.
P I bet it was the niece who talked him into it. She seemed to enjoy being on TV, too. That's the problem with programmes like that – all these boring, ordinary people turn into 'famous people'. Well, for about five minutes, anyway.
Z But I guess you could say that the programme was like a warning to people. You know, telling them to be careful, who they trust with their money, credit cards, things like that.
P Hardly.
Z But the presenter did say that at the very end.
P Yeah, I suppose so. But the saddest thing of all – the old man still thought the young woman was a 'nice girl'.
Z And the presenter did point out that many thieves are very charming.
P But doesn't everyone know that?
Z Obviously not! If I were you, I wouldn't watch that show any more.

Unit 9

3.37

TOBY Well, I'm not sure I want electronics just stuck on my skin.
ROSIE I bet it's no different from putting on a plaster when you cut yourself.
T But plasters don't have electronics in them.
R It wouldn't worry me. There are other things to worry about.
T Like what?
R Well, what was it I was reading about the other day? Yeah, there's this laboratory where they're growing meat. Synthetic meat – I find that kind of scary.
T Oh, that. Yeah, there was that scientist who made his own hamburger and ate it online.
R Yuck!
T Now, I think that's a great idea. Grow your own meat – very cool.
R But it's not natural.
T Yes, it is. It's just not grown on a cow, that's all.
R But all these tiny pieces of meat that they have to push together just to make one burger.
T Nothing wrong with that.
R And the end result is something which costs €250,000. I mean, these scientists, who are sort of like Dr Frankenstein, how can they justify that?
T Well … but they're bound to find cheaper ways to grow the meat. And what you may not realise is that it's much better for the environment.
R I don't see how it can be.
T I was reading about it … And, to produce just 15 grams of meat – that's one-five – cows need about 100 grams of vegetables. I mean, that's a really, really inefficient use of energy.
R I'm sure it takes a lot of energy to make meat grow in the laboratory.
T Not as much. And what I didn't know was that about 30% of the Earth's surface is covered with crops that we grow just to feed animals for meat.
R Yeah, I know that …
T So, if we can grow meat, we could use some of that land to grow crops for people.

R Well, yeah, I agree with you – that is a good idea. But what amazes me is that you can't see the obvious answer – become a vegetarian.
T Vegetarian? Why would I do that? I like meat.
R Well, I don't think you'd like meat that a scientist has made in a laboratory. There's no fat or blood in it, which means no flavour.
T They're working on that.
R Just like they're working on making it cheaper to produce.
T But what's really incredible is that you can get rid of all those gases.
R Gases? What do you mean?
T Cows. They produce carbon dioxide, methane, which are all harmful gases. Very bad for global warming.
R Once again, very true. But tell me one thing.
T What?
R When did you last catch the bus to work?
T Well, it was … I don't know … a couple of months ago.
R More like a year ago. You drive every day! Well, Toby, what I find strange is that if you're worried about global warming … Well, I think there are better ways of helping out than eating meat that a scientist has put together in a laboratory.
T Yeah, but the bus service is really inconvenient.
R Sure it is.
T Well, you can stick what you like on your skin. I'm going to enjoy my synthetic burger!

3.41

B … So this Swedish director was backpacking round the world trying to find a good story to tell and one of the people he talked to was one of the reporters who found Rodriguez.
A That's a coincidence.
B I know, and out of all the stories he heard from all over the world, he came to the conclusion that Rodriguez's story was the one to tell.
A So then what happened?
B Well, first of all he wanted to make sure that Rodriguez really was that popular in South Africa because of course most people doubted that he could be a superstar in one country when no one else had heard of him. But he was. People called him a legend, as big as the Rolling Stones. They estimated that he'd sold about 1.5 million records in South Africa, so of course everyone knew him. And then the director realised that this really was a story worth telling.
A Incredible. But they'd never heard about him.
B That's right, they'd never heard about him. So anyway, the director flew over to meet Rodriguez and he assumed, you know, that he would be dying to tell his story.
A He probably wondered why they'd come to see him.
B Yes, he didn't have any idea who they were, but he agreed to the interviews, although he didn't actually say much. In the film, he seems to be a very shy, modest kind of person. Like, he still lives in the same wooden house that he's lived in for the last 40 years, and he keeps to a very simple lifestyle.
A Amazing.
B But it gets even better. The director ran out of money while he was doing the film and he was aware that he might not be able to finish it. So what he did was he shot the last part of the film on his smart phone and put it together on his kitchen table.
A Wow. And he managed to do that?
B Oh yeah. He finished it and it's made a lot of money and won loads of prizes from all around the world for best documentary. So now the whole world knows about Rodriguez.
A That's amazing.
B Yeah.
A I've got to see that film.

3.43 PART 1

BECKY What's all this about? What's the big secret?
TOM We've got to be somewhere, that's all.
B But where?
T Ah … it's a surprise.
B Hmm, I'm not sure I like surprises.
T It'll be fine.
B I've no idea where we are. I've never seen this street before.
T Just wait and see.
B Where on earth are we going?
T Wait and see.
B Hang on … I know where we are.
T Do you?
B Yeah. Is there another flat available around here?
T Follow me.

3.45 PART 2

BECKY But Tom … this is the same flat.
TOM Welcome to our new home!
B Really?!
T Step right this way … What do you think?
B But didn't you say yesterday that we'd missed out?
T And we did.
B So what happened?
T The estate agent called me back – the other people changed their mind.
B Really? So it's ours if we want it?
T Um … actually … it is ours.
B What?
T I paid a deposit this afternoon.
B But, Tom, I thought we were going to talk about it first.
T Oh. Right. I sort of thought we had.
B Well, I suppose – in a way.
T And you were so disappointed when we missed out.
B Yes. Yes, I was.
T And I didn't want to miss out this time.
B But you could have said something.
T Sorry. I wanted it to be a surprise.
B Well, next time make sure you ask me …
T Well?
B It's a lovely surprise.
T You're not too annoyed?
B No. In fact, not at all.
T You did say it was the perfect flat.
B And it is. I love this space … And the view … And the kitchen is so well designed …
T Did you guess?
B In the car?
T Yeah.
B Well, I thought you were taking me to see a flat.
T But not this one?
B No, of course not.
T I thought about it a bit yesterday, you know, the different route …
B I do love it. I can't wait to move in.
T We have to sign the lease first.
B Yes, of course.
T And … oh … but there's another document that we have to sign beforehand.
B Oh. What's that?
T Our marriage licence – that's all!

3.49

TOM What do you think?
BECKY But didn't you say yesterday that we'd missed out?
T And we did.
B So what happened?
T The estate agent called me back – the other people changed their mind.
B Really? So it's ours if we want it?
T Um … actually … it is ours.
B What?
T I paid a deposit this afternoon.
B But, Tom, I thought we were going to talk about it first.
T Oh. Right. I sort of thought we had.

3.50

SPEAKER 1 I had really bad headaches, so I decided to go to a homeopathic doctor. You know, they give you these little white tablets which have a tiny amount of something which is actually poisonous. And I remember on my first visit, he spent an hour asking me questions to find out as much as he could about me, before he looked at what was wrong with me. He said the idea was to treat 'the whole person', not just the disease. I thought this was really good – my normal doctor is always in a hurry and you're lucky if he gives you more than ten minutes.
SPEAKER 2 A friend of mine had a very bad cough which wouldn't go away, so he tried a treatment called 'radionics'. The person treating you takes something that belongs to you, like a piece of clothing or something, and then turns some dials on this box. It looks a bit like a radio actually. And then they decide what's wrong with you. What a load of rubbish! I don't know how people can believe things like that.
SPEAKER 3 I had really bad pains in my knee. I tried all kinds of drugs and I even went to hospital, but nothing worked. I could walk, but I couldn't run or do sport. Then a friend recommended acupuncture. It's where they put needles into particular points or places on your body. I was a bit doubtful at first, but I tried it and the doctor put needles all round my knees. Since then I haven't had any problems at all – I can even go skiing again. I've no idea how it works, but it certainly worked for me.
SPEAKER 4 A friend of mine tried several times to give up smoking, but she always started again. Then someone recommended a doctor who used hypnosis. She told me about it, it was really interesting. She sat in a comfortable chair and he hypnotised her – he just counted to 20 and she fell into a deep sleep and when she woke up she didn't want to smoke any more. Obviously she doesn't remember what he said when she was under hypnosis, but I guess he must have told her that she didn't need to smoke. That was three months ago and she still doesn't want to smoke.

Unit 10

3.53

INTERVIEWER The story of Dan Cooper raises more questions than it answers. Today we talk to Bob Fernandez, who has written a new book on the disappearance. Bob, there are a lot of mysterious elements to this story. First of all, how did he get on the plane with a briefcase full of dynamite?
BOB Well, that's easy to answer. Remember, this was 1971 and they didn't have airport security the way they do now. Security checks came in much later, so there's no mystery there. But, of course, we have no idea whether he was really carrying dynamite – it might have just looked like dynamite.
I And who was he? Do we know that?
B We know that Dan Cooper wasn't his real name. That was easy to check and there were no Dan Coopers who'd gone missing. But who was he? No one knows. He knew a lot about planes and he also knew how to parachute, so he may have been a retired pilot or he may have had some job to do with aircraft. Certainly someone with inside knowledge. And he also knew the area where he jumped. One interesting thing is that several people claimed later that he survived and they knew him. For example, in 1982, a woman claimed that he was her husband, who'd just died. She said she'd found him in 1972 hiding in her garden with a broken foot and they'd fallen in love and got married. This was her story. But there was no way they could prove it.
I I suppose the big question is: could he have survived the jump? He jumped into a storm, at night, holding bags of dollar bills and he had to open a parachute. Is that possible?

B Well, we know that what he did was possible, because not long afterwards a stuntman repeated exactly what he'd done – successfully. And quite a few things suggest that he did land safely. For example, they never found either the body or the parachute and if you think the parachute was bright yellow and red, and they searched everywhere, that's quite something. You'd be able to see it from the air. So that suggests he might have landed and then hidden the parachute.

I One of the few clues we have is that in 1980 a boy found some of the money buried in a riverbank.

B Yes, this was one bag of Dan Cooper's money, so people thought that he might have drowned in the river. But they searched the river pretty carefully and they didn't find anything. And there are other explanations. For example, he might have lost some of the money when he landed and gone off with the rest. Or he might even have thrown it away to confuse the police and then crossed the border into Mexico. No one knows. The one thing we do know is the police never found him.

3.55

LOUISE Ever since I was a child, I've been fascinated with Africa. The thing that has always interested me most is the incredible wildlife – lions, elephants, gazelle, rhinos – I mean, there are just so many amazing animals. After I started work, I saved up money for a holiday in South Africa and went on a safari. It was fantastic, but it just wasn't enough. I remember thinking at the time, 'I wish I could stay longer.' I came back home and went back to work. I'd heard about conservation projects and the fact they often need volunteers – you know, people who go and help researchers – that kind of thing. So, I started saving, because I thought it would be great to go and volunteer for a year. It took me another six years to save up enough money to support myself for that year, but I managed to do it. My workplace lets people take leave without pay for up to six months. I should probably have done that, but I wanted to go for a full year, so I had to resign from my job.

TERRY I'm a computer technician and I used to work in the IT support department for a bank. I was there for about three years and in my final year I really began to hate the atmosphere in the team I worked in. I thought my boss wasn't a very good manager – and I felt I could have done a better job. If only I'd applied for his job when it became free. I thought I wasn't qualified enough, but I would have done a much better job than he did. Anyway, I realised there were a lot of people living in my area who needed help with computers and IT problems. And I also worked out that they'd prefer the technician to go to them at home rather than have to take it to a workshop to be fixed. So I decided to set up my own business and become my own boss. I gave up my job at the bank.

3.56

LOUISE I was really excited just before my departure. When I arrived, we stayed in a kind of hut, but there were five people sleeping in the same room and I found it a bit crowded. I wish I'd checked this before leaving, because I've heard that other conservation projects have better living conditions and I could have chosen a different project. The main part of my job was counting elephants. Sounds a bit boring, I know. But I loved it. And apart from the elephants, I saw all kinds of extraordinary wildlife. I also made some amazing new friends. It was a unique experience. I've been back now for three months and am having trouble finding a new job. I could have stayed on in Africa, but I didn't have enough money. If only I'd saved more before I left, I could have had two years there. Not to worry, I've had an amazing year and I've managed to make a dream come true. How many people can say that?

TERRY Things were quite hard to start and I wish I'd done a bit more market research before I gave up my job. For example, I found out that I got more calls at weekends, so, perhaps in the beginning, I could have worked part-time for the bank and started my business at weekends only. This would have helped my money situation. And the other thing – I should have checked out other companies doing this kind of work. I quickly found out that I wasn't charging enough, so I wasn't making enough money. Still, after two years, things are going quite well and I'm managing to make a decent living. I don't think this will make me a millionaire and getting set up was much harder than I'd thought it would be. I wish I'd done a course on starting a small business, but it's too late now! But I do have much more flexibility in my working life and, most important of all, I'm my own boss.

3.60 PART 1

TUTOR Oh hi, Tessa. I was just looking for you. Uh, can I have a quick word? It's something important. Let's go to my office.

TESSA Yeah.

BECKY I'll wait for you.

TU Don't look so worried. It's good news. We've had the results of the photo competition.

TE Oh yeah?

TU And you've won first prize. £500. Congratulations!

TE What?

TU Yes. Well done. We're very pleased for you. And it's excellent news for the college too.

TE I don't know what to say. I wasn't expecting this.

TU No, you deserved to win. I don't think you realise quite how good you are.

TE Well – no. I mean, yes, thank you.

3.61 PART 2

SAM So … two things to celebrate today. First, Becky and Tom, you've found your dream flat.

BECKY Thanks to Tom making a quick decision.

TOM We almost didn't get it.

EMMA We hope you'll both be very happy in it.

B So what's the second thing?

S The second reason to celebrate … as you've seen, business is going well. The meals have really been a success … thanks to Emma and your wonderful cooking … and to Phil, it was your idea to open late and serve meals. Brilliant! So, let's cut this cake.

B Hold on, there's something else we have to celebrate.

3.65 PART 3

BECKY Hold on, there's something else we have to celebrate. You know the photo competition? Our photos of the bridges? Well, Tessa won first prize.

EMMA That's brilliant!

SAM Yeah, great news.

E When did you find out?

TESSA I only heard this morning. I couldn't believe it, I was so surprised. First prize! I still can't get over it.

PHIL Well done, Tessa. I knew you'd win. You take such great photos.

S So that's three things to celebrate – the flat, the café and Tessa's prize.

E And you looking happy for a change – that's a fourth thing.

S OK. So can we eat this cake?

P Hang on a minute, before we start. I have got something to say … I know you won't believe this, but … I've finished my novel.

E That's great, Phil!

P I sent it off today. So, the coffee's on me.

B You can't afford to buy us coffee, you're not JK Rowling yet!

T You never know. Maybe one day? Well done, Phil. It's such a good story. And so original.

P Thanks, Tessa.

T I reckon you'll get some good news soon.

P Hope so.

T But you won't forget us when you're rich and famous?

P How could I?!

S Right, I'm going to cut this cake.

TOM Just a minute, before we start. One more thing. We've decided on a date for the wedding.

B Finally.

T Saturday the nineteenth of June … and you're all invited!

S OK, any more good news, anyone? No? Right – now I am definitely going to cut this cake.

3.67

The Valley

It is a late afternoon in September. The scene is a valley in south-western France. The river flows slowly between the steep, wooded hills. The sun is shining on the water. It is quiet. A man is sitting on a flat rock, which sticks out into the river. He is alone. He sits absolutely still. After a while he bends to look at something in the water – a fish, perhaps. As he does so, something hits the water and there is a sudden splash. He puts his hand to his ear. It is covered in blood. He falls forward into the river and disappears into its muddy water.

3.68

I picked up a piece of wood lying near my hiding place. My ear was bleeding heavily, but I tried to ignore the pain. Quietly and carefully, I crept up behind Heid. He was so busy looking at the river through his binoculars that he did not notice me. I brought the stick down on the back of his head. He fell down and rolled a little further down the riverbank. I thought I had knocked him out but, as I bent over him, he suddenly grabbed me. I felt his hands around my throat, slowly squeezing the breath out of me. The stick was still in my hand and with the last of my energy I brought it down on his head. He let go of my throat immediately. In a sudden burst of anger, I hit him again and again with the stick. As my anger left me, I realised I had gone too far. Heid was dead. I had foolishly lost my chance to find the answers to my questions. And all because of my anger.

Heid's body was now at the bottom of the riverbank. His face was in the water and the slow current of the river carried away a steady flow of blood. I pulled the body along the riverbank, to a place where some overhanging trees and low bushes hid it from any curious eyes. I need not have worried. It was evening and I knew that anyone out fishing or hiking would already be going home. The surface of the river was still, except for the occasional fish jumping for flies. Far away, a church clock struck seven. It was a perfect autumn evening.

First, I had to hide the body. Then I had to find out if it was safe to return to the house. After this attack, it would not be safe for me to stay in the village – but where should I go? And then I had to find out why Heid had come after me and who had sent him.

In the pocket of his shorts there was a set of car keys – with a registration number on the key ring. I put the keys in my pocket. There was only one place where Heid could have parked the car – outside the café. It might be useful later.

I rolled the body into the water, pushed it into a hole under the riverbank and put some large stones on top of it to hold it under the water. I picked up Heid's rifle and then set off for the village. It was almost dark by the time I reached the house.

Phonemic Symbols

Vowel sounds

Short

/ə/ teacher	/æ/ man	/ʊ/ put	/ɒ/ got
/ɪ/ chip	/i/ happy	/e/ men	/ʌ/ but

Long

/ɜː/ shirt	/ɑː/ part	/uː/ who	/ɔː/ walk	/iː/ cheap

Diphthongs (two vowel sounds)

/eə/ hair	/ɪə/ near	/ʊə/ tour	/ɔɪ/ boy	/aɪ/ fine	/eɪ/ late	/əʊ/ coat	/aʊ/ now

Consonants

/p/ pill	/b/ book	/f/ face	/v/ van	/t/ time	/d/ dog	/k/ cold	/g/ go	/θ/ thirty	/ð/ they	/tʃ/ choose	/dʒ/ jeans
/s/ say	/z/ zero	/ʃ/ shop	/ʒ/ usually	/m/ me	/n/ now	/ŋ/ sing	/h/ hot	/l/ late	/r/ red	/w/ went	/j/ yes

Irregular verbs

Infinitive	Past simple	Past participle
be	was /wɒz/ / were /wɜː/	been
become	became	become
blow	blew /bluː/	blown /bləʊn/
break /breɪk/	broke /brəʊk/	broken /'brəʊkən/
bring /brɪŋ/	brought /brɔːt/	brought /brɔːt/
build /bɪld/	built /bɪlt/	built /bɪlt/
buy /baɪ/	bought /bɔːt/	bought /bɔːt/
catch /kætʃ/	caught /kɔːt/	caught /kɔːt/
choose /tʃuːz/	chose /tʃəʊz/	chosen /'tʃəʊzən/
come	came	come
cost	cost	cost
cut	cut	cut
deal /dɪəl/	dealt /delt/	dealt /delt/
do	did	done /dʌn/
draw /drɔː/	drew /druː/	drawn /drɔːn/
drink	drank	drunk
drive /draɪv/	drove /drəʊv/	driven /'drɪvən/
eat /iːt/	ate /et/	eaten /'iːtən/
fall	fell	fallen
feel	felt	felt
find /faɪnd/	found /faʊnd/	found /faʊnd/
fly /flaɪ/	flew /fluː/	flown /fləʊn/
forget	forgot	forgotten
get	got	got
give /gɪv/	gave /geɪv/	given /'gɪvən/
go	went	gone /gɒn/
grow /grəʊ/	grew /gruː/	grown /grəʊn/
have /hæv/	had /hæd/	had /hæd/
hear /hɪə/	heard /hɜːd/	heard /hɜːd/
hide /haɪd/	hid /hɪd/	hidden /'hɪdn/
hit	hit	hit
hold /həʊld/	held	held
keep	kept	kept
know /nəʊ/	knew /njuː/	known /nəʊn/
lead /liːd/	led /led/	led /led/

Infinitive	Past simple	Past participle
learn /lɜːn/	learnt /lɜːnt/	learnt /lɜːnt/
leave /liːv/	left	left
lend	lent	lent
let	let	let
lose /luːz/	lost	lost
make	made	made
meet	met	met
pay /peɪ/	paid /peɪd/	paid /peɪd/
put	put	put
read /riːd/	read /red/	read /red/
ride /raɪd/	rode /rəʊd/	ridden /'rɪdən/
ring	rang	rung
run	ran	run
sink /sɪŋk/	sank /sæŋk/	sunk /sʌŋk/
say /seɪ/	said /sed/	said /sed/
see	saw /sɔː/	seen
sell	sold /səʊld/	sold /səʊld/
set	set	set
sing	sang	sung
sleep	slept	slept
speak /spiːk/	spoke /spəʊk/	spoken /'spəʊkən/
spend	spent	spent
stand	stood /stʊd/	stood /stʊd/
steal /stiːl/	stole /stəʊl/	stolen /'stəʊlən/
swim /swɪm/	swam /swæm/	swum /swʌm/
take /teɪk/	took /tʊk/	taken /'teɪkən/
teach /tiːtʃ/	taught /tɔːt/	taught /tɔːt/
tell	told /təʊld/	told /təʊld/
think	thought /θɔːt/	thought /θɔːt/
throw /θrəʊ/	threw /θruː/	thrown /θrəʊn/
understand	understood /ʌndə'stʊd/	understood /ʌndə'stʊd/
wake /weɪk/	woke /wəʊk/	woken /'wəʊkən/
wear /weə/	wore /wɔː/	worn /wɔːn/
win	won	won
write /raɪt/	wrote /rəʊt/	written /'rɪtən/